Asian Financial Integration

In the wake of the global financial crisis, Asia is leading the global recovery with strong economic growth. However, this book argues that, in the coming years, the region will need to play a much more active role in shaping the future global financial system and, in turn, suggests policy strategies for doing so.

Asian Financial Integration explores the lessons we can learn from Asia's experience during the global financial crisis in terms of the future direction of the region's economic policy and the challenges posed by the opening and deepening of its financial markets. The contributors deal with a number of crucial questions, including what Asia should learn from the crisis, especially with regards to financial innovation and regulation; whether global imbalances are a result of policy distortions or a natural outcome of global division of labour; what are the lessons and implications from the financial market reform and liberalization experiences of some of the region's major economies; and what should Asia do to promote regional financial integration.

This book will be welcomed by students and scholars interested in Asian economics and international economics, as well as by policy-makers working in the field.

Yiping Huang is Professor of Economics and Deputy Dean of the National School of Development at Peking University and an Adjunct Professor at the Crawford School of Public Policy at the Australian National University.

Shiro Armstrong is a Senior Research Fellow at the Crawford School of Public Policy at the Australian National University and Director of the East Asian Bureau of Economic Research, as well as the co-editor of the East Asia Forum.

Routledge Studies in the Growth Economies of Asia

1. The Changing Capital Markets of East Asia
Edited by Ky Cao

2. Financial Reform in China
Edited by On Kit Tam

3. Women and Industrialization in Asia
Edited by Susan Horton

4. Japan's Trade Policy
Action or reaction?
Yumiko Mikanagi

5. The Japanese Election System
Three analytical perspectives
Junichiro Wada

6. The Economics of the Latecomers
Catching-up, technology transfer and institutions in Germany, Japan and South Korea
Jang-Sup Shin

7. Industrialization in Malaysia
Import substitution and infant industry performance
Rokiah Alavi

8. Economic Development in Twentieth Century East Asia
The international context
Edited by Aiko Ikeo

9. The Politics of Economic Development in Indonesia
Contending perspectives
Edited by Ian Chalmers and Vedi R. Hadiz

10. Studies in the Economic History of the Pacific Rim
Edited by Sally M. Miller, A.J.H. Latham and Dennis O. Flynn

11. Workers and the State in New Order Indonesia
Vedi R. Hadiz

12. The Japanese Foreign Exchange Market
Beate Reszat

13. Exchange Rate Policies in Emerging Asian Countries
Edited by Stefan Collignon, Jean Pisani-Ferry and Yung Chul Park

14. Chinese Firms and Technology in the Reform Era
Yizheng Shi

15. Japanese Views on Economic Development
Diverse paths to the market
Kenichi Ohno and Izumi Ohno

16. Technological Capabilities and Export Success in Asia
Edited by Dieter Ernst, Tom Ganiatsos and Lynn Mytelka

17. Trade and Investment in China
The European experience
Edited by Roger Strange, Jim Slater and Limin Wang

18. Technology and Innovation in Japan
Policy and management for the 21st century
Edited by Martin Hemmert and Christian Oberländer

19. Trade Policy Issues in Asian Development
Prema-chandra Athukorala

20. Economic Integration in the Asia Pacific Region
Ippei Yamazawa

21. Japan's War Economy
Edited by Erich Pauer

22. Industrial Technology Development in Malaysia
Industry and firm studies
Edited by Jomo K.S., Greg Felker and Rajah Rasiah

23. Technology, Competitiveness and the State
Malaysia's industrial technology policies
Edited by Jomo K. S. and Greg Felker

24. Corporatism and Korean Capitalism
Edited by Dennis L. McNamara

25. Japanese Science
Samuel Coleman

26. Capital and Labour in Japan
The functions of two factor markets
Toshiaki Tachibanaki and Atsuhiro Taki

27. Asia Pacific Dynamism 1550–2000
Edited by A.J.H. Latham and Heita Kawakatsu

28. The Political Economy of Development and Environment in Korea
Jae-Yong Chung and Richard J Kirkby

29. Japanese Economics and Economists since 1945
Edited by Aiko Ikeo

30. China's Entry into the World Trade Organisation
Edited by Peter Drysdale and Ligang Song

31. Hong Kong as an International Financial Centre
Emergence and development 1945–1965
Catherine R. Schenk

32. Impediments to Trade in Services
Measurement and policy implication
Edited by Christoper Findlay and Tony Warren

33. The Japanese Industrial Economy
Late development and cultural causation
Ian Inkster

34. China and the Long March to Global Trade
The accession of China to the World Trade Organization
Edited by Alan S. Alexandroff, Sylvia Ostry and Rafael Gomez

35. Capitalist Development and Economism in East Asia
The rise of Hong Kong, Singapore, Taiwan, and South Korea
Kui-Wai Li

36. Women and Work in Globalizing Asia
Edited by Dong-Sook S. Gills and Nicola Piper

37. Financial Markets and Policies in East Asia
Gordon de Brouwer

38. Developmentalism and Dependency in Southeast Asia
The case of the automotive industry
Jason P. Abbott

39. Law and Labour Market Regulation in East Asia
Edited by Sean Cooney, Tim Lindsey, Richard Mitchell and Ying Zhu

40. The Economy of the Philippines
Elites, inequalities and economic restructuring
Peter Krinks

41. China's Third Economic Transformation
The rise of the private economy
Edited by Ross Garnaut and Ligang Song

42. The Vietnamese Economy
Awakening the dormant dragon
Edited by Binh Tran-Nam and Chi Do Pham

43. Restructuring Korea Inc.
Jang-Sup Shin and Ha-Joon Chang

44. Development and Structural Change in the Asia-Pacific
Globalising miracles or end of a model?
Edited by Martin Andersson and Christer Gunnarsson

45. State Collaboration and Development Strategies in China
The case of the China–Singapore Suzhou Industrial Park (1992–2002)
Alexius Pereira

46. Capital and Knowledge in Asia
Changing power relations
Edited by Heidi Dahles and Otto van den Muijzenberg

47. Southeast Asian Paper Tigers?
From miracle to debacle and beyond
Edited by Jomo K.S.

48. Manufacturing Competitiveness in Asia
How internationally competitive national firms and industries developed in East Asia
Edited by Jomo K.S.

49. **The Korean Economy at the Crossroads**
Edited by MoonJoong Tcha and Chung-Sok Suh

50. **Ethnic Business**
Chinese capitalism in Southeast Asia
Edited by Jomo K.S. and Brian C. Folk

51. **Exchange Rate Regimes in East Asia**
Edited by Gordon de Brouwer and Masahiro Kawai

52. **Financial Governance in East Asia**
Policy dialogue, surveillance and cooperation
Edited by Gordon de Brouwer and Yunjong Wang

53. **Designing Financial Systems in East Asia and Japan**
Edited by Joseph P.H. Fan, Masaharu Hanazaki and Juro Teranishi

54. **State Competence and Economic Growth in Japan**
Yoshiro Miwa

55. **Understanding Japanese Saving**
Does population aging matter?
Robert Dekle

56. **The Rise and Fall of the East Asian Growth System, 1951–2000**
International competitiveness and rapid economic growth
Xiaoming Huang

57. **Service Industries and Asia-Pacific Cities**
New development trajectories
Edited by P.W. Daniels, K.C. Ho and T.A. Hutton

58. **Unemployment in Asia**
Edited by John Benson and Ying Zhu

59. **Risk Management and Innovation in Japan, Britain and the United States**
Edited by Ruth Taplin

60. **Japan's Development Aid to China**
The long-running foreign policy of engagement
Tsukasa Takamine

61. **Chinese Capitalism and the Modernist Vision**
Satyananda J. Gabriel

62. **Japanese Telecommunications**
Market and policy in transition
Edited by Ruth Taplin and Masako Wakui

63. **East Asia, Globalization and the New Economy**
F. Gerard Adams

64. **China as a World Factory**
Edited by Kevin Honglin Zhang

65. **China's State Owned Enterprise Reforms**
An industrial and CEO approach
Juan Antonio Fernandez and Leila Fernandez-Stembridge

66. **China and India**
A tale of two economies
Dilip K. Das

67. Innovation and Business Partnering in Japan, Europe and the United States
Edited by Ruth Taplin

68. Asian Informal Workers
Global risks local protection
Santosh Mehrotra and Mario Biggeri

69. The Rise of the Corporate Economy in Southeast Asia
Rajeswary Ampalavanar Brown

70. The Singapore Economy
An econometric perspective
Tilak Abeyshinge and Keen Meng Choy

71. A Basket Currency for Asia
Edited by Takatoshi Ito

72. Private Enterprises and China's Economic Development
Edited by Shuanglin Lin and Xiaodong Zhu

73. The Korean Developmental State
From dirigisme to neo-liberalism
Iain Pirie

74. Accelerating Japan's Economic Growth
Resolving Japan's growth controversy
Edited by F. Gerard Adams, Lawrence R. Klein, Yuzo Kumasaka and Akihiko Shinozaki

75. China's Emergent Political Economy
Capitalism in the dragon's lair
Edited by Christopher A. McNally

76. The Political Economy of the SARS Epidemic
The impact on human resources in East Asia
Grace O.M. Lee and Malcolm Warner

77. India's Emerging Financial Market
A flow of funds model
Tomoe Moore

78. Outsourcing and Human Resource Management
An international survey
Edited by Ruth Taplin

79. Globalization, Labor Markets and Inequality in India
Dipak Mazumdar and Sandip Sarkar

80. Globalization and the Indian Economy
Roadmap to a convertible rupee
Satyendra S. Nayak

81. Economic Cooperation between Singapore and India
An alliance in the making
Faizal Yahya

82. The United States and the Malaysian Economy
Shakila Yacob

83. Banking Reform in Southeast Asia
The region's decisive decade
Malcolm Cook

84. Trade Unions in Asia
An economic and sociological analysis
Edited by John Benson and Ying Zhu

85. Trade Liberalisation and Regional Disparity in Pakistan
Muhammad Shoaib Butt and Jayatilleke S. Bandara

86. Financial Development and Economic Growth in Malaysia
James Ang

87. Intellectual Property and the New Global Japanese Economy
Ruth Taplin

88. Laggards and Leaders in Labour Market Reform
Comparing Japan and Australia
Edited by Jenny Corbett, Anne Daly, Hisakazu Matsushige and Dehne Taylor

89. Institutions for Economic Reform in Asia
Edited by Philippa Dee

90. Southeast Asia's Credit Revolution
From moneylenders to microfinance
Aditya Goenka and David Henley

91. Economic Reform and Employment Relations in Vietnam
Ngan Thuy Collins

92. The Future of Asian Trade and Growth
Economic development with the emergence of China
Linda Yueh

93. Business Practices in Southeast Asia
An interdisciplinary analysis of Theravada Buddhist countries
Scott A. Hipsher

94. Responsible Development
Vulnerable democracies, hunger and inequality
Omar Noman

95. The Everyday Impact of Economic Reform in China
Management change, enterprise performance and daily life
Ying Zhu, Michael Webber and John Benson

96. The Rise of Asia
Trade and investment in global perspective
Prema-chandra Athukorala

97. Intellectual Property, Innovation and Management in Emerging Economies
Edited by Ruth Taplin and Alojzy Z. Nowak

98. Special Economic Zones in Asian Market Economies
Edited by Connie Carter and Andrew Harding

99. The Migration of Indian Human Capital
The ebb and flow of Indian professionals in Southeast Asia
Faizal bin Yahya and Arunajeet Kaur

100. Economic Development and Inequality in China
The case of Guangdong
Hong Yu

101. The Japanese Pharmaceutical Industry
Its evolution and current challenges
Maki Umemura

102. **The Dynamics of Asian Labour Markets**
Balancing control and flexibility
Edited by John Benson and Ying Zhu

103. **Pakistan – The Political Economy of Growth, Stagnation and the State, 1951 to 2009**
Matthew McCartney

104. **Korean Women Managers and Corporate Culture**
Challenging tradition, choosing empowerment, creating change
Jean R. Renshaw

105. **Trade Liberalisation and Poverty in South Asia**
Edited by Prema-Chandra Athukorala, Jayatilleke S. Bandara and Saman Kelegama

106. **Pro-poor Growth and Liberalization in Developing Economies**
The case of Nepal
Sanjaya Acharya

107. **China and the Global Economy in the 21st Century**
Edited by John Saee

108. **State Structure and Economic Development in Southeast Asia**
The political economy of Thailand and the Philippines
Antoinette R. Raquiza

109. **An Economic History of Indonesia**
1800–2010
Jan Luiten van Zanden and Daan Marks

110. **Taxation in ASEAN and China**
Local institutions, regionalism, global systems and economic development
Edited by Nolan Cormac Sharkey

111. **Macroeconomic and Monetary Policy Issues in Indonesia**
Akhand Akhtar Hossain

112. **Economic Reform Processes in South Asia**
Toward policy efficiency
Edited by Philippa Dee

113. **Manufacturing Enterprise in Asia**
Size structure and economic growth
Dipak Mazumdar and Sandip Sarkar

114. **Managers and Management in Vietnam**
25 years of economic renovation (doi moi)
Vincent Edwards and Anh Phan

115. **New Models of Human Resource Management in China and India**
Alan R. Nankervis, Fang Lee Cooke, Samir R. Chatterjee and Malcolm Warner

116. **Sustaining Development and Growth in East Asia**
Edited by Timo Henckel

117. **Small and Medium Enterprises in India**
Infirmities and asymmetries in industrial clusters
Satyaki Roy

118. Workforce Development and Skill Formation in Asia
Edited by John Benson, Howard Gospel and Ying Zhu

119. Understanding Management in China
Past, present and future
Malcolm Warner

120. Reform and Productivity Growth in India
Issues and trends in the labour markets
Dibyendu Maiti

121. Intellectual Property Valuation and Innovation
Towards global harmonisation
Edited by Ruth Taplin

122. Marketing and Consumption in Modern Japan
Kazuo Usui

123. Economic Growth and Employment in Vietnam
David Lim

124. Asian Financial Integration
Impacts of the global crisis and options for regional policies
Edited by Yiping Huang and Shiro Armstrong

Asian Financial Integration
Impacts of the global crisis and options for regional policies

Edited by
Yiping Huang and Shiro Armstrong

Routledge
Taylor & Francis Group
LONDON AND NEW YORK

First published 2014
by Routledge
2 Park Square, Milton Park, Abingdon, Oxon OX14 4RN

and by Routledge
711 Third Avenue, New York, NY 10017

Routledge is an imprint of the Taylor & Francis Group, an informa business

British Library Cataloguing in Publication Data
A catalogue record for this book is available from the British Library

Library of Congress Cataloging in Publication Data
Asian financial integration : impacts of the global crisis and options for regional policies / edited by Yiping Huang and Shiro Armstrong.
pages cm -- (Routledge studies in the growth economies of Asia ; 124)
Includes bibliographical references and index.
. Asia--Economic integration. 2. Asia--Economic policy. 3. Finance--Asia. 4. Global Economic Crisis, 2008-2009. I. Huang, Yiping, 1964-, editor of compilation. II. Armstrong, Shiro, editor of compilation. III. Series: Routledge studies in the growth economies of Asia ; 124.
HC412.A765 2014
332'.042095--dc23
2013038180

ISBN: 978-0-415-74887-2 (hbk)
ISBN: 978-1-315-79643-7 (ebk)

Typeset in Sabon by Sam Highley, Canberra, Australia

Contents

Figures

Tables

Abbreviations

ABCP	asset-backed commercial paper
ABFI	Asian Bond Fund Initiative
ACFB	Asian Central Bank Forum
AFSB	Asian Financial Stability Dialogue
AIG	American International Group
AMF	Asian Monetary Fund
ASEAN	Association of Southeast Asian Nations
BCLMV	Brunei, Cambodia, Laos, Myanmar, Vietnam
BIS	Bank for International Settlements
BOJ	Bank of Japan
BSA/s	bilateral swap arrangement/s
CAI	comparative advantage index
CAL	capital account liberalization
CDIS	Coordinated Direct Investment Survey (IMF)
CDS	credit default swap
CDO/s	collateralized debt obligation/s
CEEMA	Central and Eastern Europe, Middle East and Africa
CMI	Chiang Mai Initiative
CMIM	Chiang Mai Initiative multilateralization
CPI	consumer price index
CPIS	Coordinated Portfolio Investment Survey (IMF)
CRA/s	credit rating agency/ies
ECB	European Central Bank
EME/s	emerging market economy/ies
EU	European Union
FAI/s	fixed asset investment/s
FCAC	full capital account convertibility
FDI	foreign direct investment
FDIC	Federal Deposit Insurance Corporation (USA)
FE/s	fixed effect/s
FSA	Financial Services Agency (Japan)/Financial Services Authority (UK)
FSB	Financial Stability Board

FY	fiscal year
G20	The Group of Twenty: the Finance Ministers and Central Bank Governors of Argentina, Australia, Brazil, Canada, China, the European Union, France, Germany, India, Indonesia, Italy, Japan, Mexico, Russia, Saudi Arabia, South Africa, the Republic of Korea, Turkey, the United Kingdom and the United States of America
GAO	Government Auditing Office (USA)
GDP	gross domestic product
GFC	global financial crisis
GMM	generalized method of moments
GSE/s	government-sponsored enterprise/s
IMF	International Monetary Fund
IT/s	information technology/ies
LDC/s	less-developed country/ies
LIBOR	London Interbank Offered Rate
NPL/s	non-performing loan/s
OECD	Organisation for Economic Co-operation and Development
OIS	overnight indexed swap [interest rate]
PBOC	People's Bank of China
PN/s	Participatory Note/s
RBI	Reserve Bank of India
RCC	Resolution and Collection Corporation (Japan)
RER	real exchange rate
RMB	renminbi
RMBS/s	residential mortgage-backed security/ies
SMEs	small- and medium-size enterprises
SOB/s	state-owned bank/s
SOE/s	state-owned enterprise/s
TIPS	Treasury Inflation-Protected Securities (USA)
VAR	value-at-risk
WTO	World Trade Organization

Contributors

Shiro Armstrong is a Senior Research Fellow in the Crawford School of Public Policy at the Australian National University and Director of the East Asian Bureau of Economic Research, as well as the co-editor of the East Asia Forum.

Weijiang Feng is Assistant Research Fellow at the Institute of Asia–Pacific Studies, Chinese Academy of Social Sciences, Beijing.

Prasanna Gai is Professor of Macroeconomics at the Business School of the University of Auckland, New Zealand.

Donald Hanna is Managing Director of global liquid markets research in the Fortress Investment Group, Singapore.

Yiping Huang is Professor in Economics and Deputy Dean of National School of Development at Peking University and an Adjunct Professor in the Crawford School of Public Policy at the Australian National University.

Kazumasa Iwata is President of the Japan Center for Economic Research in Tokyo.

D.M. Nachane is Director of the Indira Gandhi Institute of Development Research in Mumbai.

Shinji Takagi is Professor at the Graduate School of Economics, Osaka University, Japan.

Jianwei Xu is Assistant Professor at the School of Economics and Management, Beijing Normal University.

Yang Yao is Professor of Economics and Deputy Director of the China Center for Economic Research, Peking University, Beijing.

Yu Yongding is Director of the Institute of World Economics and Politics, Chinese Academy of Social Sciences, Beijing.

Chai Yu is Director of the Institute of Asia–Pacific Studies in the Chinese Academy of Social Sciences, Beijing.

Preface

Much of emerging Asia sailed through the global financial crisis (GFC) relatively unscathed. The crisis shortened the trajectory that will see China surpassing the United States as the world's largest economy and, with India, Indonesia and the rest of Asia, has launched the Asian century earlier and in a bigger way than anyone expected. Asia is now the growth centre of the global economy, with Europe embroiled in a crisis of its union, and only slow recovery in the United States.

Asian financial markets were not deeply integrated into global financial markets when the GFC hit and were sheltered from the financial contagion of the crisis. Yet, for Asian growth and development to continue, and for more of emerging Asia to become prosperous, Asia's financial systems will need to be liberalized and opened-up. There are important lessons to be learned from past reform experience in the region, as well as from the crisis itself.

With careful sequencing of reforms and liberalization, and with regional cooperation, Asian financial integration can be a stabilizing force for the global financial system. The alternative is the risk that China or another Asian economy could be the cause of the next great financial crisis.

The chapters in this volume look at the lessons of the GFC and the challenges that face Asia, and most importantly China, in opening and deepening its financial markets. It examines policy strategies for moving forward after the crisis.

The work on this volume began at a conference held in Beijing in May 2009, in the immediate aftermath of the GFC. The conference was co-hosted by the Institute of World Economics and Politics in the Chinese Academy of Social Sciences, and the East Asian Bureau of Economic Research, which is centred in the Crawford School of Public Policy at the Australian National University.

The volume benefited greatly from the input of participants at the original Beijing conference and from comments received on chapters in the years since. The rapidly changing global financial and economic landscape has led to new chapters being added and research directions changing. The result is that chapters are not specific to a certain time or circumstance but, rather, provide policy-makers and researchers with analyses and a set of policy recommendations that address the longer-term challenges and priorities of Asia.

The East Asian Bureau of Economic Research and South Asian Bureau of Economic Research supported the project and publication through funding from the Australian Agency for International Development and the Australian Research Council.

Yiping Huang and Shiro Armstrong
January 2013

1 New challenges for Asian financial integration

Yiping Huang and Shiro Armstrong[1]

Asian economies have been actively promoting regional financial cooperation for the past decade. This was first triggered by their painful experiences during the Asian financial crisis. No internal or external mechanism was available to mitigate violent adjustments of their external accounts: foreign exchange reserves were insufficient to fight market forces while the International Monetary Fund (IMF) was not a reliable lender of last resort. Since then, Asian nations have introduced a range of regional initiatives, including reserve pooling, Asian bond funds, currency-swap arrangements and macro-economic-policy surveillance.

Individually, the regional economies also made significant progress in improving their economic structure and policy in order to better withstand future external shocks. Most economies increased flexibility in their exchange rates, reduced overseas borrowing, promoted current account surpluses and accumulated more foreign-exchange reserves. Many also tried to reorientate economic growth toward domestic demand to reduce dependence on export markets.

However, when the global financial crisis (GFC) hit the region in late 2008, most of the new mechanisms did not help to shield Asian economies. Almost all economies suffered a sharp collapse of economic activities. Some economies, such as India, Indonesia and Korea, were close to another major disruption to their financial systems when foreign portfolio flows reversed almost overnight. There were various reasons why this happened. In Korea, for instance, despite earlier efforts that reduced external borrowing, the country's short-term debt actually increased significantly again during the years leading up to the GFC. India and Indonesia opened their capital markets to foreign portfolio investment, which was, by nature, subject to quick and sharp corrections. And some of the newly devised regional mechanisms, such as reserve pooling, did not work, since they are based on conditionality similar to that applied by the IMF.

The region's experiences during the GFC raise a range of important questions about the future direction of its economic policy and financial cooperation. For instance, what should Asia learn from the GFC, especially with regard to financial innovation and regulation? Are global imbalances a result of distorted policy or a natural outcome of global division of labour? What are the implications of the experiences of some of the region's major economies, such as Japan and China? What should Asia do to promote regional financial integration, especially cooperation on currency matters?

The GFC that started with the US subprime mortgage crisis and spread globally after the collapse of Lehman Brothers in September 2008 was the largest global economic downturn since the Great Depression in the 1930s. The crisis exposed weaknesses in the global financial system, marked a turning point in the way global financial institutions operate and changed the global financial architecture as we knew it. The crisis further elevated policy challenges that had already been escalating, the most important of which were global imbalances, financial sector reform, international economic governance and reform of global institutions.

As Asia, prominently China, leads the global recovery, there are important reforms under way around the world; but reforms are also needed at a national level to make the recovery sustainable. As we move into the next phase of dealing with the GFC, the structural dimensions of medium- to long-term economic performance come into sharper focus. Fixing structural problems lies at the heart of all solutions, as does completing financial reforms. To overcome the unprecedented and unsustainable global imbalances, domestic structural and financial reforms are necessary. Merely saying that Chinese domestic consumption needs to grow and American saving has to increase is not helpful. Both these changes require fundamental reforms to the structures of the Chinese and American economies and financial systems. The imbalance issue is not, of course, a bilateral problem with a bilateral solution. It is a global-scale problem requiring a global solution.

For Asia, the key policy shift should be towards increasing domestic consumption but, in order to do that, a whole menu of complicated reforms must be carried out in each country. For example, in China it is necessary to provide a social safety net so that consumers do not need to save as much for health contingencies or old age; the state-owned enterprises (SOEs) have to be reformed and their profits distributed so that their savings are not high; and the financial system has to be reformed so that small- and medium-size enterprises can have access to capital. Financial reform is key policy in China as private enterprise has difficulty in accessing the formal financial market. China is not the only Asian economy where the domestic capital market is suppressed.

Japan is dealing with a completely different set of issues; a demographic problem, stalled structural reforms and learning to live with a declining labour force. While the list of reforms in each country is not the same, as the unique circumstances of China illustrate, the crisis has changed priorities and brought urgency to financial and other reforms in all countries.

It appears that unprecedented fiscal-stimulus spending has saved the global economy from a much deeper downturn and serious depression. Although the coordination of this was a large success and a story in itself, the fiscal stimulus was the easy part.

The crisis has brought about a rethinking of the sequencing of reforms and recognition of the need for a new approach. One question is: which should come first, floating of the exchange rate followed by reform and adjustment elsewhere (as was the case in Australia) or financial deepening, with exchange-rate flexibility a much lower priority (as was the case in some other Asian countries)? One common element in financial reforms, for example in India and China, is that capital-account controls remain. Thus, there is a problem of net domestic savings not being converted into productive foreign investment.

The diverse experience in the region can provide helpful lessons. The Japanese experience of capital-account and foreign-exchange liberalization over too long a period proved highly costly to Japan. The lesson from the completion of Japan's capital-account liberalization is that financial liberalization focusing only on the external side has costs, so policy-makers should synchronize domestic and foreign financial liberalization, conducting both at the same time. A point that is made repeatedly in this volume is that countries should be thinking 'domestic' to get the 'regional' and 'international' right. That is, domestic financial liberalization is necessary for efficient integration into international financial markets. Proceeding with capital-account and foreign-exchange liberalization at the same time can limit the loss from proceeding with them one at a time, but regional experience has shown there is need to proceed cautiously.

A medium-term priority in financial integration for the region is exchange-rate cooperation, but coordination of macro-economic policy and a focus on domestic reforms and developments are needed to get there. Financial cooperation is one of the best approaches to promote financial development and further financial integration. Although all of these are domestic reforms at heart, there are useful experiences that can benefit some countries that are trying to implement difficult reforms. The most successful example in the region is China, which used external pressure to liberalize its domestic financial system through the World Trade Organization (WTO) accession agreements.

While the instincts of some were to retreat from financial integration after the crisis, the solution to many of the problems of the crisis, and a priority for many countries in pursuit of development, is to liberalize capital and current accounts and deepen financial markets at home at the same time as cooperating, coordinating and integrating at the regional and global levels.

Asia will lead the global recovery with strong economic growth, but it will need to step up and play a much more active role in shaping the future financial system. As Asia's effects on and role in the global economic system increase, a process that the crisis has accelerated, it is in Asia's interest to lead the financial reform, especially as the international community now expects a larger role of Asia. Asia, and especially the larger countries like China and India, can no longer afford to be free riders on the international financial regime. The Group of 20 (G20) countries have thrust Asia's developing countries – China, India and Indonesia, and the region's developed countries – Japan, Korea and Australia, onto the world stage to contribute to solutions in the exit phase of the GFC. But these countries have to strengthen regional institutions and cooperate, as well as undertake domestic reforms consistent with the regional and global agenda.

This volume is divided into three sections. First, it reviews some lessons from the GFC. Second, it looks at particular and important Asian experiences from the crisis and some of the policy responses, as well as some forthcoming challenges they present. Finally, the volume lays out some strategies for financial integration in Asia.

LESSONS FROM THE GLOBAL FINANCIAL CRISIS

While the GFC will change the growth model for economies and shift paradigms of international economic interaction, this volume focuses on aspects directly relevant to financial integration in the Asian region.

The volume starts, in Chapter 2, with Don Hanna's review of some of the early lessons that Asia can take from the crisis. Hanna provides a comprehensive account of the policies that have been implemented and the global response to the financial crisis. This is done to set the scene for discussion of future challenges and risks. In his discussion, Hanna warns that policymakers should let market disciplines work, and not interfere where those disciplines may be working to fix the problems. Also, in the new regulatory frameworks, it is important not to over-regulate but to improve on prudential regulation. The most important of the policy recommendations are: to have greater and more effective international cooperation in financial regulation; and to coordinate regulatory reforms. This broad look at global policy initiatives, past and present, sets the scene for the rest of the volume.

In Chapter 3, Jianwei Xu and Yang Yao explore the question of whether the global imbalances are a result of international division of labour between the surplus and deficit countries. This analysis goes to the core of understanding one of the underlying causes of the GFC. Understanding the global imbalances that played a large role in the GFC is important in understanding what policy measures can and cannot, or should not, be taken in correcting imbalances.

Global imbalances are a result of the structure of the interaction between the countries with strong financial sectors and those with strong manufacturing or resource sectors, the former being the deficit countries and the latter being the surplus countries. The starting point is that, for both surplus and deficit countries, there are substantial gains from trade. But it requires robust financial intermediation to underpin and therefore sustain the imbalances, and efficient financial intermediation to maximize the gain.

Xu and Yao remind us that the imbalances are created by long-term factors and cannot be easily corrected by short-term measures, such as adjustments to exchange rates. This is an important message that is often forgotten in public discussion and is critical to thinking about policy prescriptions. Exchange rate adjustments should be a part of any package of reforms. The structural characteristics that led to the imbalances require structural adjustments over time, both in individual economies and the global economy.

A quick fix such as creating an international currency will not work, according to Xu and Yao, as the US financial system still dominates the global financial system. Financial markets and systems in China and the rest of Asia will need to be strengthened and deepened to move towards any credible global currency, and that is a longer term issue.

Finally, Xu and Yao remind us that, due to the structure of China's economy, China's export-led growth model will continue in the medium term. They recommend accelerating the pace of urbanization and improving the financial system as measures to promote a move away from the export-led growth model. The analysis shows that the structural problems all require difficult structural adjustment, and avoidance of quick fixes that will not help in the medium term.

The crisis has reinforced the importance of measuring systemic risk, of having adequate crisis warning, and of coordinating and communicating that warning. Prasanna Gai reviews, in Chapter 4, the various tools for measuring systemic risk and what some of those models tell us in hindsight about the subprime market, Lehman Brothers and the banking system leading up to the crisis. This review of the literature helps understanding of just how well the models measured the systemic risk. The second generation of models that are widely used are, according to Gai, rudimentary and have obvious weaknesses, such as the lack of micro-foundations.

The models currently used to measure systemic risk, despite their weaknesses, have an important role to play internationally, in helping to understand the interdependencies of systems and bank balance sheets. However, as Gai states, to be fully effective, the stress-testing of the models needs to be coordinated at the supranational level, with the Financial Stability Board taking a leading and coordinating role. Such a role was not adopted anywhere by any supranational authority, leading up to the crisis. As the crisis has shown, the management of this systemic risk cannot be ignored.

THE EXPERIENCE OF ASIAN ECONOMIES

Kazumasa Iwata provides in Chapter 5 a sobering warning that, considering Japan's experience in the 1980s and 1990s, the demographic shift in China might make it the next candidate for a major economic crisis. Korea also faces this problem and is destined to follow Japan and face the consequences of a demographic crisis, perhaps even before China. The longer term demographic drag is one thing but an under-appreciated, medium-term problem facing policy-makers is the interaction between demographic patterns and savings in one country and the availability of cheap funds in others. In an open capital market, there is a powerful interaction between how demographics play into the flow of savings, savings imbalances across borders, and asset price bubbles and crises. Demographic changes play a significant role in creating asset price bubbles, as was shown in Japan, and even the USA. If future decline in the working-age population is anticipated, it can cause the long-term interest rate to remain low, encouraging an asset price bubble. Iwata explains that the larger the fall in the working-age population from its peak, the larger and more prolonged is the damage from the burst of the bubble, as happened in Japan.

Unless there are financial and other reforms, Iwata warns, the demographic transition in East Asia will deliver the next big bubble in China 4–5 years from now. There are signs that policy-makers in China, Korea and Japan are beginning to think about the economic and social adjustments that flow from the demographics in Northeast Asia. Iwata alerts us to the need to think more about demographic shifts and their impact on global savings and spending in the present and medium-term contexts, as well as in the longer term. The region is diverse, with economies at different stages of development and with different institutional systems. The experience of economies that have gone through crises and undergone major reforms is extremely valuable for neighbouring countries, especially if there are signs of imminent crisis, such as those in demographic trends highlighted by Iwata.

Iwata draws important lessons from Japan's experience on exiting a downturn and moving from an unconventional policy regime of expansionary fiscal policy, even when there is a liquidity trap. Before regulation of financial markets, it is important to introduce transparency to identify toxic assets and fair-value price them. That will make regulation easier and help evict the toxic assets from the system. Another lesson from Japan is the need to clean up bank balance sheets as quickly as possible, to avoid delaying recovery.

Iwata also reminds us of the important yet difficult point of having a clear and credible exit strategy from an unconventional policy regime. And he reminds us of the importance of relying on market mechanisms wherever appropriate, and of information sharing between regulators and the central bank for coordination in implementation of macro-prudential policy.

Following on from Japan's experience and lessons for China and elsewhere, Yu Yongding looks in Chapter 6 at China's immediate policy responses to the GFC. In a succinct but comprehensive survey of economic policy leading up to the crisis, Yu reviews the major policy trends and, with the benefit of hindsight, highlights weaknesses in, and lessons from, China's performance. One major weakness in the economy was rampant overcapacity, hidden by the high growth in fixed asset investment and the even higher growth-rate in exports. This reliance on what ultimately was an external (US) bubble, and the collapse of external demand, meant that overcapacity turned to overproduction that suddenly transformed inflation into deflation, aggravated by the fact that policy-makers had been focusing on an inflation problem and pursuing contractionary policies.

Yu explains that the Chinese stimulus spending was successful and the reason for the economy's starting to bottom out in early 2009. He warns, however, that the recovery was achieved at the expense of a worsening in some structural problems. The medium- to long-term outlook for Chinese growth depends on the structural health of the economy, and Yu concludes that structural reforms have to be accelerated. Furthermore, the growth strategy, which has been so successful until now, has to be adjusted. Yu reviews expansionary policies in this context, before addressing two important issues of regional and global significance. First, he examines China's policy options in managing the risks associated with its foreign-exchange reserves. Second, he discusses the need for reform of the international monetary system, and the related longer term issue of the role of the Chinese renminbi (RMB) in the international monetary system. His argument supports the view that China has a large role to play in regional financial cooperation and internationalization of the RMB.

China's increasing role in the international financial system and the burgeoning role of the RMB in the international currency system require continuing and deeper reforms to the financial system in China. In Chapter 7, Chai Yu and Weijiang Feng provide an overview of the history of those reforms since the beginning of China's reform period in 1979. They do this in an attempt to understand the drivers of change and reform in the past, and to highlight current trends and priorities in Chinese financial reform. The history of the reforms and their drivers is crucial to understanding where the financial system in China is at present and for progressing deeper reforms.

The banking sector has undergone drastic changes but the legacy of centralization and monopolization by the state still result in financial repression. Yu and Feng warn of the high level of non-performing loans and continued financial repression being large risks for the banking sector. They also review the financial market and foreign-exchange administration reforms. The common theme is that there has been great progress in liberalization, but that capital controls, distortions, other restrictions and large-scale financial repression, mean that the job of deepening financial markets, making them efficient, liquid and robust remains a huge and daunting task for Chinese policy-makers. While the Chinese financial system is still very small, as Chapter 7 describes, how Chinese domestic financial reforms progress will significantly affect neighbouring countries, the region and, increasingly, the global financial system. Yu and Feng also remind us of the importance of the sequencing of these reforms.

The benefits of capital account liberalization are questioned from a theoretical perspective, in Chapter 8 by Nachane. Nachane presents a warning about India's embarking on capital account liberalization and removing the restrictions on inward and outward capital flows. One danger is the increased vulnerability to financial crises and the sudden reversal of hot money flows (short-term capital flows), as Southeast Asian countries experienced in the Asian financial crisis in 1997–98. While describing the benefits of capital account liberalizations, of which there are many, such analysis is timely, as China and India look at liberalizing their capital accounts in the next phase of their financial reform and development. Policy-makers in India are enthusiastic about liberalizing the capital account, but Nachane warns that lessons from the GFC have to be taken into account. He points to the fact that, while the economics profession is reviewing the lessons from the recent crisis, the enthusiasm of Indian policy-makers has not been dampened by the crisis. He sees this as a dangerous sign.

FINANCIAL INTEGRATION IN ASIA

For Asia, maintaining the status quo in financial integration is an unsustainable policy option. In Chapter 9, Takagi explains how financial integration has not kept pace with real-sector integration (trade in goods and services) as the latter has led integration in the region. Indeed, the lack of financial integration of some countries saved them from larger exposure to the crisis. Nevertheless, as Takagi warns, the potential gains from further financial integration are too great for those countries to remain inward-looking. How Canada and Australia responded to the GFC shows that robust financial and banking sectors can weather external shocks and that countries can benefit from integration with the global financial system. The deepening of regional financial integration will facilitate further real-sector integration, reduce the dependence on other financial centres (Europe and North America) and more efficiently allocate the region's savings to investment.

Asia has much to gain from financial cooperation and integration at regional and global levels. Asia's stake in international regulatory cooperation shows that Asia has a significant role to play in the new global financial architecture. Takagi goes further, to say that financial integration in Asia is necessary for the region to intermediate more of its own resources for productive use in the region. He suggests that further financial integration could overcome some of the inefficiencies of the current hub-and-spokes structure of world trade and finance, which is a source of instability. Asia should lead the transition away from that, Takagi concludes.

How this financial integration really gets going, according to Gai in Chapter 4, is by defining new international standards for macro-prudential regulation. He reviews systemic risk-measurement for a more complex set of financial instruments and arrangements in a more intricately interconnected financial world, and suggests some fundamental changes to how this should be done.

The global financial architecture does not have a global institution with rules and constraints at its peak, unlike the trading system, which has the WTO. This is despite financial integration being driven by trade and affecting individual economies as well as the global system, with heavy interactions across borders. Asia, with its high reliance on the external sector and highly integrated trade, has much to gain from contributing, and where necessary leading, the changing of the 'rules of the game' in the international system. The G20, with the establishment of the Financial Stability Board and relevant Asian countries at the global table, is the arena in which Asia can contribute. Gai proposes areas in which Asian policy-makers can promote the self-confidence and therefore effectiveness of the Financial Stability Board, as well as other areas where they can help to advance financial stability through management of systemic risk.

The focus of Yu and Feng in Chapter 7 is China's financial reforms, and the authors set all of China's challenges in the context of regional financial cooperation. Effective regional financial cooperation can reduce the incentive for China to hold enormous foreign-exchange reserves, it can act as a buffer against shocks and provide mechanisms to mitigate them, and benefit the Chinese financial market greatly. The same can be said for all financial systems in the region. Successful international financial cooperation in East Asia would improve China's policy-making environment, Yu and Feng note. China and, by implication, other East Asian countries, should each provide regional public goods according to their capacity.

Some see a single currency as the pinnacle of regional financial and monetary cooperation, but a single currency in Asia is a long-term goal, and integration in Asia is taking a different shape and form from that in Europe. And while exchange-rate stability will help many countries in Asia, flexibility is critical for individual economies, given the different levels and speeds of development in the region. The goal of monetary integration requires close coordination of regional currencies, if not their pegging to a common currency or currency basket, and would also require a level of political cooperation that seems distant for the region. It is for these reasons, Yiping Huang explains in Chapter 10, that the region should focus on more realistic and useful cooperation measures, such as enhancing reserve funds and improving policy-making, rather than specific currency arrangements.

To play a meaningful role in regional financial markets, Asia must enhance regional cooperation in managing foreign-exchange reserves. Huang argues that the Asia Reserve Fund needs to be increased to make any significant contribution to regional financial markets, but that it should be only a small part of a broader effort towards regional monetary integration. An Asian Financial Stability Dialogue (AFSD) needs to complement the Financial Stability Board (FSB) at the global level. Cooperation around the AFSD or an Asian Central Bank Forum would foster policy dialogue and eventually reduce the total reserves in the region by pooling a smaller amount.

Huang stresses that Asia must contribute to the reform of the international monetary system, just as regional cooperation in the AFSD can contribute to cooperation at the global level through the FSB.

A common theme throughout the volume is that regional financial integration involves both regional cooperation and policy reforms by individual countries. Stronger domestic financial systems are necessary to reap the opportunities for significant gains from financial integration. Financial dialogue and cooperation at the regional level, closely compatible with cooperation more broadly at the global level, will benefit the economies in the region. Dialogue and cooperation around regional financial integration also helps to communicate potential risks early, helps to reduce the chance of further crises and can help the region respond to both internal and external shocks.

NOTE

1 Yiping Huang, National School of Development, Peking University, Beijing; Shiro Armstrong, Crawford School of Public Policy, Australian National University, Canberra.

2 The global financial market crisis

Policy lessons for Asia

Donald Hanna[1]

INTRODUCTION

From what began as a crisis in a small portion of the US mortgage market, subprime lending has morphed into the worst economic shock since the Second World War. Trillions of dollars in wealth has been destroyed around the world as home prices, equity prices and bond spreads have suffered. In the USA alone, households have lost wealth equivalent to almost two years of disposable income. Hopes that the crisis could be contained by the government backstopping of mortgage guarantee agencies Fannie Mae and Freddie Mac, and by the government assistance to the acquisition of Bear Stearns, came to naught, with the essentially simultaneous and world-wide flight from risk following the collapse of Lehman Brothers in early September 2008. Financial markets seized up and with them global goods markets shuddered. Liquidity, something that had been plentiful – perhaps too plentiful in recent years – became frightfully dear. Global trade and industrial production fell at a pace similar to that of the Great Depression (Figure 2.1). Global financial institutions were shaken and, in their newly found caution, are at the heart of a process of de-leveraging and that looks set to persist even as the global economy shows signs of healing.

Policy-makers around the globe have responded to the collapse in economic and financial market activity with a breadth and depth of policy easing that is itself extraordinary.

Broad public support has been given to financial intermediaries – capital infusions, liability guarantees, access to credit lines and to foreign-exchange swaps, lower interest rates, eased regulations on provisioning standards and loss recognition, programmes to provide liquidity for distressed assets and/or to shift them to public balance sheets (Table 2.1).[2] Beyond prudential financial and monetary policies, governments have also expanded fiscal deficits in a direct effort to support aggregate demand through a mix of higher spending and/or tax rebates. Across the Organisation for Economic Co-operation and Development (OECD), for example, 2009 fiscal deficits will likely be some 6.3 per cent higher than in 2007, with some 2.5 per cent of the increase the direct effect of programmes targeted at softening the economic damage of the recession (OECD 2009). Asian governments have followed similar policies, with expansions of deficits in 2009 centred on 2 per cent of gross domestic product (GDP) (Table 2.2).

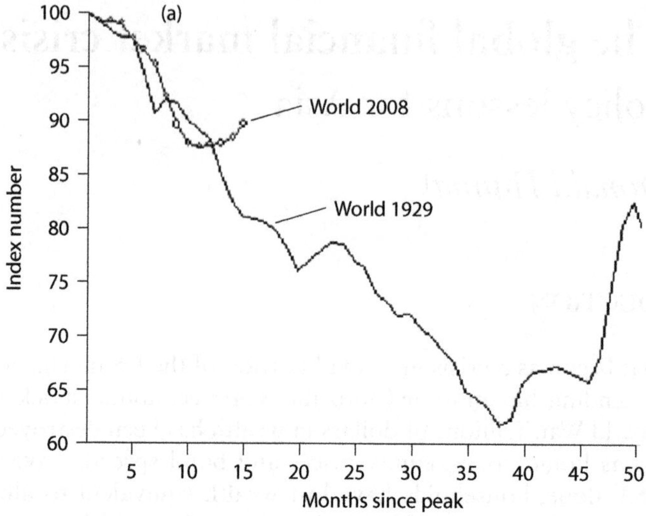

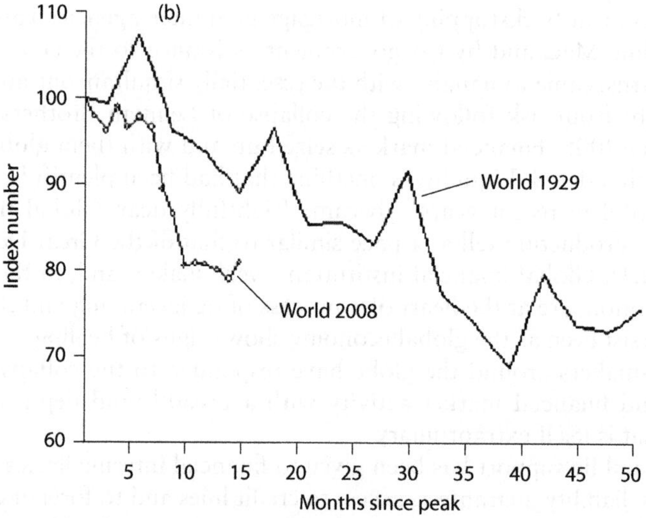

Figure 2.1 World industrial production (a) and trade (b), 1929 versus 2008. Source: Eichengreen and O'Rourke (2009).

The economic policy challenges that result from this sudden lurch from easy financial conditions to extraordinarily tight ones are perhaps the most significant we have faced in generations. Much has already been said and written.[3] The G20 at its meeting in April 2009 issued a nine-page statement outlining the policy initiatives governments are embarked on to right their wobbling economies. There are two broad but interconnected areas of policy focus. The first is on the particulars of managing a financial system that efficiently intermediates savings and minimizes risks. The second is

Table 2.1 Fiscal balances (% of GDP) of the central governments in Asia

	2000–04 average	*2004*	*2005*	*2006*	*2007*	*2008*	*2009*[6]
Cambodia[1]	–5.3	–4.5	–2.5	–2.7	–2.9	–1.7	–3.2
China, People's Rep. of[1]	–2.2	–1.3	–1.2	–0.8	0.6	–0.4	–3.0
Hong Kong, China[4]	–2.4	1.6	1.0	3.9	7.5	0.1	–3.9
Indonesia	–1.2	–1.1	–0.2	–0.9	–1.2	0.0	–2.5
Korea, Rep. of[5]	1.5	0.7	0.4	0.4	3.8	1.2	–2.2
Malaysia[2]	–5.0	–4.1	–3.6	–3.3	–3.2	–4.8	–7.6
Philippines	–4.4	–3.8	–2.7	–1.1	–0.2	–0.9	–3.2
Singapore[1,4]	7.0	6.9	9.0	8.3	13.9	6.5	–3.5
Taiwan, China[1]	–3.3	–2.4	–1.6	–0.7	–0.4	–1.4	–3.6
Thailand[4]	–0.4	0.3	0.2	0.1	–1.1	–0.3	–3.5
Vietnam[3]	–4.5	–4.9	–4.9	–5.0	–4.9	–4.5	–4.8

Sources: National sources; *Asian Development Outlook* (various issues), Asian Development Bank; *Article IV consultation reports*, International Monetary Fund; and CEIC Data Company.

Notes
1 Refers to general government balance.
2 Refers to federal government balance.
3 Refers to state budget balance.
4 Fiscal year.
5 Balance including social security funds.
6 Budget deficit estimates in 2009 budgets of respective countries, except for Cambodia (International Monetary Fund projection); China, People's Rep. of (maximum government estimate); Philippines (revised government target), and Thailand (government estimate).

on framing a set of macro-economic policies that promotes long-run GDP growth and minimizes the volatility of that growth.

There appears to be broad agreement on a range of issues concerning the first focus area:

- capital standards for financial institutions need to rise and move counter-cyclically;
- the management of liquidity risk needs to improve;
- the array of financial intermediaries subject to regulatory oversight needs to mesh with the roles those intermediaries play in the economy, not their legal structure;
- credit rating agencies need to improve their methodologies and alter their governance structures;
- the disclosure of information needs to widen;
- prudential and regulatory changes need to be synchronized and, to the extent possible, standardized;
- central banks need a broader set of regular tools for supporting market liquidity; and
- central banks need a broader – but more streamlined – method for intervening in and resolving crisis-stricken financial intermediaries.

Table 2.2 Asian government responses to the global financial crisis

Emerging Asia	*Capital support*	*Liquidity support*	*Credit guarantee schemes*	*Regulatory forbearance*	*Deposit guarantees*	*Foreign-exchange intervention & swap arrangements*	*Stock-market intervention*
China, People's Rep. of		X		X		X	X
Hong Kong, China	X	X	X	X	X	X	
Indonesia	X		X	X	X	X	X
Korea, Rep. of	X	X	X	X		X	X
Malaysia		X	X	X	X	X	X
Philippines		X		X	X	X	
Singapore		X			X	X	
Thailand				X	X	X	X
Taiwan, China		X	X	X	X	X	X
Vietnam			X	X		X	X

Sources: *Asian Economic Monitor* December 2008, Asian Development Banks; *The State of Public Finances: Outlook and Medium-term Policies After the 2008 Crisis*, International Monetary Fund; ADB Office of Regional Economic Integration staff, country write-ups; news releases; and national budget documents.

There is also consensus on key elements of the second set of macro-economic management challenges. In particular, G20 governments have all called for avoiding beggar-thy-neighbour trade and exchange-rate policies, pledging ongoing commitments to open trade (G20 2009). The absorption of private claims onto public balance sheets has been essentially universal, as has the easing of monetary policy. Fiscal easing, however, has been more constrained by the initial dynamics of public debt in particular countries and the scope those dynamics create for additional fiscal easing in the short run.[4] Indeed, concerns about how to manage the medium-term fiscal consequences of this crisis are an oft-cited element in current debates.[5]

Other points are more contentious:

- What should be the scope for innovation in financial markets?
- Should central banks have regulatory oversight of financial institutions? If so, should it be only macro-prudential or also micro-prudential?
- How should institutions that are too big to fail be handled?
- What role did global imbalances play in the crisis?

With these points as background, we provide a slightly different take on the mix of conditions, both macro-economic and industry-specific, that contributed to the current turmoil. From that analysis, we draw some lessons for policy-makers in emerging financial markets in Asia that either dovetail with or diverge from the list above.[6]

BACKGROUND TO THE CURRENT POLICY DEBATE

The recent credit bubble was driven by the interaction of four sets of factors:

1. macro-economic stability that expanded risk appetite;
2. excess demand for US housing that drove up home prices;
3. financial innovation in structured credit and mortgage finance that spread risk but also increased it, introducing a fundamental element of uncertainty associated with any innovation; and
4. structural elements of the financial system that amplified movements in risk appetite.

Macro-economic contributors

First, a variety of macro-economic factors – the Great Moderation, low short-term interest rates, improved corporate and emerging market fundamentals, and robust global savings – contributed to a general environment of strong risk appetite in financial markets. The lower macro-economic volatility, for both real output and inflation (Figures 2.2–2.5), implied less risk of loss. As the period of low macro-economic volatility extended and the number of countries broadened, investors became increasingly bold.

At the same time, the rise in global saving and fall in the levels of inflation helped produce lower interest rates.[7] However, the fall in inflation also implied lower nominal global growth, even as real growth was rising.[8] Lower nominal interest rates combined with lower volatility encouraged the 'search for yield', an effort to maintain high nominal returns in the face of falling nominal global growth. Investors took two avenues in pursuit of the 'search for yield': investments in riskier assets such as those in emerging markets; or leveraged investments in safe assets, such as highly rated structured credit. At least initially, the improving emerging market fundamentals helped to realize strong gains from those investors who pursued that avenue.[9] Those who chose leverage saw tougher times sooner. However, in the aftermath of the Lehman collapse, the seizure of interest trade finance and the wholesale flight from risk sucked emerging markets' economies and markets into the morass, by vastly expanding the level of uncertainty over counterparty risk and the associated rush to liquidity and safety.[10]

Real and financial factors affecting US housing demand

Second, the interaction between rising demand – driven largely by demographics – and constraints on supply, generated upward pressure on US housing prices. The ageing of the population expanded housing demand, even

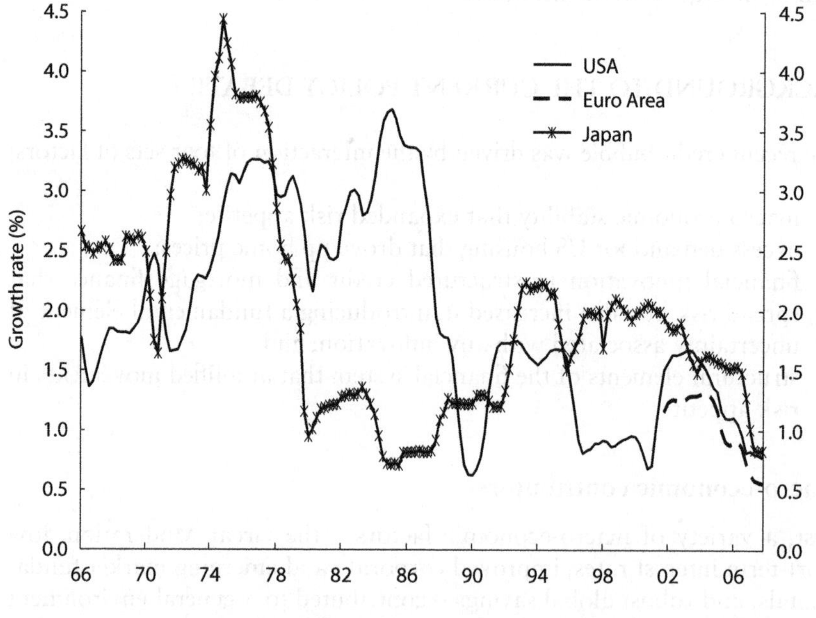

Figure 2.2 Growth volatility, 1966–2007 (4th quarter), Euro area, Japan and USA. Sources: Haver Analytics and author's calculations.

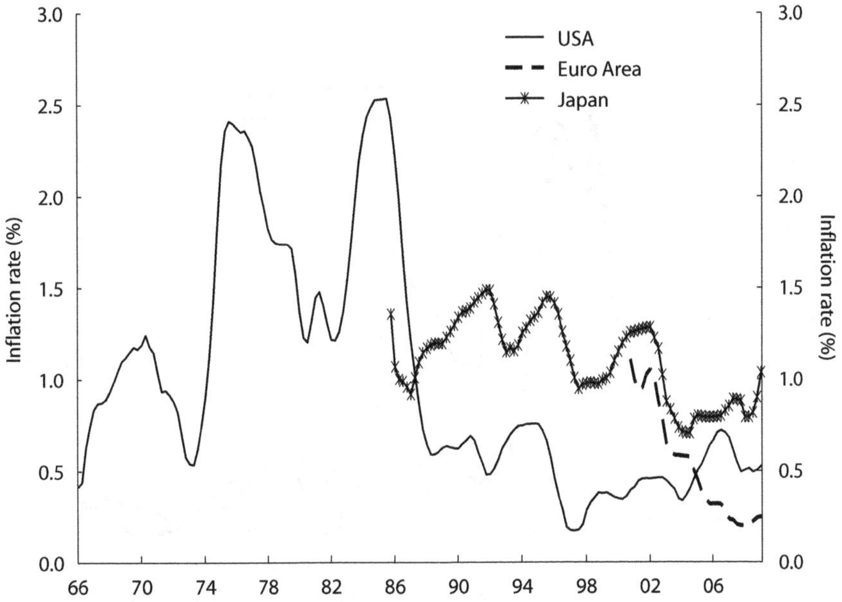

Figure 2.3 Inflation volatility, 1966–2009 (1st quarter), Euro area, Japan and USA. Sources: Haver Analytics and author's calculations.

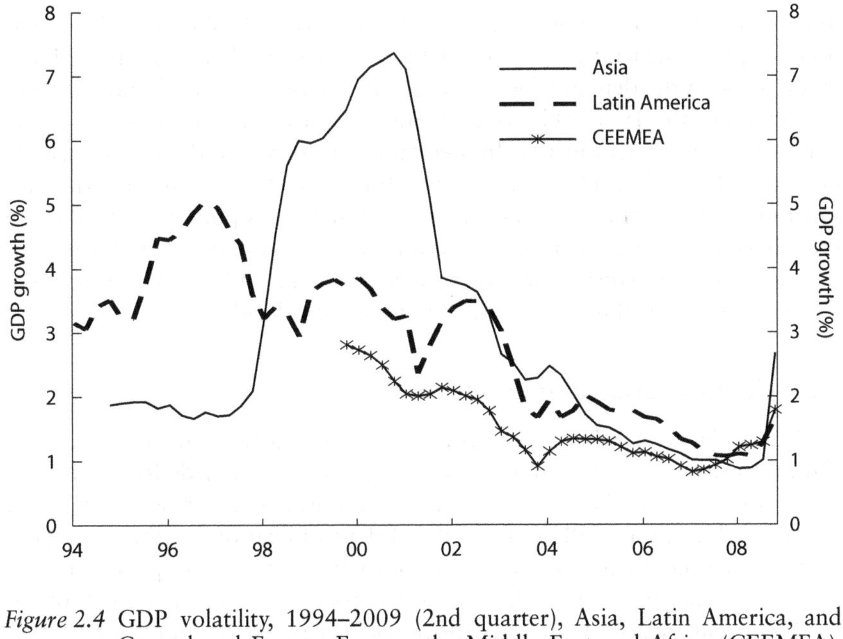

Figure 2.4 GDP volatility, 1994–2009 (2nd quarter), Asia, Latin America, and Central and Eastern Europe, the Middle East and Africa (CEEMEA). Sources: Haver Analytics and author's calculations.

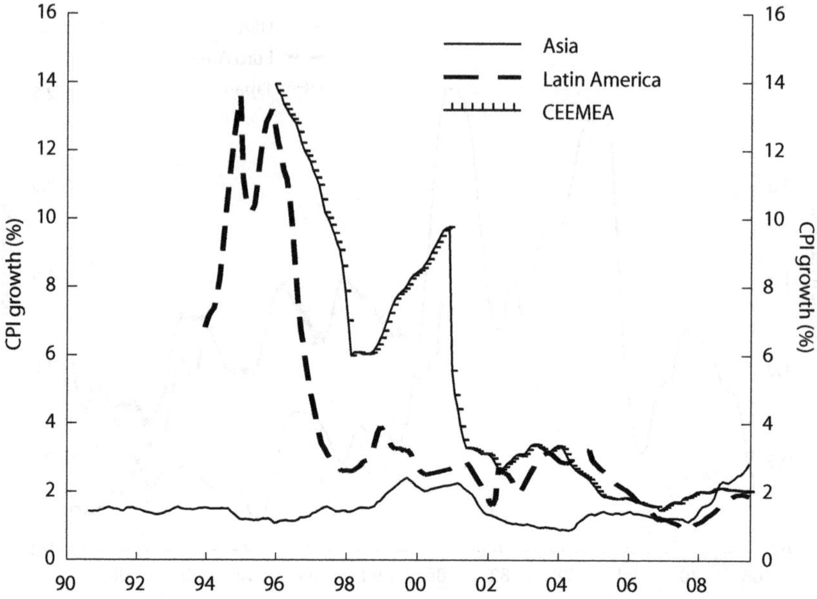

Figure 2.5 CPI volatility, 1991–July 2009, Asia, Latin America, and Central and Eastern Europe, the Middle East and Africa (CEEMEA). Sources: Haver Analytics and author's calculations.

though, over time, one would expect to see a slower *rate* of household formation. People in their fifties are the chief buyers of second homes. This led to a gradual rise in the demand for housing that mirrored the rise in home prices over much of the 1990s (Figure 2.6). Supply constraints on housing, largely due to zoning restrictions that limited land use, also played a role in driving up prices. Cities like Houston, famous for the lack of zoning restrictions, saw much lower home price increases than other metropolitan areas like San Francisco or Boston, where zoning laws are a bigger constraint. Areas with the most rapid expansion of homes were abundant in land (Las Vegas, the Central Valley in California and the west coast of Florida).

Financial innovation and incentives

In the 2000s, the US housing market received a further boost from financial innovation. The combination of easing credit standards for lending to households with higher credit risk and the burgeoning of new-structured credit products, especially collateralized debt obligations (CDOs), created a ready market for an ever larger pool of mortgages. The proportion of the US population owning homes went from 67.4 per cent in 2000 to 69.0 per cent in 2006[11], just as the stock of residential mortgage-backed securities rose from US$3.1 trillion to $6.6 trillion.[12]

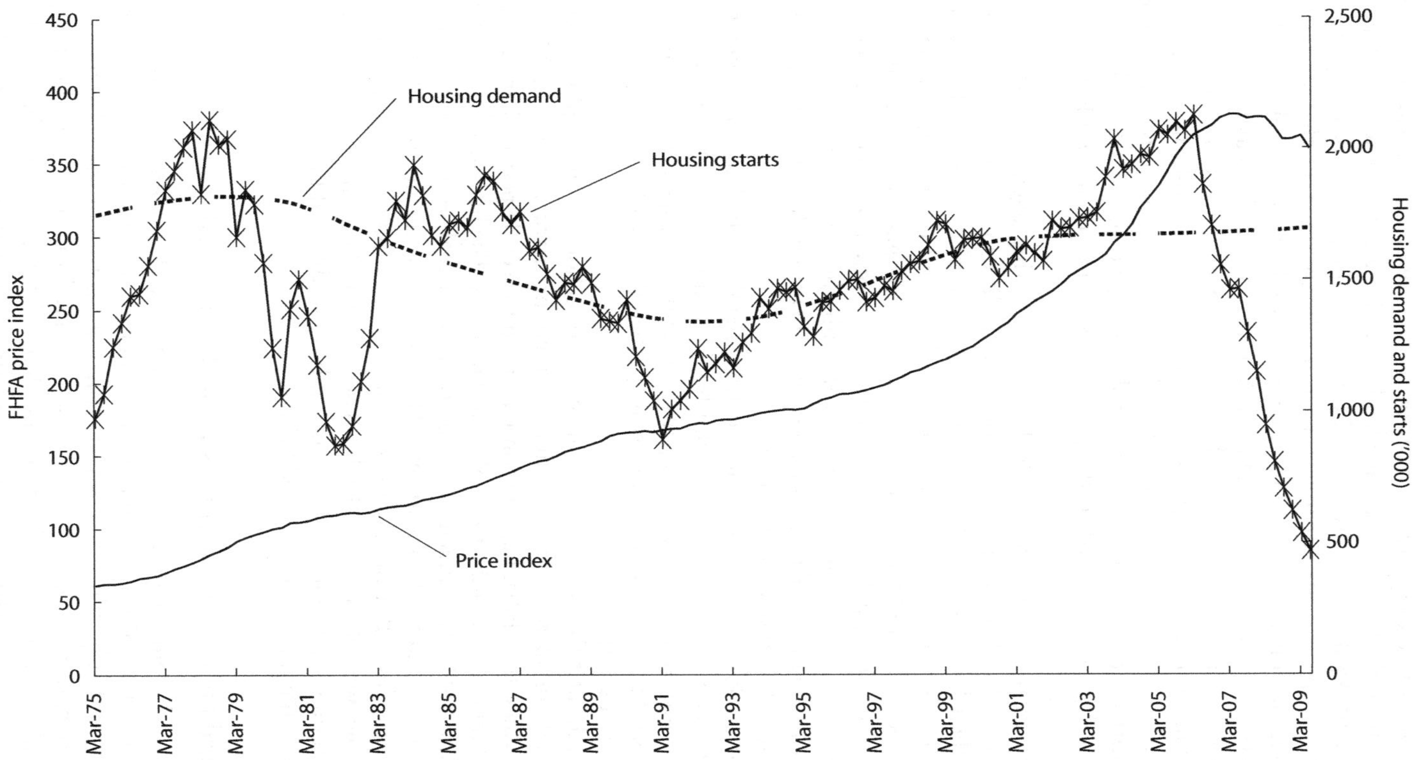

Figure 2.6 US housing prices (Federal Housing Finance Agency (FHFA) price index), and housing demand and starts, 1975 (1st quarter) – 2009 (2nd quarter). Sources: Haver Analytics and author's calculations.

However, these two interacting processes of financial innovation – the expansion of alternative mortgage lending and the development of structured credit products – were pushed too far. CDOs, by breaking up risk, offered the opportunity for investors to hold only the risks they desired. However, meeting the demand for CDOs required, at some level, underlying assets to securitize.[13] Mortgage brokers and banks increasingly eased lending conditions, emboldened by the low macro-economic volatility, the demand for their product and the fact that they would not hold the credit risk for securitized mortgages. Low licensing requirements and high short-term gains also helped push mortgage brokers to originate riskier mortgages, at a cost to the purchasers and to their own long-term viability.

In the meantime, investors relied on credit rating agencies (CRAs) to assess the risks of the increasingly complex credit products they were putting on their books, rather than on their own assessments of risks. The same CRAs were integral to the structuring of CDOs and residential mortgage-backed securities (RMBSs), employed by the originators to evaluate the credit risk of the tranches. However, CRAs were often competing with one another to provide ratings for issuers, with only the winning rating (i.e. the strongest) being paid. This created a conflict between the long-run reputation of the CRA and its short-run gain.

Lulled by low macro-economic volatility, emboldened by low interest rates and lenders that were flush with liquidity, and dismissive of the fundamental uncertainties that accompany any truly new financial innovation, originators, brokers, CRAs and investors pushed the use of structured credit to vertiginous extremes.

Throughout this giddy expansion there are echoes of the explosion of syndicated commercial bank lending to emerging markets in the 1970s, a time in which the global macro-economic need to recycle petrodollars met a financial innovation in the form of loan syndicates. The internet/tech bubble of the late 1990s was much more the result of a real sector innovation – the internet – than a financial one. The accompanying macro imbalance is not so obvious. But the excess to which financial intermediaries pushed the bubble was clear in hindsight. The parallels here are important to understanding what policy reforms might be desirable and their likely effectiveness; something that is treated below.

Structural factors and incentives in the US financial system

When the disconnect between the underlying credit quality of subprime lending and that of the structured credit built on it came to light between February and July 2007, a series of structural factors in the USA and, to a large extent, the global financial system, served to amplify the bursting of the bubble. The work of Adrian and Shin (2008), among others, highlights a number of structural aspects of the current financial system that tend to amplify swings in risk appetite and asset prices. Chief among these are value-at-risk (VAR) risk management, mark-to-market accounting for assets, investment mandates with credit ratings cut-offs and index benchmarking by investors.

VAR risk management as used by major financial institutions is pro-cyclical. The co-variances used in VAR analysis tend to cover a rolling period of recent history. Hence, as booms take hold and volatility subsides, VAR limits on risk-taking gradually loosen. At the top of a bubble, VAR risk limits will be at their easiest. However, as a bust takes hold, the opposite occurs, with shrinking risk limits forcing more selling and increasing volatility, thereby exacerbating the crash.

Mark-to-market accounting for assets has a similar pro-cyclical effect. As booms raise the price of assets, mark-to-market gains bolster earnings and capital, promoting an expansion of intermediaries' balance sheets and stronger asset demand. However, when markets fall, the implied losses engender just the opposite.

Investors whose mandates are guided by credit ratings can also produce herd effects. Since ratings are highly pro-cyclical, upgrades expand during a boom, which increases the demand for newly upgraded assets. However, as a downturn takes hold, downgrades multiply and investors with ratings thresholds are forced to sell.

Finally, benchmarking adds to the pro-cyclical nature of asset markets. Institutional fund managers may chase a rising or falling market out of concern that the tracking risk they run by not doing so is too large, even if their estimates of asset and market values diverge. Institutional, long-only fund investors, who are the primary users of benchmarks, are especially loath to diverge from their benchmark because redemptions can come at any time. Benchmarking therefore leaves the quantum of assets invested largely in the hands of the investors, not the investment managers. With the complexity and opacity of investments rising, it is likely that the ability of investors to gauge risks properly will fall.

Beyond the pro-cyclicality embedded in the industry practices in the US financial market, a shift in the regulatory regime towards a greater reliance on market discipline probably inadvertently abetted the bubble. Market discipline assumes that participants will act on available information to protect their long-run interests. Facing the right set of information and incentives, then, market discipline can supplant regulatory oversight. Subordinated debt, for example, has been held out as a means of disciplining bank owners since it creates a class of lenders who will only suffer from excessive risk taking (they gain a fixed return but suffer conversion to equity if risky bets sour).[14]

However, the effectiveness of market discipline depends both on the quality and interpretation of information. The short-sighted behaviour of mortgage brokers and banks, and the failure of investors to assess diligently the risks they faced from structured products, point to a world in which expectations and/or information undermined the effectiveness of market discipline. Furthermore, financial innovations, or any innovations, by virtue of being innovations, introduce elements of uncertainty that complicate the assessment of risks and, thereby, the imposition of market discipline.

The unwind

When the bubble burst, it set off a negative feedback between losses for financial institutions, contracting credit and leverage, and falling asset prices. Structured credit products concentrated these losses on the books of some major institutions in ways that neither the institutions nor the market had anticipated. This happened largely in two ways. First, off-balance-sheet investment vehicles (structured investment vehicles and conduits) set up by major financial institutions were reabsorbed onto balance sheets of those financial institutions due to the reputation costs were they to fail. Second, a number of banks had begun investing in the senior tranches of structured credit rather than acting solely as brokers, a move of which the market was generally unaware.[15] This exposed the institutions to large credit losses as the value of these tranches plummeted.

Major institutions responded to their new balance-sheet problems by tightening the terms on which they supplied credit to other market participants. This led to a general de-leveraging throughout the financial system, which had a significant impact on a wide range of asset prices. The largest effects were felt in markets that had depended on a high degree of leverage; that is, markets for high-grade assets. The disruptions to markets for high-grade assets and leveraged financing vehicles created new strains on the balance sheets of major institutions, prompting further pressures to reduce leverage.

The complexity and relative opacity of many of the new credit products and financing vehicles exacerbated the market reaction. Some of the structured credit products were so complex that the only institutions capable of assessing their fundamental value were the underwriters and the agencies rating the products. The perception of increased counterparty risk also exacerbated the contraction in market liquidity. This became especially extreme in the aftermath of the failure of Lehman Brothers, when the settlement of billions of dollars of trades and positions became uncertain. Counterparty risk suddenly became an issue for a wide array of financial institutions around the globe.

In a near simultaneous fashion, banks began husbanding liquidity and constraining credit expansion. Asset markets tumbled, not just in the USA, but around the globe, and even in emerging markets that had been relatively protected until then. Global trade plummeted in a fashion worse than that of the 1930s (see Figure 2.1). By the fourth quarter of 2008, GDP growth, measured on a seasonally adjusted quarter-on-quarter basis was negative in all but a handful of countries around the globe. Even in those that maintained positive growth, the deceleration was large (Figure 2.7).

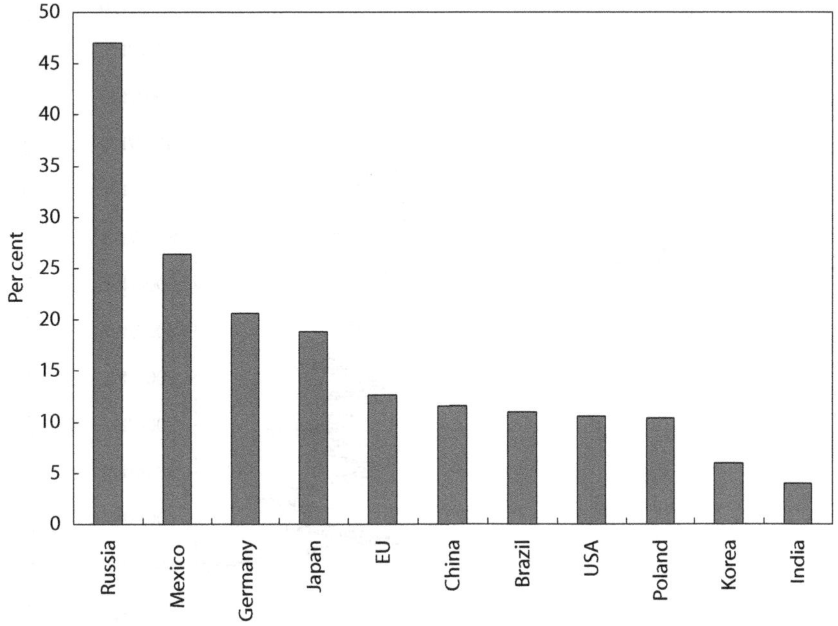

Figure 2.7 Drop in quarterly seasonally adjusted annualized GDP growth from peak to first quarter 2009. Sources: Haver Analytics and author's calculations.

We have already cited the unprecedented flurry of macro and financial policy measures that governments commenced or accelerated in the last quarter of 2008. It is worth noting, however, that the collapse of Lehman Brothers came in the aftermath of easing by the US Federal Reserve and capital-raising by major international banks in the northern spring and summer of 2008. These measures were, nevertheless, not adequate given the tsunami of panic the Lehman's plunge into bankruptcy triggered. The distress was easily evident in measures of liquidity risk, such as the difference between three-month LIBOR[16] rates and overnight interest rate swaps (Figure 2.8). It was in part the failure of the first round of measures to forestall the deepening of the crisis that has heightened the resolve among policy-makers to be very aggressive in combating the collapse in late 2008. Concern to avoid the early withdrawal of stimulus, a contributing factor to the return to recession in 1937 (see Eichengreen and O'Rourke 2009), also informs policy-makers' current focus on tail risks and consistent adherence to the need to maintain accommodative policy.[17]

Balance-sheet problems that were at the core of the system remain. The balance sheets involved are not just those of households burdened with excessive mortgage debt, or of banks lumbered with crippled mortgage securities. Banks that had funded themselves in wholesale markets with short-term money across a variety of countries came under pressure.

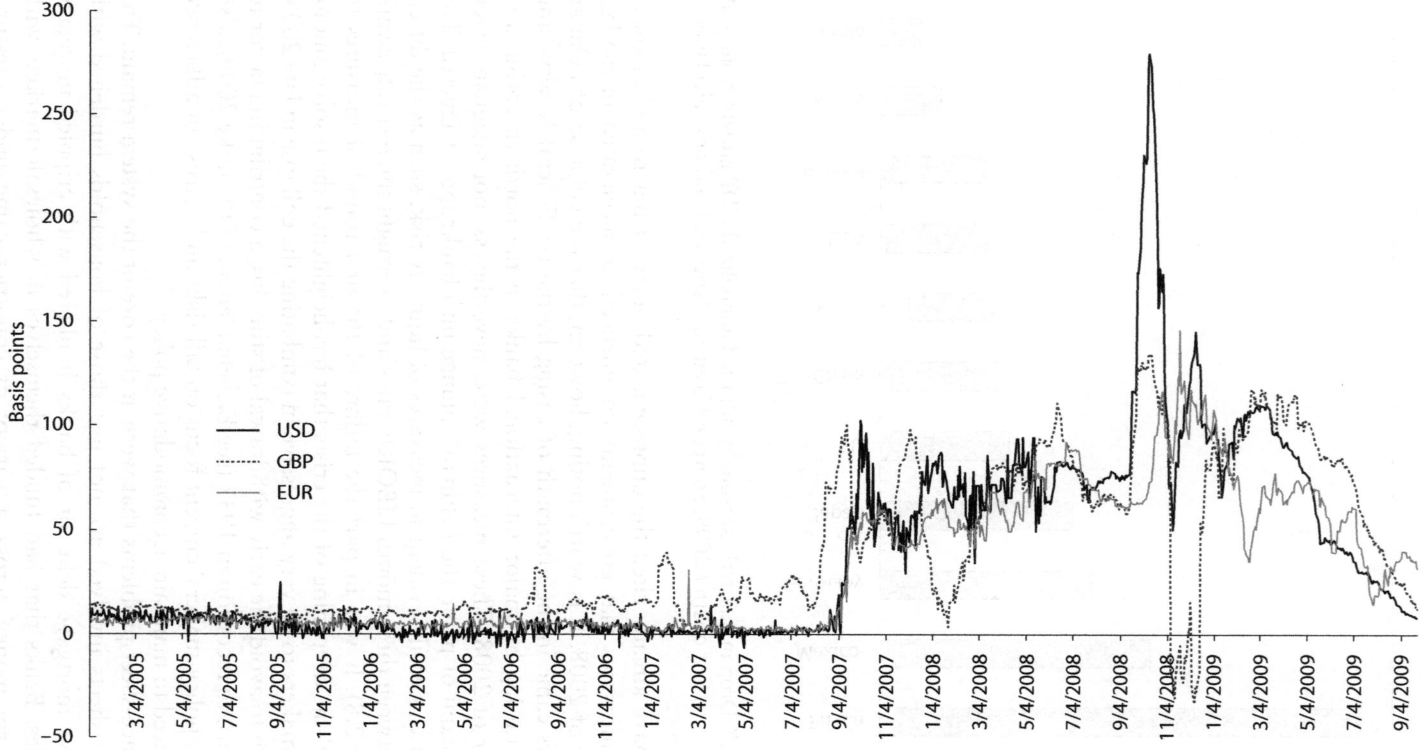

Figure 2.8 Spread between the 3-month London Interbank Offered Rate and overnight interest rate swaps (basis points). Source: Bloomberg.

Government interventions or support were needed in Ireland, Iceland, the UK, Belgium, Russia, Sweden, Indonesia, Korea and Hong Kong. The near collapse of major global financial institutions brought many countries' public balance sheets into play in ways that, while of paramount importance in quelling panic, have raised concerns about medium-term fiscal balance (IMF 2009b).

The extraordinary policy measures in the face of the extraordinary collapse seem to be gaining traction. World industrial production is not continuing down the path followed in the 1930s. Measures of illiquidity in financial markets – the LIBOR–OIS[18] spread, for example – have moved back to far less extreme levels (Figure 2.8). So have the prices for protection of the credit risk of major financial institutions. Many of the world's stock markets are up over 40 per cent in the year through August, while investment-grade and high-yield bond spreads have all narrowed markedly.

In short, we are experiencing a gradual normalization of financial intermediation after a near cataclysmic shock. In the aftermath, the contraction of leverage probably means that financial institutions will play a less important role in standing between savings and investment. The sheer scale of the adjustments will take time as financial market participants find a new equilibrium with a different distribution of assets and liabilities and a different constellation of asset prices. Intermediation is likely to be costlier in future, putting greater pressure on lending rates and tending to curtail investment and growth, unless firms can generate higher returns, or reforms can strengthen the linkages between investment and growth.

PRIORITIES FOR REGULATORY REFORM

With this background on the nature of the current stresses at the core of the global financial system, we now turn to the question of reforms. At the outset, a few points are worth highlighting. Liquidity matters; now more than ever. First, more and more financial intermediation is taking place through markets. This means that the liquidity of those markets is becoming increasingly important to the system overall. Second, the globalization of finance, and with it the increase in the correlation of financial markets, makes disruptions to liquidity a wider problem. Third, banks are special. The institutions that provide credit to other financial institutions play a particular role in the system. Losses on the books of those institutions create specific problems by endangering asset values and the process of financial intermediation and investment globally.

So what should be done in response to this evolving credit crunch so as to create a sounder global financial system and a less volatile global economy? First, we concentrate on some things to avoid, with Hippocrates' maxim[19] firmly in mind. We then turn to some general concepts that should help reduce future risks.

Where feasible, policy-makers should let market discipline work

In the heat of a crisis, it is important to avoid efforts to fix problems that the market itself may already be solving. This is perhaps most applicable to the questions of incentive incompatibilities that are at the heart of many reform agendas (the 2008 Infrastructure Stimulus Fund, for example). The normal process of market discipline is already having a big impact. Most of the institutions responsible for the origination of subprime mortgages have gone out of business. The survivors are likely to have put a much higher premium on the quality of their loans in order to be able to stay in business over time. Here, prudence should add to the stability of the system without the need for proposals that shift risk back to originators. The evidence of incompetence, however, does support adequate licensing to ensure that brokers understand what they are selling. The evidence of fraud argues that anti-fraud laws need to cover new forms of intermediation adequately and to be enforced aggressively.

The issuance of new, structured credit products has collapsed. Looking ahead, market participants have strong incentives to correct the particular institutional failings – such as the lack of transparency in structured credit products or the incentive/information problems associated with the originate-to-distribute model – that were the proximate causes of the turmoil.

Letting markets fix the problems that private actors, once armed with a better understanding of risks, will naturally fix, still leaves an important role for policy-makers, which is to avoid exacerbating panic. Efforts to 'let the market find its level' in an environment of fear and uncertainty make a recipe for an exaggerated collapse of asset prices that risks significant losses for those not directly involved in the initial imprudent behaviour. The risks of systemic collapse and, with it, significant macro-economic distress, can warrant government efforts to mitigate panic.

Some have argued that government efforts to cushion financial collapses – as was done widely across the globe either through direct intervention, guarantees or orchestrated takeovers – generate moral hazard (Buiter 2008a,b). Investors, it is argued, know that they will be 'bailed out' and therefore take more risk than they should. This argument simply implies, however, that there are costs to maintaining financial stability. It is not an argument against intervention, only a plea to temper it with a sense of the overall costs and benefits.

One should not exaggerate the costs of moral hazard. Certainly, shareholders in the major global commercial and investment banks, who have seen the value of their investments shrink as much as 90 per cent, have paid a heavy price, even if they were not wiped out completely. Surely the loss is large enough to have demonstrated the errors in the practices of the banks in the go-go period up to 2007.

The foregoing argument also implies that governments, in good times, need to be circumspect about the support they provide financial institutions.

If the dictates of financial stability demand government intervention in times of crisis, regulatory oversight and fees are also necessary to restrict the probability of crises occurring. In the case of government-sponsored enterprises (GSEs), both the ambiguous nature of the government sponsorship and the weak oversight were problems that could have been avoided. Furthermore, the justification for the existence of the GSEs – deepening US mortgage markets – was clearly outdated. It was an excess of mortgage securitization, not its scarcity, which was at the root of recent traumas.

Others argue that the problem is not so much one of moral hazard, but of principal-agent problems in financial institutions, problems that were exacerbated by the opacity of the new financial instruments (UN 2009). They would argue that, while it was not in the interest of shareholders (principals) to bet the bank on CDOs or other structured credit products, it was in the interests of some individual bankers (agents). Asymmetric information about the risks of the structured credit then allowed individual agents to enrich themselves at the expense of shareholders and, ultimately, taxpayers.

But principal-agent problems and asymmetric information are at the heart of any modern financial system. Eliminating principal-agent problems at their core means aligning agents' incentives with those of owners. In many institutions in the USA, this was done. The much maligned bonus payments, for example, were often done with a preponderance of stock payable over 3–5 years. These structures for bonuses were designed to align the interests of the agents with the principals. The structures were a manifest failure. That failure, however, is more likely to have sprung from the fundamental uncertainty that accompanies dealing in innovative products than from conniving agents. Neither bankers nor shareholders fully understood the risks that they were taking. They could not, because there was no history against which to assess the products.

It is this uncertainty springing from innovation that, beyond incentive structures and inflation asymmetries, creates limits to the effectiveness of market discipline. I now turn specifically to the question of financial market innovation.

Treat financial innovation most cautiously not when it starts, but when it becomes materially important to the financial system

Financial crises are a regularly recurring phenomenon. However, in understanding why they come repeatedly, the unique aspects of these events – the innovations and their associated surprises – are just as important as the similarities.

One of the key issues is how financial markets handle innovation. The recent turmoil was, to a significant degree, the result of two intersecting and self-reinforcing processes of financial innovation – the expansion of mortgage credit and the development of structured credit products – that simply were pushed too far. These processes generated Knightian uncertainty that risk-management systems failed to contain.

Such risks are inherent in any process of financial innovation. One of the important challenges for both the official sector and financial institutions is to better manage the risks of this sort that will inevitably be associated with the next round of financial innovation.

What is particularly difficult is that experience suggests that the big problems do not arise at the early stages of innovation, but rather after financial institutions (and regulators and supervisors) have had some experience with new products and/or markets. Initial success appears to breed complacency that subsequently leads to mistakes. We know from psychology and behavioural finance that people tend to overreact to small amounts of information (Tversky and Kahneman 1974; Barberis *et al.* 1998). This may help to explain how financial innovations that are initially seasonable and successful are often pushed beyond reasonable limits. This general problem is wholly independent of the specifics of the subprime mortgage excesses, CDO opacity, or the failings of the rating agencies. The reform process should tackle this general problem and not focus exclusively on the specific details of the recent troubles.

It would likely be a mistake to conclude that forestalling financial innovation in the wake of the current debacle is prudent, as some emerging market policy-makers have argued (Khor and Kee 2008). Rather, greater caution in the expansion of financial innovation, not in its introduction, would seem warranted. In the specific case of structured credit, the very examples of the failures and excesses in the USA, and the likely market adaptations, provide emerging market financial systems that adopt structured credit with a more robust basis for doing so.

Consider how policies perform over the cycle

When considering changes in financial regulation, particularly changes to capital requirements and mandates for managing liquidity risk, how policies will perform over the entire boom/bust cycle of risk appetite will be important.

Because of the pro-cyclical bias of a number of attributes of the global financial system, it is worth considering ways to make the system less pro-cyclical. It may make sense to reconsider the appropriate accounting treatment for very complex assets that are hard to trade *in extremis*. When risk appetite declines, the market value of such assets is likely to be volatile downward. Rather than marking such assets to market over the cycle, it may make sense to replace market pricing with higher capital charges.

It is also important to note that making the capital system more sensitive to risk can cause problems over boom/bust cycles. Risk-based capital systems may be efficient in a static sense; i.e. they impose higher capital standards for institutions that take on more risk. However, they can exacerbate swings in risk appetite by expanding balance sheet capacity when risks appear low, and reducing it when risk appears to increase.

This raises the obvious question of whether capital adequacy standards should have an explicitly countercyclical element to them. If such an element were generalized, it would be akin in many ways to monetary tightening. However, if that is the case, then perhaps monetary policy itself is a better policy tool, so long as it is wielded with due regard for asset cycles (see later section, 'Macro-prudential regulation is a must …').

Any consideration of major regulatory changes – particularly changes in capital standards and mandates for managing liquidity risk – needs to weigh carefully how policies operate over boom/bust cycles of risk appetite. In particular, the imposition of new, pro-cyclical regulations in the midst of a financial crisis is probably ill-advised. A bleeding car-crash victim with a bad heart must still have his severed arteries repaired before doctors can turn to open-heart surgery!

Encourage the use of exchanges and clearing-houses

The rapid growth of over-the-counter markets of various forms has tended to increase the importance of counterparty risk. Under normal circumstances, this has not been a significant problem. However, when major institutions are at risk, it can become a significant problem, as it was for Bear Stearns and, even more so, after the failure of Lehman Brothers.

Greater uses of exchanges and clearing-houses can mitigate this problem. When financial institutions trade on an exchange with a clearing-house arrangement, their exposure is to the exchange, rather than an individual institution. Many instruments, including standard derivatives contracts, could be traded on such exchanges. Expanding the use of exchanges could materially reduce counterparty risk and shrink the number of institutions that are truly 'systemically' significant. Trading on exchanges also fosters standardization, which, in turn, improves transparency and allows for easier oversight.

Exchanges also make it easier to collect information and monitor systemic risks. This can be especially important in dampening the panic that ensues during a bust, when market participants try to come to grips with the size and extent of the problem. Better aggregate information could also allow for a more cautious appraisal of booms, to gather credibility earlier in a cycle, dampening the ultimate cost.

Greater, more effective, international cooperation in financial regulation is necessary

Unilateral attempts to tighten regulatory standards will be problematic because of the ease with which financial intermediation can shift between jurisdictions. In order to be effective, any significant tightening of regulation and supervision will have to be agreed upon and implemented globally (and, given cyclical issues, probably gradually).

It is worth remembering that the original impetus to the creation of the Basel I capital rules was the perceived need to level the competitive playing field for globally active banks, not to safeguard the system from default.

International coordination of regulatory reforms needs to accommodate the differing institutional capacities of countries

Note that all of the judgements in favour of housing macro-prudential regulation in central banks are conditioned on a general institutional assessment. The particulars of individual countries can differ. This brings up a crucial element of coordinating policy reform: taking account of the institutional capacities and constructs of different countries. The international uniformity of regulations that affect the profitability and risk of financial products presupposes that the regulatory structure will determine profitability and risk. Yet it is obvious that, even with the same rules, elements like oversight and implementation will also matter. In coordinating reforms, then, it is likely better to aim for minimums rather than uniformity and to temper calls for 'international best practice' with an understanding of local capacity.

Within Asia, to the extent that there is greater regional coherence in regulatory capacity and financial structure, it is likely worth tailoring global standards laid out by entities like the Financial Stability Board to such regional realities. This could be done under the direction of an existing central bank grouping such as the Executives' Meeting of East Asia–Pacific Central Banks, augmented by national supervisory authorities outside of Asian central banks, or under the Economic Review and Policy Dialogue that ASEAN+3 has been carrying out.

Monetary policy should take into account the natural boom/bust characteristics of asset markets

Conventional monetary policy can, and in many cases should, be aggressive in responding to the asset market dynamics that characterize the collapse of a credit bubble. If a credit bubble collapses with inflation well-contained, the choices are somewhat easier. In this circumstance, an aggressive response, as was taken across Asia, would seem warranted. However, the sheer instability of financial markets in these circumstances will present special challenges. The collapse of a credit bubble can be thought of as a discrete shift from one asset market equilibrium to another that is likely to have much more adverse consequences for the economy.

Today, the transmission of monetary policy works largely through the prices of long-term financial assets and the process of financial intermediation.

Of course, empirical work has shown that financial asset prices tend to be excessively volatile, probably reflecting fluctuations in risk appetite. The inconvenient truth about modern monetary policy is that it must work with and through the expectations of financial markets – what Keynes trenchantly termed 'animal spirits'.

In order to contain the collapse of a credit bubble with conventional monetary policy tools, central banks may have to send a relatively unequivocal signal that they are prepared to do 'whatever it takes' to offset the deflationary consequences of the fundamental shift in investors' risk preferences. Note that clear, and relatively unequivocal, communication of policy intentions is likely to be critical to the success of policy in this case.

Obviously, if a credit bubble collapses in an environment where inflation risks are *not* well-contained, central banks face a more complicated set of choices. Under these circumstances, central banks may want to take advantage of the deflationary consequences of a collapsing credit bubble – indeed, it may be part of the consequences of past monetary tightening. Again, the non-linear dynamics of asset markets in these circumstances will make it difficult to get just a little bit of opportunistic disinflation. The issue is even more complicated when one realizes that quantitative easing, especially when associated with the purchase of government securities, is designed to generate *expected* future inflation. It is that expectation that reduces ex-ante real interest rates and helps restore aggregate demand. But generating expected future inflation can erode the central bank's credibility in the absence of a strong market consensus that risks are skewed toward deflation in the absence of action.

In these circumstances, central banks will have to consider the risks of alternative policies. The experience of the USA since August 2007 is a cautionary tale in this context. There was nothing preordained about the collapse of Lehman and about the Federal Reserve's extraordinary actions in its aftermath. It is possible that a more aggressive easing of conventional monetary policy could have led to a different set of financial market outcomes that would have meant the Reserve could have avoided the unusual policy decisions that it was forced into in dealing with the market collapse of September 2008. Of course, there is no way to know for sure about this.

Innovations in central bank money market operations have been an important alternative tool for dealing with the stresses associated with the collapse of a credit bubble. To the extent that they can ease financial stress by improving the functioning of markets, they are useful and important tools. However, it would be a mistake to think that they improve the output–inflation trade-off that central banks face. The primary channel for monetary policy's impact on inflation expectations is through the expected path for the economy. It is by no means obvious that aggressive monetary easing through conventional means, which merely offsets the deflationary economic consequences of a collapse in risk appetite, is likely to elevate inflation expectations in a meaningful and lasting way. Similarly, if improved central bank money market operations ease financial pressures, they will have the same inflationary impact as an easing of financial pressures achieved through conventional means.

Macro-prudential regulation is a must, most likely carried out by the central bank

The complications of managing asset bubbles through monetary policy lead to a natural conclusion that macro-prudential instruments should be used to deal with such bubbles. The use of such instruments presupposes that macro-prudential oversight occurs.

In Asia, governments and central banks have a long history of incorporating asset market conditions into the formulation of policy, and of using prudential regulations in the pursuit of macro-economic goals. Even very market-orientated administrations like that of Hong Kong have used instruments like loan-to-value ratios or other specifics of lending conditions to temper house price appreciation. Governments in China, Korea and Taiwan have on various occasions used government pension funds, listing requirements and margin calls to influence stock markets. In this, calls for consideration of the stability of the overall financial system, not simply individual institutions, are preaching to the converted.

There is still the question of where macro-prudential regulation can best be housed. Here I tend to favour, for three reasons, those who support its inclusion under the responsibilities of the central bank. First, central banks in many countries tend to have the deepest technical economic and crisis-management skills and implementation ability. Second, they already have a broad set of information on the macro-economy that, when combined with institution-level prudential data, provides the grist for even macro-prudential oversight. Third, central banks tend to have the institutional authority needed to carry out policies that may be unpopular (as pricking asset bubbles almost universally is).

Some argue that macro-prudential oversight can conflict with inflation control. In my experience it is generally the lack, rather than the presence, of macro-prudential oversight that constrains monetary policy. Central bankers can defer from tightening out of concern that higher interest rates will set off a financial collapse the likelihood of which would be much lower were macro-prudential regulation more strict. Indeed, it is a version of this problem that confronted Thailand and other Asian central banks in 1997 as they battled to hold the line on exchange rates through interest rate increases in the face of weakening financial institutions and crumbling asset markets.

Others argue that macro-prudential regulation or, more precisely, a mandate to provide financial stability, can undermine the independence of the central bank by forcing it into acquiring and absorbing the net losses of weakened financial intermediaries. This, in turn, erodes the central bank's balance sheet and forces a recapitalization that can require, at a minimum, an infusion from the finance ministry and, often, legislative approval. This was again a situation that affected central banks in Asia – in particular the Philippines and Indonesia.

The argument seems flawed on two fronts. First, it misses the point that one needs to make a trade-off between the efficacy and costs of identifying and dealing with an asset bubble and its aftermath. Housing responsibility for systemic financial stability in an institution that is less effective than the central bank in identifying instability may generate a false economy. Second, central bank independence is always politically constrained. A central bank that is empowered to protect financial stability, but which does it so poorly as to bankrupt itself, may well be an institution in need of reform.

The debate over macro-prudential regulation and where it should be housed does, however, highlight the need for effective structures for oversight and for resolution of failing institutions. It also brings into focus the question of institutions that are too big or too connected to fail, since these are often the source of major costs for central banks or other government entities empowered to resolve failing banks. One lesson of the latest crisis is that bank size in relation to government fiscal resources is a crucial element that can feed panic. The complications of handling the banking crisis in Iceland stemmed in no small part from the size of Icelandic banks relative to the Icelandic Government's balance sheet. Here, calls for higher capital charges and more stringent liquidity standards to reflect the implicit government subsidy seem sensible.[20] Such measures will naturally tend to limit the size of institutions by reducing the profitability of scale.

Institutions that are too big or too complicated to fail are also often active internationally or regionally. Hence, their presence is another impetus to coordinated and comprehensive global and regional regulation.

NOTES

1 Managing Director, Global Macro Research, Drawbridge Liquid Markets, Fortress Investment Group, 20 McCallum Street, #19-01, Singapore, 069046, Singapore; <dhanna@fortress.com>.
2 For a more complete rundown of public support for financial systems around the globe see the BIS (2009).
3 See FSB (2008, 2009), President's Working Group on Financial Markets (2008) or the G30 (2008) for three reform agendas. An analysis of the financial market breakdown and an agenda for reform can also be found in IMF (2008a, 2009a), G20 (2009) and UN (2009). A specific reform agenda for Asia is contained in ADB (2009).
4 In Central Europe, for example, fiscal polices were more likely to tighten due to high initial fiscal deficits and debt levels that compromised the ability to run higher current deficits without engendering rising domestic interest rates or destabilizing the exchange rate. See Chopra (2009) and IIF (2009) for a discussion of the crisis and policy response in Central Europe and the Baltics.
5 On this see the comments of Rogoff (2009), or the paper on fiscal policy by Auerbach and Gale (2009) presented at the same conference.
6 This analysis draws on work in Alexander and Hanna (2009).

7 On the rise in global saving, see Bernanke (2005).
8 Lower nominal interest rates also contributed to increased demand for commodities. Emerging market countries' efforts to forestall appreciation, which contributed to the rise in global savings and lower interest rates, also implied that emerging market demand was stronger than it otherwise would have been. Both of these factors then contributed to higher rates of inflation in 2008 and the ugly macro-economic trade-off between growth and inflation many central banks faced as the crisis began to broaden during the late summer of 2008.
9 Returns on emerging market bonds were double digit from 2004–07 and while being sold off in 2008 were still outperforming US investment grade bonds. See Citigroup (2008b). Local market returns in emerging markets have been higher still in many cases, supported by currency appreciation.
10 The performance of emerging markets has generated an ongoing debate about whether and to what extent emerging markets have decoupled from developed markets. Those arguing that decoupling, in the sense of asynchronous GDP growth, is incorrect include Citigroup (2008a) and Rose (2009). Proponents of decoupling include Anderson (2009) and IMF (2008b).
11 See US Census Bureau, *Housing Vacancies and Homeownership*, available at http://www.census.gov/housing/hvs/, accessed 4 October 2012.
12 See Federal Reserve, *Federal Reserve Bulletin*, various issues available at http://www.federalreserve.gov/econresdata/releases/mortoutstand/current.htm, accessed 4 October 2012.
13 One should not stretch this point too far. As the expansion of structured credit gathered steam, CDOs built on CDOs (CDOs squared and CDOs cubed) flourished.
14 See, for example, Benink and Calomiris (1999).
15 Rather than originate to distribute, some banks were originating and holding. They held largely the 'super senior' tranches of CDOs, believing that, in a market 'searching for yield', the price at which these tranches could be sold was too low in relation to the risk embodied in them. That judgement proved disastrous. The behaviour, however, should give pause to those that argue for banks to hold a portion of all securitized obligations they originate. While this will align the banks' incentives to monitor the credits with those of other investors, it will not save either the bank or investors from starry-eyed assessments of credit risk!
16 London Interbank Offered Rate.
17 The commitment to accommodative policy is apparent in the statements from central bankers at the Kansas City Fed Meeting at Jackson Hole in August 2009, available at http://www.kc.frb.org/home/subwebnav.cfm?level=3&theID=11163&SubWeb=10660.
18 Overnight indexed swap [interest rate].
19 'Above all else, do no harm'.
20 Such provisions are included in the US Treasury's draft law on financial sector reform (US Department of the Treasury 2009).

REFERENCES

ADB (Asian Development Bank) (2009) *Asia Economic Monitor*, July, Office of Regional Economic Integration, available at http://www.aric.adb.org/asia-economic-monitor/.

Adrian, Tobias and Hyun Song Shin (2008) 'Liquidity and leverage', *Federal Reserve Bank of New York Staff Report*, No. 328.

Alexander, Lewis and Don Hanna (2009) 'The US financial market distress: policy lessons for emerging markets', *Asian Economic Papers*, 8(1): 46–62.

Anderson, Jonathan (2009) *Emerging Economic Perspectives: the Real Decoupling*, UBS Investment Research, Global Economic Research, Hong Kong, 17 August 2009.

Auerbach, Alan J. and William G. Gale (2009) 'Activist fiscal policy to stabilize economic activity', paper presented at a conference on *Financial Stability and Macro-economic Policy* sponsored by the Federal Reserve Bank of Kansas City, Jackson Hole, Wyoming, 20–22 August 2009.

Barberis, Nicholas, Andrei Shleifer and Robert Vishny (1998) 'A model of investor sentiment', *Journal of Financial Economics,* 49(1998): 307–343, available at http://www.lingnan.org/cferm/files/amodelofinvestorsentiment.pdf.

Benink, Harald and Charles Calomiris (1999) 'Pushing for a sub debt requirement', *The Banker*, 17–18 September.

Bernanke, Ben (2005) 'The global saving glut and the U.S. current account deficit', speech at the *Sandridge Lecture*, Virginia Association of Economics, 10 March 2005, Richmond, VA, available at http://www.federalreserve.gov/boarddocs/speeches/2005/200503102/default.htm.

BIS (Bank for International Settlements) (2009) *Annual Report 2009*, available at http://www.bis.org/publ/arpdf/ar2009e.htm.

Buiter, Willem (2008a) 'Moral hazard, here we come!', *Maverecon Blog*, 25 March 2008, available at http://blogs.ft.com/maverecon/2008/03/moral-hazard-here-we-come/.

—— (2008b) 'There is never a right time to tackle moral hazard ...', *Maverecon Blog*, 19 July 2008, available at http://blogs.ft.com/maverecon/2008/07/there-is-never-a-right-time-to-tackle-moral-hazard/.

Chopra, Ajay (2009) 'The global crisis and emerging Europe: why the script differs from the Asian crisis', 19 August, blog entry, available at http://blog-imfdirect.imf.org/2009/08/19/the-global-crisis-and-emerging-europe-why-the-script-differs-from-the-asian-crisis/.

Citigroup (2008a) *Prospects for Emerging Markets,* unpublished manuscript, December 2008, New York: Citigroup.

—— (2008b) *Global Economic Outlook and Strategy*, December, New York: Citigroup available at http://www.citi.com/slovakia/homepage/slovak/docs/20081023ea.pdf.

Eichengreen, Barry and Kevin H. O'Rourke (2009) 'A tale of two depressions', 1 September 2009, blog entry, available at http://www.voxeu.org/index.php?q=node/3421.

FSB (Financial Stability Board) (2008) *Report of the Financial Stability Forum on Enhancing Market and Institutional Resilience*, 7 April 2008, available at http://www.financialstabilityboard.org/publications/r_0804.pdf.

—— (2009) *Progress since the Pittsburgh Summit in Implementing the G20 Recommendations for Strengthening Financial Stability, Report of the Financial Stability Board to G20 Finance Ministers and Governors,* 7 November, available at http://www.financialstabilityboard.org/publications/r_091107a.pdf.

G20 (Group of Twenty) (2009) *London Summit – Leaders' Statement*, 2 April 2009, available at http://www.wcoomd.org/files/1.%20Public%20files/PDFandDocuments/Highlights/G20_Final_London_Communique.pdf.

G30 (Group of Thirty) (2008) *The Structure of Financial Supervision: Approaches and Challenges in a Global Marketplace*, Washington, DC: Group of Thirty.
IIF (Institute for International Finance) (2009) *Regional Overview: Emerging Europe*, May, available at http://www.iif.com/emr/article+254.php.
IMF (International Monetary Fund) (2008a) *Global Financial Stability Report*, October, Washington, DC: IMF, available at http://www.imf.org/external/pubs/cat/longres.cfm?sk=22027.0.
—— (2008b) *World Economic Outlook: Financial Stress, Downturns and Recoveries*, October, Washington, DC: IMF, available at http://www.imf.org/external/pubs/ft/weo/2008/02/.
—— (2009a) *Global Financial Stability Report*, April 2009, Washington, DC: IMF, available at http://www.imf.org/external/pubs/ft/gfsr/2009/01/.
—— (2009b) *The State of Public Finances: Outlook and Medium-Term Policies After the 2008 Crisis*, 6 March 2009, Washington, DC: IMF, available at http://www.imf.org/external/np/pp/eng/2009/030609.pdf.
Khor, Hoe Ee and Kee Rui Xiong (2008) 'Asia: a perspective on the sub-prime crisis', *Finance & Development*, 45(2) (June), available at http://www.imf.org/external/pubs/ft/fandd/2008/06/khor.htm.
OECD (Organisation for Economic Co-operation and Development (2009) *OECD Economic Outlook 85*, June, available at http://www.oecd.org/dataoecd/36/57/43117724.pdf.
President's Working Group on Financial Markets (2008) *Policy Statement on Financial Market Developments*, March, available at http://www.treasury.gov.
Rogoff, Kenneth (2009) 'Comments on "The 'surprising' origin and nature of financial crises: a macroeconomic policy proposal"', by Ricardo J. Caballero and Pablo Kurlat', presented at a conference on *Financial Stability and Macroeconomic Policy* sponsored by the Federal Reserve Bank of Kansas City, Jackson Hole, Wyoming, 20–22 August 2009, available at http://www.frbkc.org/publicat/sympos/2009/papers/rogoff.08.23.09.pdf.
Rose, Andrew K. (2009) 'Business cycles become less synchronised over time: debunking "decoupling"', 1 August 2009, blog entry available at http://www.voxeu.org/index.php?q=node/3829.
Tversky, Amos and Daniel Kahneman (1974) 'Judgment under uncertainty: heuristics and biases', *Science*, 185, 1124-1131, available at http://www.hss.caltech.edu/~camerer/Ec101/JudgementUncertainty.pdf.
UN (United Nations) (2009) *Report of the Commission of Experts of the President of the United Nations General Assembly on Reforms of the International Monetary and Financial System*, 21 September 2009, New York: UN, available at http://www.un.org/ga/econcrisissummit/docs/FinalReport_CoE.pdf.
US Department of the Treasury (2009) *Financial Regulatory Reform, a New Foundation: Rebuilding Financial Supervision and Regulation*, Washington, DC: US Treasury, available at http://www.financialstability.gov/docs/regs/FinalReport_web.pdf.

3 International division of labour and global imbalances

Jianwei Xu and Yang Yao[1]

INTRODUCTION

The current financial crisis has its roots in global imbalances, but the causes of global imbalances are still a mystery and their linkage with the crisis unclear. Although there were discussions before the crisis, the current consensus seems to ubiquitously suggest that the imbalances were caused by the deficit countries' excessive consumption and the surplus countries' excessive savings. Both academics and policy-makers are quickly gathering together to propose and plan for the 'right' cures; that is, to increase consumption in the surplus countries and to increase savings in the deficit countries. Indeed, some encouraging signs have emerged from the deficit countries; for instance, domestic savings in the USA have increased since the crisis broke out. Taking this as evidence for a turning point for the USA, which is the largest deficit country to shift away from excessive consumption, many people begin to doubt whether there is a chance of sustaining the export-led growth model of the surplus countries. After all, if Americans do not want to consume too much, where will the surplus countries, especially China and Japan, sell their products?

The central idea of this chapter is that the real cause of global imbalances rests in the long-term economic factors that have shaped the new international division of labour that started immediately after the Second World War and accelerated after the fall of the Berlin Wall. Even a casual glance at the countries on both sides of the imbalance reveals a pattern in this new wave of division of labour. On the deficit side, we have the USA, UK and Australia, all of which have adopted the Anglo-Celtic model of capitalism that places finance in the centre of the economy. The surplus side is more diverse, but we can still see a pattern. There are three groups of countries: the old manufacturing giants, namely Germany and Japan; the newly emerged 'world factories', especially China and Brazil; and the oil exporters. Because this pattern of division of labour is determined by slowly changing factors that shape countries' comparative advantages, we should not expect that the imbalances will disappear quickly after the crisis has passed. Most of the measures taken by either the international organizations or individual countries, because they are based on wrong or partial understanding of the causes of the imbalances, are not likely to produce long-lasting results. America's rising saving rates will be temporary, and the surplus countries will continue on the export-led growth model, regardless of whether or not they like it.

The chapter is organized as follows. In the next section we discuss how global imbalances are linked with countries' comparative advantages and provide evidence for it using data of 40 countries for the period 1991–2006. We also discuss how global imbalances could lead to financial crisis. In the third section, we present proposals for the international community to correct global imbalances and for the Chinese Government to correct China's external imbalances. We conclude the chapter by recapitulating several important implications emerging from it.

INTERNATIONAL DIVISION OF LABOUR AND GLOBAL IMBALANCES

The story

There are four existing explanations for global imbalances. The first proposes that government deficits in some countries are the causes for those countries' current account deficits. However, empirical studies do not find strong evidence for this explanation (e.g. Backus *et al.* 2005). The second explanation puts the view that manipulation of the exchange rates by some countries is the cause for global imbalances. For example, undervaluation of a country's currency may lead to current account surpluses in that country. However, this may not be a major cause for global imbalances even if it does have an effect. Germany and Japan have a floating system but both countries have very large surpluses. The third explanation links global imbalances to the variable rates of economic growth and different paces of demographic transition in the world (Henriksen 2005). Countries with higher rates of economic growth have more optimistic expectations for the future and thus consume more today. Additionally, countries with a lower age-dependency ratio tend to have a relatively large supply of labour and consume less. Proponents of the last explanation realize the importance of financial sector variability in the world. Willen (2004) shows in a theoretical model that a country with a less complete financial sector will save more. Mendoza *et al.* (2009) also note the importance of the heterogeneous development of the financial sector. They show in their theoretical model that global financial integration induces countries with more advanced financial sectors to reduce domestic savings and increase international borrowings. An important corollary of their model is that countries with strong financial sectors gain from global imbalances whereas countries with weak financial sectors lose. However, Chinn and Ito (2006) find in a cross-country panel study that the strength of the financial sector has explanatory power for developed countries only and not for underdeveloped countries.

Our explanation is an extension of that of Mendoza *et al.* (2009). Instead of focusing on the single factor of financial development, we centre on the combined comparative advantage of finance and manufacturing. In the single-factor model of Mendoza *et al.*, countries with weak financial sectors lose in global financial integration. In our framework of comparative advantage, all countries gain.

The Anglo-Celtic model of capitalism strongly favours the financial sector. The Harvard economist Andrei Shleifer and his co-authors (La Porta *et al.* 1998) have found strong evidence that the common-law countries (or the Anglo–Celtic countries) have better developed capital markets than do countries with other legal origins. Whether legal origins provide the right explanation is still debatable, but it is clear that the USA and UK are more dependent on the capital market to raise capital, and their banking sectors are much more dynamic, than in those countries such as Germany, Japan and France. That is, the Anglo–Celtic countries have a comparative advantage in finance and, for that reason, they naturally specialize in finance. On the other hand, their manufacturing sectors have experienced deep 'hollowing out'.

Germany and Japan, the old manufacturing giants, continue to have a comparative advantage in manufacturing, because they have accumulated strong manufacturing capacities in both physical and human capital. This has much to do with the history they have inherited from the first wave of division of labour. At that time, their roles were already cemented in manufacturing goods for the consumption in the USA. Their current strengths lie in sophisticated consumer products and intermediate inputs.

The newly emerged manufacturers like China export mainly low-end consumer products. Their comparative advantage lies in their relatively cheap but educated labour force. Joining in the world system helps those countries to tap into the potentials of their abundant labour force. In the case of China, accession to the World Trade Organization in 2001 has made a big difference. Between 2001 and 2007, China's exports grew by 28 per cent per annum, compared with 15 per cent in the 1990s. Not surprisingly, China's burgeoning foreign-exchange reserves also began to build up over that period. Comparing developments in India with those in China often leaves people puzzled. India has similar demographics to China, but India's current account registers deficits. This may be caused by India's reluctant embrace of globalization. India has more restrictive labour market regulations than China, and Indian intellectuals are more critical of globalization than their Chinese counterparts. Indeed, if we trace both countries' trade dependency ratios (that is, the ratio of trade to gross domestic product (GDP)) against the years when their respective reforms began in 2003, we find that India has closely followed China's trajectory of opening to international trade.

The oil exporters have traditionally provided oil dollars to the United States. These countries have small manufacturing sectors, but their oil income is more than enough for them to import consumer goods. What is surprising is that in the past decade Russia has joined the ranks of these countries. Being a traditionally strong manufacturer has not immunized

Russia from catching the Dutch disease. Its economy has been singularized and its inflation rate has seldom fallen to single digits.

In summary, this round of globalization has a strong tendency to specialize countries in specific economic activities in which individual countries enjoy a comparative advantage. This is evident in Figures 3.1 and 3.2. Figure 3.1 shows the amounts of stock market transactions divided by GDP in several major countries, and Figure 3.2 the shares of manufacturing in GDP in those countries. Clearly, the USA and UK have larger capital markets and smaller manufacturing sectors, and China, Germany, Japan and Russia have smaller capital markets and larger manufacturing sectors.

Why then does specialization lead to imbalance of payments, with some countries having net surpluses and others having net deficits? Economic theory predicts that, normally, a surplus country would enjoy an increase of wealth, so it would import more and its current account would end up with being roughly balanced again. Economic theory also predicts that a deficit country would usually face high interest rates and would cut borrowings and rebalance its current account. In reality, however, we have observed persistent imbalance on both sides.

That this is so, has much to do with the pattern of specialization we've just seen. It is not a coincidence that none of the surplus countries has a highly developed financial market. They specialize in either manufacturing or oil exporting. That is why the 'manufacturing' of finance is concentrated in New York and London. Like other activities, finance also finds its way to concentrate in places where it is done in the most efficient way. As a result, hard-earned money flows from the surplus countries to the deficit countries;

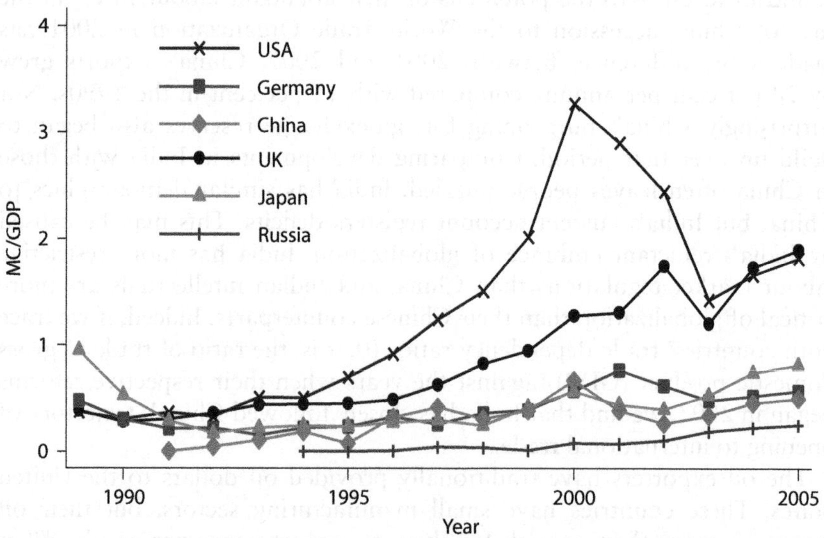

Figure 3.1 The development of stock markets (market capitalization/GDP) in various countries.

that is, the financial markets in the surplus countries are incapable of channelling savings earned on exports to domestic investment or consumption. This observation has an ironic implication for the current debate, which often lays blames on the American financial market for causing the financial crisis. While the American financial market may be too fluid, the financial markets in the surplus countries are too static.

However, there is still one question left unanswered: how can current account deficits be sustained in a deficit country? Put in another way, how can a country consume more than it produces for a long period without violating its inter-temporal budget constraint? This is the so-called 'dark substances' question. Here we would like to propose one kind of 'dark substance' – the wealth effect of consumption caused by optimistic expectations for future income growth. Although the liquidities flowing to the deficit countries are not real wealth, they do have the effect of increasing those countries' real wealth by suppressing the interest rates. Both the real economy and the prices of financial assets grow faster under cheaper credits. As a result, people consume more than they produce.

Empirical evidence

In this section, we present evidence for our theory. We collect data from 40 major countries for the period 1990–2006 and study how the comparative advantage of finance over manufacturing affects a country's current account surplus (deficit). Our data sources include the Penn World Table,

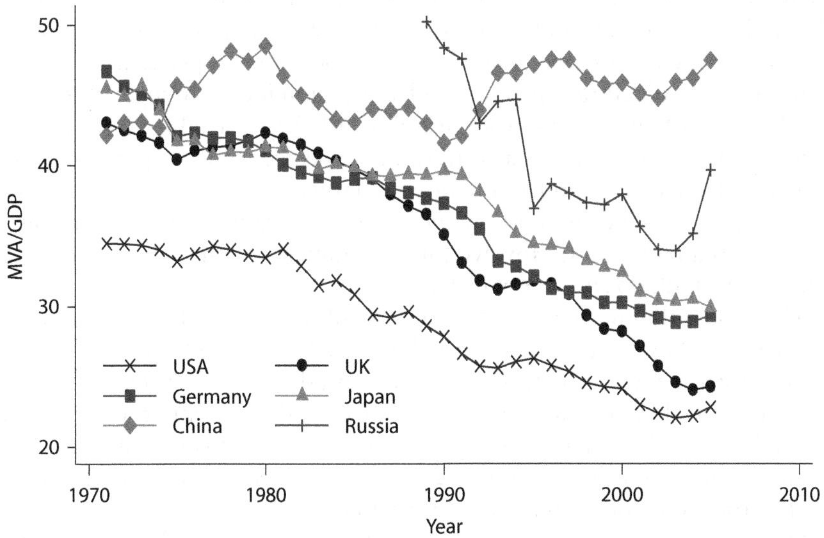

Figure 3.2 The development of the manufacturing sector (manufacturing value-added/GDP) in various countries.

World Bank Development Indicators, International Financial Statistics, and Beck (2006). One of our innovations is to create an index measuring the relative strength of finance over manufacturing in a specific country:

$$CAI = \frac{\text{capitalization of the capital market}}{\text{value-added of manufacturing}}$$

Here the capitalization includes the values of stocks, bonds and debts. We have data for comparative advantage index (*CAI*) for each country in each year, from which we estimate the following fixed-effect (FE) panel model:

$$Current_{it} = \alpha + \beta \ln CAI_{it} + \delta X_{it} + f_i + f_t + u_{it}. \quad (1)$$

In the model, $Current_{it}$ is the ratio of country *i*'s current account surplus to its GDP in year *t*; CAI_{it} is its comparative advantage index in that year; X_{it} is a set of control variables; f_i and f_t are country and year fixed effects, respectively; and u_{it} is an i.i.d. (independent identically distributed) error term. In X_{it} we have included variables to account for the predictions of other theories, including the degree of currency undervaluation, the rate of GDP growth and the age-dependency ratio. The degree of currency undervaluation comes from Rodrik (2008).

Table 3.1 presents the results of several regressions based on model (1). In FE_1 we include ln*CAI* as the sole explanatory variable. The result shows that doubling a country's comparative advantage of finance over manufacturing will lead to an increase of 3.3 times in the share of current account deficit in a country's GDP. This is a very significant effect, but is smaller than that which has been observed in the USA. Between 1991 and 2001, its *CAI* index increased from 8 to 12, or by 50 per cent, but its current account deficit increased from 1 per cent of GDP to more than 3 per cent.

In FE_2 we added the currency undervaluation index (in logarithm), and in FE_3 the other two control variables. All three variables have significant estimates, all of which also have the expected signs. In particular, the estimates for currency undervaluation are large. If undervaluation increases by 100 per cent, the share of current account surpluses in GDP increases by more than 11 times. However, most countries, if they overvalue their currencies at all, do so by very little.

The last column presents the results of the generalized method of moments (GMM) estimation with the lagged dependent variable added. Except for the GDP growth rate, the magnitudes of the estimates have all dropped, but they remain significant. However, the estimate for the lagged dependent variable is large; by its value, the long-run effect of each variable should be increased by a factor of 2.5. This will basically raise the effect of *CAI* to the levels found in the FE estimations.

Strictly speaking, our definition of *CAI* does not reflect the comparative advantage between countries, because it is defined for only one country. To correct it, we define the following index, using the USA as a reference:

$$\widehat{CAI}_{it} = \frac{CA_{it}}{CA_{US,t}} \tag{2}$$

It measures country *i*'s comparative advantage of finance over manufacturing with respect to the USA. We then investigate how this measure affects a country's trade surplus with the USA. The specification is still the one defined in Model (1). Now the dependent variable is country *i*'s trade surplus with the USA divided by its own GDP; CAI_{it} is replaced by $\widehat{CAI}_{it}$ (still in logarithm). In addition, the currency undervaluation index is replaced by a country's real exchange rate (RER) with the US dollar (direct price) because the index does not measure bilateral undervaluation well. The other two variables are redefined as relative values with respect to the USA. The results of three regressions are shown in Table 3.2.

The first two regressions are standard FE estimations, one with only the comparative advantage index, the other with RER added. The last regression adds other control variables and is estimated by GMM. Most of the results are qualitatively the same as those shown in Table 3.1, although the GMM regression does not provide a significant result for $\widehat{CAI}_{it}$. The GMM does not provide stable results when the size of cross-sectional units is small. Our case falls in this category because we have data for only 39 countries.

Table 3.1 Fixed-effect (FE) panel estimations based on model (1)

	FE_1	*FE_2*	*FE_3*	*GMM*
Logarithm of *CAI*	–3.30***	–2.99***	–2.95***	–1.23***
	(–0.52)	(0.48)	(0.47)	(0.34)
Logarithm of currency undervaluation index		11.43***	11.38***	6.64***
		(1.09)	(1.06)	(0.77)
Growth rate of real per-capita GDP(%)			–0.17***	–0.35***
			(0.04)	(0.03)
Age-dependency ratio (%)			–0.17***	–0.08*
			(0.06)	(0.05)
Lagged dependent variable				0.61***
				(0.03)
Country dummies	Yes	Yes	Yes	Yes
Year dummies	Yes	Yes	Yes	Yes
Sample size	556	499	499	442
R^2	0.18	0.35	0.39	

Notes
GMM = generalized method of moments.
The dependent variable is the share of current account surplus in GDP.
Currency undervaluation index takes values in [–4, 5]. Positive values indicate undervaluation, and negative values overvaluation.
*, ** and *** indicate significance at the 10%, 5% and 1% significance levels, respectively.

Table 3.2 Finance–manufacturing comparative advantage and a country's trade surplus with the USA

	FE_1	*FE_2*	*GMM*
Logarithm of $\widehat{CAI}_{it}$	–1.62***	–1.74***	–0.28
	(0.23)	(0.21)	(0.21)
Logarithm of RER		0.06	–0.10
		(0.06)	(0.07)
Per-capita GDP growth rate relative to the USA		–0.03	–0.01***
		(0.02)	(0.10)
Age-dependency ratio relative to the USA		–0.30***	–0.10***
		(0.03)	(0.03)
Lagged dependent variable			0.68***
			(0.04)
Country dummies	Yes	Yes	
Year dummies	Yes	Yes	
Sample size	567	508	
R^2	0.26	0.41	

Notes
The dependent variable is a country's share of trade surplus with the USA in its own GDP.
*, **, and *** indicate significance at the 10%, 5% and 1% significance levels, respectively.

Using the results of the GMM regression, we assess the relative strengths of different factors in contributing to China's trade surplus with the USA between 2001 and 2004. The results, presented in Table 3.3, are very illuminating. First, 40–53 per cent of China's trade surplus with the USA can be attributed to its comparative disadvantage of finance over manufacturing (or comparative advantage of manufacturing over finance) relative to the United States. Second, another 22–24 per cent of the surplus can be explained by China's advantage of lower dependant burdens relative to the USA. Third, the contribution of the RER has never been larger than 2 per cent, and the contribution of per-capita GDP growth is also small. In summary, about two-thirds of China's trade surplus with the USA can be explained by the two long-term factors defining the two countries' finance–manufacturing comparative advantages and demographics. This conclusion has major implications for policies aiming at reducing global imbalances and China's trade surplus with the USA.

Global imbalances and the financial crisis

The last two subsections show how global imbalances come into place. However, if the financial markets in the deficit countries, particularly the USA and UK, could properly digest the 'excessive' supply of money from the surplus countries, then imbalance would not have mattered. It might even have disappeared. In a frictionless world, i.e. a world free of cross-border restrictions and endowed with strong legal protections and able actors who have all the relevant information to make the right decisions, we should have

Table 3.3 Factor contributions to China's trade surplus with the USA, 2001–04

Factor	*2001*	*2002*	*2003*	*2004*
Finance–manufacturing comparative advantage (%)	53.26	47.70	44.53	41.17
RER (%)	1.88	1.69	1.59	1.42
Per-capita GDP growth rate (%)	−3.33	−3.05	−2.05	−1.25
Age-dependency ratio (%)	22.95	23.07	24.33	24.41
Unexplained factors (%)	25.24	30.59	31.60	34.25

Note
The estimates of FE_2 in Table 3.2 are applied in making the calculations.

seen the banks in Wall Street open subsidiaries in Germany, Japan, China and Russia, so those countries would not need to export their hard-earned surpluses. Of course, the world is full of frictions so we end up with the imbalance. Nevertheless, imbalances did not necessarily lead to the financial crisis. If the American financial market had not been overly concentrated in the housing and commodity markets, there would have been no asset bubbles and no crisis. There seem to be numerous opportunities for high-return investments in other parts of the world. For example, investing in infrastructure in Africa and India should be profitable in view of the low quality of infrastructure in those places. Unfortunately, the financial sector is the most sensitive industry in terms of demands for legal protection and information so, unsurprisingly, it is the most home-biased industry despite its fluidity. Bankers prefer doing their business in their home countries, where they feel easy with the legal system. It is not an accident that the deficit countries have the best legal framework for financial market development. As a result, money flows there and mostly stays there. Unfortunately, there are not many new technologies or other productive activities to invest in those countries. In the end, their financial sectors flourish on creating their own 'productive' assets, which are basically assets on paper, accumulated as derivatives and other sorts of financial innovations.

POLICY RESPONSES TO GLOBAL IMBALANCES

Conventional wisdom

The crisis seems to have bottomed and there appears to be a light at the end of the tunnel, signalling a recovery. However, there will be no corrections to global imbalances even if the world economy recovers. We will quickly go back to business as usual. The proposals currently on the table are not going to offer a cure.

Many people criticise the inflexible exchange-rate regimes in some surplus countries, particularly China. However, our empirical results show that the exchange rate is only a minor contributor to global imbalances. Germany and Japan both have a floating exchange regime, but both countries run very large surpluses. In particular, Japan has remained a strong exporter despite the Plaza Accord forcing the yen to float and revalue. China's own experience since 2005 also rejects the claim. Between 2005 and 2008, the renminbi appreciated by about 20 per cent, but China's trade and current account surpluses both surged.

The proposal to replace the US dollar with an international currency will not work either, at least not in the short run. Even if all tradable goods and services were denominated in the international currency, or any other currency for that matter, the fundamental forces determining the international division of labour would remain, and global imbalances would continue. The effect of the dollar dominance is to concentrate excessive liquidities in the US market. In the long run, liquidities will probably disperse to other countries if the position of the dollar is weakened. However, we have to realize that the strong dollar and the strong American financial system reinforce each other. That is, the dollar is likely to remain strong as long as the American financial system continues to lead the world. Since there are no signs, even after the financial crisis, that the American financial system is going to become weaker relative to other countries, we should not expect the dollar to become substantially weaker either.

Another mainstream proposal is for the surplus countries to increase consumption, but the chances of this working are small. Most of the growth in savings in the surplus countries has been contributed by corporate profits and government revenues, although residential saving rates remain high there. The problem is not so much a lack of residential consumption as a lack of corporate investment and government spending. The Chinese Government is being urged to spend more on social security and health care. While this will have a direct effect on government spending, the government has to be careful not to over-commit itself to social security and health care. Public money becomes cheap at a time of fast economic growth and concomitant rapid growth in government revenues, which often leads governments to over-commit in public spending. Japan and the USA are two examples of this. In addition, the induced residential consumption should not be exaggerated. Both Germany and Japan have good social security and health-care systems, but residential consumption in both countries is still relatively low, especially compared with other industrialized countries.

If the adjustments in the surplus countries are unlikely to happen or at least take time to happen, we cannot expect that the adjustments in the deficit countries will happen quickly either. Money is still going to be cheap and borrowing is still optimal to finance consumption.

In the end, economics wins the game. Unless we reject free trade, and the free flow of capital and division of labour associated with it, we will have to live with global imbalance for a long time. The problem facing us is not how to correct the imbalance, rather how to neutralize its negative consequences.

To do that, we have to realize that either side of the imbalance is incapable of finishing the business on its own. We have to find a global solution.

Policy recommendations for international organizations

The solution for international organizations is to create non-country-specific financial assets and make them sufficiently profitable for the surplus countries to invest in. The special drawing rights of the International Monetary Fund (IMF) can be such an asset. Most of the world is still very poor and desperately needs investment. If the arrangements are right, this investment can be profitable, and surplus countries will be willing to contribute. In this respect, the IMF can work with the World Bank to enlarge and strengthen both institutions' current operations to accommodate more contributions from the surplus countries. The latest round of IMF capitalization is a good start and should be continued. The recent move of the Asian countries to create an Asian fund is also a step in the right direction.

In the short run, however, the spread of liquidity to more countries will not reduce global imbalances. Instead, it will be akin to a relocation of the current account deficits from the traditional deficit countries to future deficit countries. Nevertheless, we should see a moderation in the level of imbalances in the long run. This is because investments in the new deficit countries will enhance those countries' domestic manufacturing capacities and thus reduce their reliance on imports. That is, the reduced deficits in the traditional deficit countries will not be fully picked up by the new deficit countries, and global imbalances will be reduced.

The traditional deficit countries can also act to help reduce global imbalances. For example, they can allow more companies from other countries, including the surplus countries, to be listed on their stock markets, so that excessive liquidities can be spread more evenly across the globe.

Policy recommendations for the Chinese Government

China has to undergo serious structural changes in order to reduce its external imbalances. Among them, accelerating the pace of urbanization and reforming the financial sector are the two most critical.

In terms of its income level, China lags behind in urbanization. China's per-capita GDP was US$5,500 in nominal terms in 2011, and its urbanization rate was 50 per cent. In comparison, the Philippines has a per-capita GDP of US$2,200, but an urbanization rate of 48 per cent. Domestically, agriculture contributes only 10 per cent of the national GDP, but 30 per cent of the national labour force is in the countryside. If all the rural residents worked in agriculture and the urban–rural income gap were to remain at 3.3 to 1, then China's urbanization rate should be 71 per cent.

Urbanization increases domestic consumption in two ways. First, urbanization increases people's income and consumption almost for free. Currently, an average urban resident consumes as much as 2.6 times of an average rural resident. Second, urbanization leads to the development of the services sector, which is better able to generate employment than is manufacturing. When employment increases, labour income also increases. The share of labour income in GDP has been declining rapidly in the past decade (Bai and Qian 2009) and is one of the most important factors leading to China's external imbalances (Yao and Yu 2009). By increasing labour income, urbanization boosts consumption and reduces China's external imbalances.

While urbanization corrects China's external imbalances by reducing China's exports, reforming the financial sector does that by better utilizing the savings accumulated by exports. In recent years, China's trade surplus has reached 9 per cent of its GDP, most of the surplus accruing to China's burgeoning official foreign reserves. This is a wasteful process. The return on capital in China is over 10 per cent (CCER Research Team 2007) whereas China's foreign reserves can get a return of only 2 per cent on the treasury bills and other bonds in the American market. China's inadequate financial sector should take most of the blame. Two major deficiencies make it incapable of fully utilizing China's national savings.

The first is the lack of small and medium-size banks. China has only 16 major commercial banks and 110 regional banks. There are many rural credit unions, but most of them are running badly. In comparison, the USA has 7,500 commercial banks, 9,900 credit unions, 886 savings and loan associations, and 400 mutual savings banks. One of curious things amid China's abundance of savings is that small and medium enterprises (SMEs) still suffer the problem of lack of credit. This has a lot to do with China's dearth of smaller banks. Large banks often chase large firms because they demand larger loans, which reduces bank operating costs. Smaller banks cannot compete with large banks and have to serve SMEs. The lack of credit constrains SME expansion, but SMEs are more efficient than large firms in generating employment. Therefore, the lack of smaller banks suppresses labour income and contributes to China's external imbalances.

The second deficiency of the financial sector is the lack of regional capital markets. Each province in China equates to a medium or large country in terms of population and territory, but none of them has a functioning capital market. The two national stock markets currently accommodate only about 1,500 companies, a tiny fraction of China's total number of firms. This distorted structure not only hinders the growth of SMEs, but also sets barriers for ordinary citizens to share the benefits of rapid economic growth. This is particularly relevant for China's lack of corporate bond markets. The Chinese stock market is unusually volatile, and very risky for ordinary citizens to invest in. For most people, fixed-income assets should be the first choice of investment. Without such an option, many people opt to invest in the informal financial market, facing the risk of frauds.

Reforming the financial sector requires that the government improve its regulatory framework. This will be a daunting task. The government made mistakes in the 1990s when regional capital markets began to emerge. There was a great deal of fraud and the government closed all the markets. Next time, by implementing regulatory controls, the Chinese Government should not miss the opportunity again.

CONCLUSIONS

In this chapter we propose and test the hypothesis that global imbalances are the result of international division of labour between countries with strong financial sectors (the deficit countries) and countries with strong manufacturing or resource sectors (the surplus countries). Our theory and empirical evidence have strong implications for the literature on global imbalances and the policies applied to correct them. It is worthwhile to recapitulate some of them.

First, global imbalances mask potentially substantial gains from trade. Both the deficit countries and the surplus countries gain from the division of labour behind the imbalances. Second, since it is determined by long-term factors, the phenomenon of global imbalances cannot be easily corrected by short-term measures such as adjustments to exchange rates. To minimize the costs associated with imbalances, international organizations and individual countries must encourage structural changes in the global economy and national economies. Third, so long as the American financial system still leads the world, creating an international currency, an idea currently being considered, will likely not work. Fourth, China will continue its export-led growth model in the next decade because of its comparative advantage in manufacturing and its abundant labour supply. To lower the costs coming with this model, China should accelerate its pace of urbanization and improve its financial system to accommodate more banks and regional capital markets.

NOTE

1 Jianwei Xu: School of Economics and Management, Beijing Normal University, Beijing. Yang Yao: National School of Development and China Center for Economic Research, Peking University, Beijing.

REFERENCES

Backus, D., E. Henricksen, F. Lambert and K. Telmer (2005) 'Current account fact and fiction', NBER Working Paper, No. 15525, Cambridge, MA: National Bureau of Economic Research.

Bai, Chong-en and Zhenjie Qian (2009) 'The factor allocation of national income: a story behind statistical data', *Jingji Yanjiu* [Economic Research], 44(3): 27–41.

Beck, T. (2006) *A New Database on Financial Development and Structure (1960–2006)*, Washington, DC: World Bank.

CCER (China Center for Economic Research) Research Team (2007) 'Zhongguo ziben huibaolv guce' ['The profit rates of Chinese enterprises'], *CCER Working Paper*, No. C2007002.

Chinn, M. and H. Ito (2006) 'What matters for financial development? Capital controls, institutions, and interactions', *Journal of Development Economics*, 81(1): 163–192.

Henriksen, E. (2005) 'A demographic explanation of U.S. and Japanese current account behavior', Carnegie Mellon University, unpublished manuscript.

La Porta, R., F. Lopez De Silanes, A. Shleifer and R. Vishny (1998) 'Law and finance', *Journal of Political Economy*, 106(6): 1113–1155.

Mendoza, E., V. Quadrini and J. Ríos Rull (2009) 'Financial integration, financial development, and global imbalances', *Journal of Political Economy*, 117(3): 371–416.

Rodrik, D. (2008) 'The real exchange rate and economic growth', *Brookings Papers on Economic Activity*, 2008: 365–412.

Willen, P. (2004) 'Incomplete markets and trade', *Working Paper*, Federal Reserve Bank of Boston.

Yao, Yang and Miaojie Yu (2009) 'Labor, demography, and the export-oriented growth model in China', National School of Development and China Center for Economic Research, Peking University, available at http://mjyu.ccer.edu.cn/research/LDE.pdf.

4 Measuring systemic risk

Implications for financial stability and Asian policy-makers[1]

Prasanna Gai[2]

INTRODUCTION

'The signal difference between the Asian crisis and the current crisis is complexity.'

Andrew Sheng, Third Dr KB Lall Memorial Lecture, 7 February 2009

Modern financial systems link households and firms to a variety of financial institutions such as banks, insurance companies and hedge funds. Although enabling risk-sharing, the resulting balance sheet interdependencies have led to a global financial system that is increasingly vulnerable to system-wide breakdown, as the recent global financial crisis made all too clear.[3]

The global financial crisis does, however, provide an opportunity to revisit the 'rules of the game' needed to tackle financial crises in the 21st century. The micro-economic frictions that lie at the heart of the present crisis (network externalities, fire-sale externalities, information failures and misaligned incentives for risk management) cut across international borders and, naturally, invite multilateral solutions.[4] As Krugman (2008) reminds us, there are large welfare gains to financial policy coordination; gains far in excess of those predicted by the standard analyses of macro-economic policy coordination.[5]

The G20 meeting in London established a Financial Stability Board (FSB), elevating the mandate of the existing Financial Stability Forum to monitor global financial stability and promote medium-term reform, while at the same time broadening its membership. Although it remains a secretariat, collaborating with the International Monetary Fund (IMF) on early-warning exercises, it is arguably the prototype for a global macro-prudential regulator. The formation of a largely independent multilateral agency charged with tackling future financial crises is the belated recognition by policy-makers that balance sheets interact (including at the national level) and that the free flow of capital severely limits the scope of national authorities to safeguard financial stability.

But what might such a multilateral body do? And how might Asian members of the G20, namely China, India, Indonesia, Japan and Korea, along with Australia, best contribute? The influential Geneva Report on Financial Regulation (Brunnermeier *et al.* 2009) points to the important role that the

FSB can play in giving forewarning of crises, and in preventing and managing them. In this chapter, I draw on the formal analysis of systemic risk to highlight some lessons and challenges facing the new Board and regional policy-makers in the areas of crisis warning and prevention. The debate on systemic risk measurement and management is not an arcane exercise in finance and must be taken seriously by the region. The outcomes will likely influence the shape of the international financial architecture and materially affect financial integration, development and economic growth. Asia's stake in international regulatory cooperation has increased substantially with the financial crisis, and regional policy-makers will need to play a major role in helping define new international standards for macro-prudential regulation. Accepting Sheng's (2009) proposition that 'Asians do not have the global reach to change global conditions' is simply not good enough.

MEASURING SYSTEMIC RISK

The Geneva Report makes clear that the main cause of systemic financial collapse is endogenous risk caused by key micro-economic externalities fuelling self-amplifying spirals. It recommends existing macro-prudential stress-testing practices be overhauled and that 'completely new techniques ... based on models and endogenous risk spillover measures ... be devised to explore the implications of risk for the system'.[6]

Stress-testing models are used to gauge financial sector resilience by central banks, and form the basis for the Financial Sector Assessment Program reports conducted with the IMF. As Figure 4.1 shows, traditional 'macro' stress-testing models link macro-econometric models to banks' balance sheets, with a view to estimating credit and market losses. Total losses are then calculated by aggregating credit and market losses, with expected losses being compared with buffers of capital and profits to gauge the overall impact of the stress scenario on the financial system.

Such a toolkit is not fit-for-purpose, however. Traditional stress-testing tools fail to capture default or the financial frictions that trigger spillovers

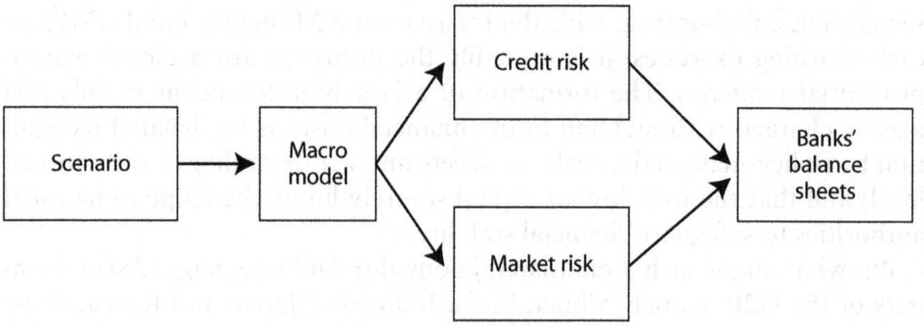

Figure 4.1 The traditional approach to stress-testing.

and contagion. No account is taken of network externalities or the fire sale of assets by institutions facing default. The potential feedback to the macro-economy from the behavioural responses of financial market participants individually and collectively to balance sheet distress is also ignored.

A growing number of policy-makers are, therefore, beginning to advocate 'dynamic systemic stress tests' as a way of helping internalize some of the key amplifying mechanisms of the present crisis. On this view, the regulator compiles the balance sheets of the relevant participants, taking into account the externalities, and aggregates the behaviour of the system to common (and extreme) risk scenarios. These common stress scenarios are then used to derive loss distributions for the financial system as a whole. The results of such stress tests are played back to financial firms, enabling them to use system-wide information to revisit their risk management practices and assess the effect of their own and others' actions. Such an iterative approach to stress testing has already been implemented in the Netherlands and is becoming influential in the UK.[7]

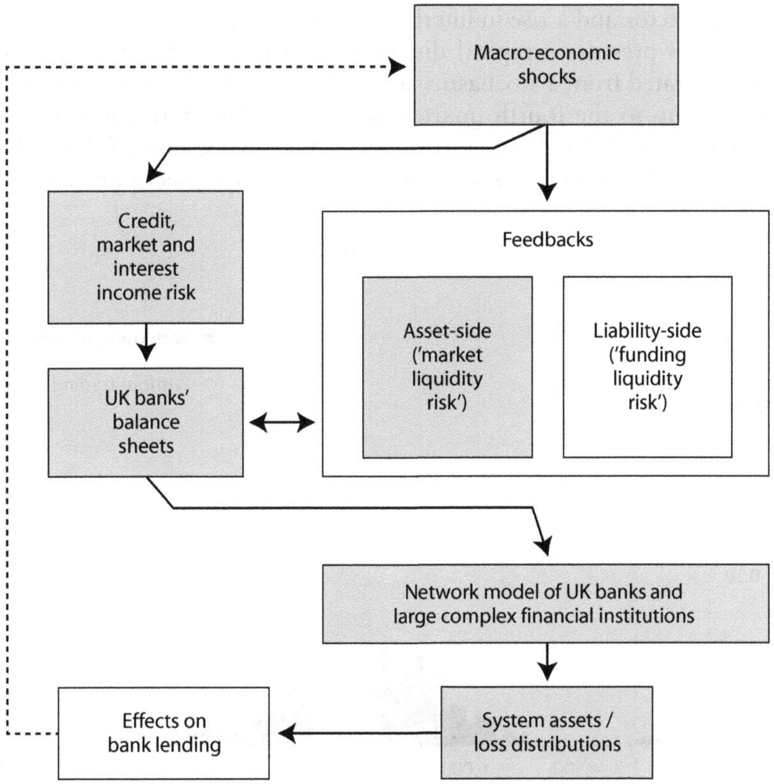

Figure 4.2 The stress-testing approach of Alessandri *et al.* (2009) and Aikman *et al.* (2010).

Work that the author was involved in while at the Bank of England (Alessandri *et al.* 2009; Aikman *et al.* 2010; Anand *et al.* 2012) has made some progress towards an empirical framework for financial stability assessment and systemic stress testing. Figure 4.2 illustrates how models of the macro-economy and banks' balance sheets might be brought together and integrated with models of the interbank network and asset-side feedbacks, to generate forecast distributions for system-wide banking assets over arbitrary horizons. The transmission dynamics hinge crucially on two factors – the nature of the shocks and the structural characteristics of the financial system, such as the heterogeneity of balance sheets and the connectivity of the interbank network.

The model suite illustrated in Figure 4.2 is a useful tool for risk assessment and stress-testing exercises. For example, it can yield point estimates for system and bank-specific losses. And it can be used to generate conditional distributions by imposing shock parameters and/or a set of macro-economic variables in any period. Alessandri *et al.* (2009) illustrate both exercises – considering the impact on UK banks of a macro-economic environment similar to the 1990s recession, and scenarios involving distress in the US household sector and a rise in interbank borrowing costs.

Figure 4.3 presents a typical distribution of future UK banking system assets, generated from a stochastic simulation of the macro-economic model using data up to the fourth quarter of 2005. A thousand simulations are run on a 3-year forecasting horizon stretching to the end of 2008. Each simulation is driven by a sequence of macro-economic shocks drawn from a

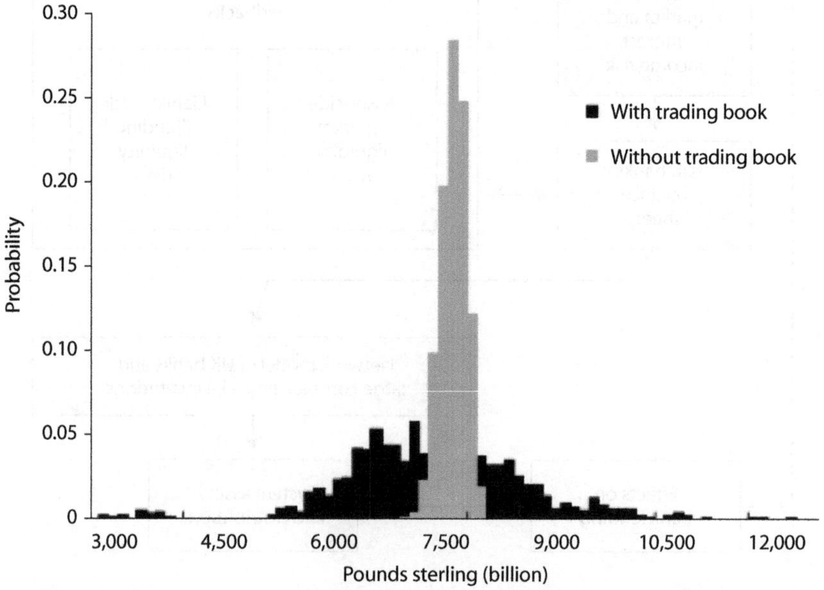

Figure 4.3 System asset distribution. Source: Alessandri *et al.* (2009).

multivariate normal distribution. Despite the joint normality of the risk factors, the model generates a bi-modal asset distribution. This is as one might expect of a system in which losses on interbank exposures, and pressures on asset prices and market liquidity from failing firms, are transmitted through the financial system, triggering a default cascade.

Bankruptcy costs, which erode the assets of defaulting banks, play a vital role in the model because they create a large discrete loss at the point of default. But network effects and asset-price feedbacks are also important contributors to systemic losses. If default occurs, and especially if contagion breaks out, the cumulative bankruptcy costs yield a system-wide outcome that is significantly worse than if the initial default is just avoided.

Comparing Lehman Brothers with banks that have just avoided default helps illustrate the point. Upon the failure of Lehman Brothers in September 2008, its creditors will have incurred a range of legal and other expenses. Over time, financial institutions may also suffer from the cheap fire sale of assets, which can represent a real cost if the fire sale is due to a disruption in longstanding bank–borrower relationships. On their own, these losses represent a deadweight cost that would not have been incurred if Lehman Brothers had just survived. But it was the contagion from the failure of Lehman Brothers that caused a major amplification in system-wide distress and arguably moved the entire banking system from a precarious, but sustainable position, to a full-blown crisis.

Figure 4.4 illustrates what happens to the tail of the system asset distribution as the network and fire sale externalities are switched 'on and off' in

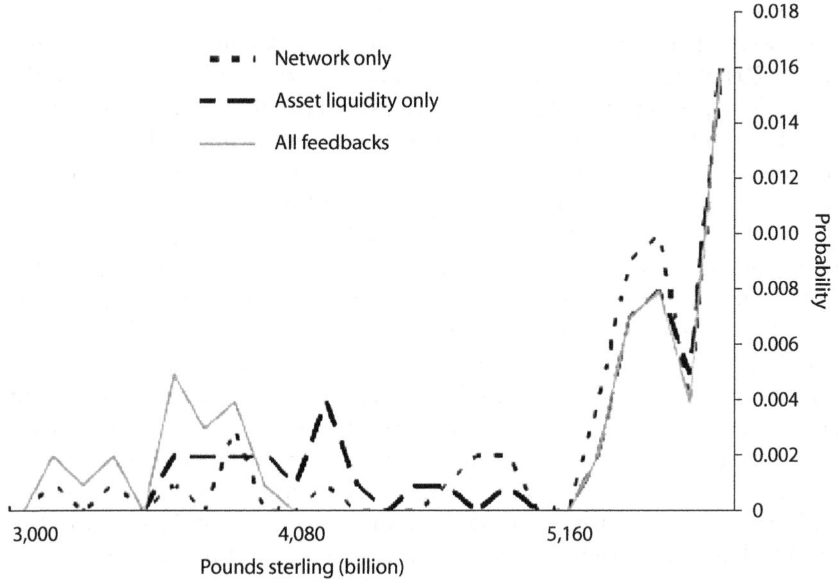

Figure 4.4 Tail of the system asset distribution. Source: Alessandri *et al.* (2009).

the model. Network and asset-price feedbacks independently contribute to the shaping of the tail of the distribution, and each externality, on its own, is capable of generating contagion. When combined, however, the effect is much more potent, generating a much more substantive amplification effect. It underscores why an understanding of the interaction of externalities is a matter of prime importance to financial stability regulators.

Figure 4.5 plots the conditional system-wide asset distribution that obtains from a scenario that mimics the distress in the US household/corporate sector and rising interbank borrowing costs. While imposing a specific path for all the macro-economic variables associated with this stress scenario delivers a point estimate of its impact, some randomness in the model can be retained by imposing priors on a subset of risk factors and parameters (e.g. real equity prices and US mortgage default rates). Relative to the baseline, it is clear that banks are adversely affected – the entire distribution shifts to the left. The greater mass in the tail under the stress scenario also reflects a higher incidence of default. It is worth noting that although the results presented are for the UK banking system in aggregate, the model produces a rich set of information to assess the vulnerability of particular institutions under stress. As such, it can be used to feed directly into internal institution-specific risk assessment work undertaken by regulators.

In the crisis triggered in 2008, much of the action took place on the liability side of the balance sheet. The deteriorating balance sheets of many banks increased their future funding costs, raising the risk that some banks could be shut out of the short-term funding markets altogether. If these then fail and their assets are sold at fire sale prices, funding liquidity feedbacks and asset-side feedbacks can interact to generate default cascades. Aikman *et al.* (2010) extend the work of Alessandri *et al.* (2009) to examine this issue. They project individual bank ratings and use these results to calibrate how the funding costs of a bank rise as its position weakens. The onset of a funding crisis is then calibrated to particular institutions, based on a series of indicators drawn from previous episodes of funding stress. The distribution of UK system assets remains bi-modal, with a main peak associated with a healthy banking sector and a small peak in the left tail (Figure 4.6).

The global financial network is vastly more diverse and complex than models dominated by bank balance sheets imply. Figure 4.7 illustrates a stylized version of such a global system – tracing the propagation of a shock through is clearly a challenge. The financial linkages created by credit risk transfer and other off-balance-sheet transactions are frequently unrecorded, and there is little information on the balance sheets of other financial institutions (such as hedge funds and insurance companies) and firms. So it is natural to ask if models like those of Alessandri *et al.* (2009) that rely on rich, country-specific, banking sector data are of much use when assessing global financial stability. The lack of information on financial sector exposures has been an important reason why the IMF

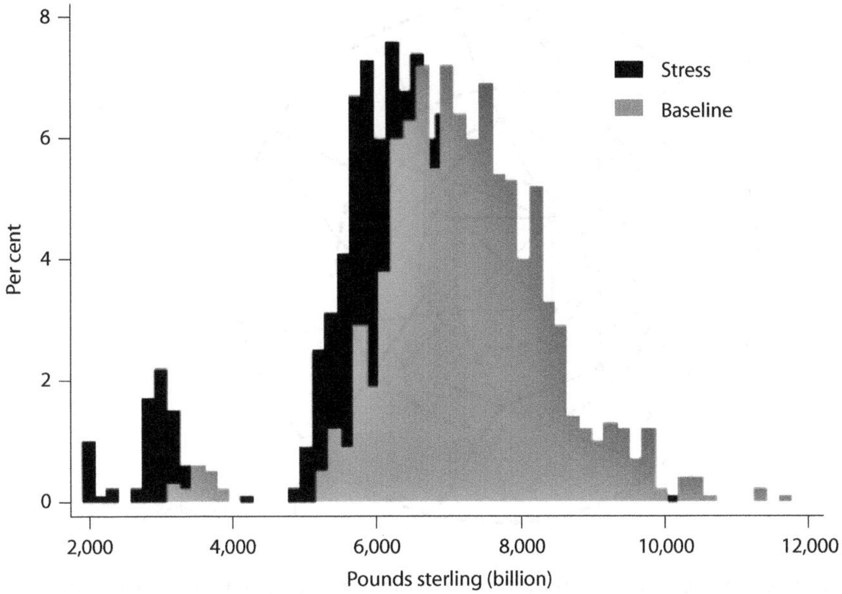

Figure 4.5 System asset distributions under a stress scenario. Source: Alessandri *et al.* (2009).

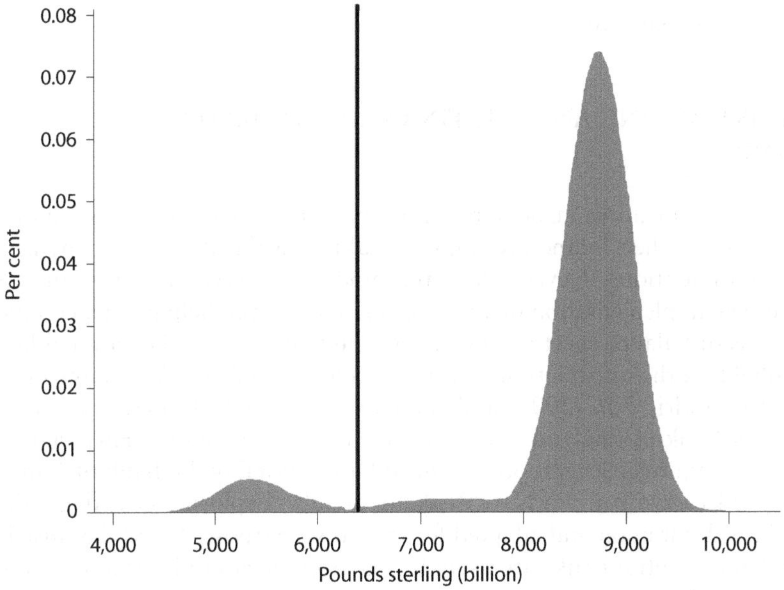

Figure 4.6 System asset distribution with funding liquidity effects. Source: Aikman *et al.* (2010).

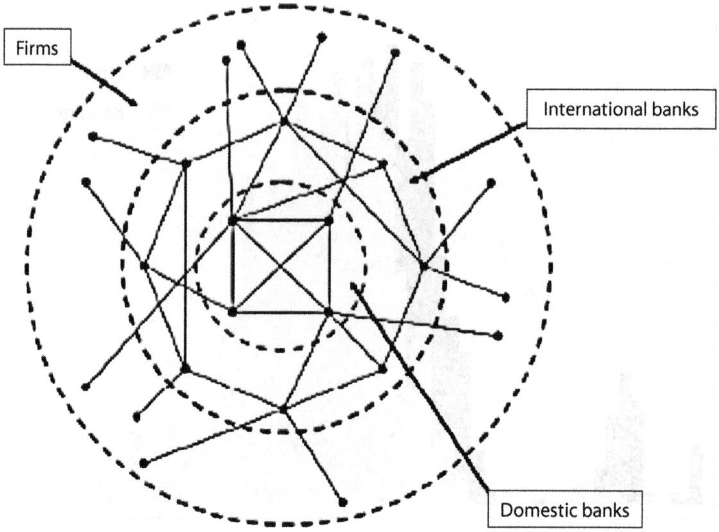

Figure 4.7 Stylized representation of the global financial system. Source: based on Anand *et al.* (2012).

and international regulators have been left to concentrate on asset-pricing approaches to systemic risk measurement. Anand *et al.* (2012) draw on methods from the science of complexity to show how progress can still, nevertheless, be made.

CRISIS WARNING AND THE FINANCIAL STABILITY BOARD

Despite the advances made in recent years, public-sector stress-testing models remain in their infancy. A notable weakness is the absence of convincing micro-foundations. Nevertheless, the models do serve an important purpose. The implementation of stress-testing models can help build a common analysis of balance sheet positions between regulators at the national level, highlighting the information gaps that need to be filled.[8] The analysis from the Alessandri *et al.* (2009) and Aikman *et al.* (2010) framework is being used by Bank of England senior management, including the Financial Stability Committee. Several other central banks, notably the Bank of Canada and the Reserve Bank of New Zealand, are also exploring how these ideas might be built upon and adapted for their own purposes.[9] And the Austrian and Dutch central banks are using formal approaches to inform their internal policy debate on systemic risk.

Systemic risk models also have a role to play at the international level, including at the FSB. As 'second-generation' models of systemic risk gain traction, they contribute towards a shared understanding of the implications of balance sheet interdependence for the world economy. It is important that policy-makers do not fall prey to a fallacy of composition, in which it is assumed that the system as a whole is safe simply because national financial systems are reportedly resilient.[10] Dynamic stress-testing supported by such models needs to be coordinated at the supranational level, with the FSB taking the lead in setting the stress scenario, and also becoming involved in the iterative dialogue between firms and national regulators. The results of these exercises could then be published in an early warning report of the kind envisaged in the Geneva Report, with countries being held to public account for their policy positions. Apart from filtering risks, the analysis would also help prioritise medium-term reform to international financial sector regulation.

The ability of a body such as the FSB to deliver the public good of dispassionate information on financial system risk depends, however, on its internal governance. The Board is envisaged as a secretariat and this is likely to limit its scope to do any meaningful and independent monitoring. This lack of resources means that any crisis warning must be delivered jointly with the IMF, opening it up to potential politicization. To minimize this, early warning messages need to be produced by the staff of the FSB and the IMF without country interference. And it is in this regard that Asian policy-makers can help to make a difference.

SYSTEMIC RISK ISSUES FOR THE REGION

Although Asia and Australia have experienced adverse macro-economic effects from the global financial turmoil, regional financial intermediaries and markets have remained resilient. Loretan and Wooldridge (2008) identify several factors responsible for this relative stability, notably:

- restrictions on cross-border financial activities in some countries, and lower capital mobility relative to other emerging market economies;
- limited uptake of the 'originate-to-distribute' model of banking, coupled with very low exposure by banks in the region to structured credit products;[11] and
- greater reliance on deposits rather than wholesale funds, with banks in some countries (e.g. Malaysia and Thailand) being net creditors on the interbank market. In part, this reflects the shallowness of these markets.[12]

Recent Financial Stability Reports in Australia, India and China confirm this general picture and add weight to the role of proactive regulatory policies in securing greater resilience.

A general lesson that emerges from the formal analysis of systemic risk is that, in the presence of fat tails, past resilience to financial shocks is no guarantee against future financial instability. Two very similar size shocks can have very different consequences for the financial system, depending on where they hit the network. A shock that strikes at particular pressure points associated with underlying structural vulnerabilities can be very damaging indeed. And, as Alessandri *et al.* (2009) and Anand *et al.* (2012) demonstrate, even relatively small shocks can have a major impact if the liquidity of the market for key financial assets is impaired. So policy-makers in the region would be unwise to draw too much comfort from the strong fundamentals of their financial institutions and the relative stability of key regional asset markets.

McCauley and Zukunft (2008) argue that the crisis has, indeed, brought new vulnerabilities in the Asian interbank markets to light. In recent years, foreign banks have used foreign currency to fund Asian local currency claims. Such carry trade activity has been relatively cheap and extremely profitable.[13] But it exposes domestic capital markets to potential instability in the event that foreign banks choose to suddenly withdraw funding, because of their own need for liquidity in offshore capital markets. Some evidence of vulnerabilities of this kind was seen in the government bond market in Korea, where foreign bank activity was significant during December 2007.

An accurate picture of Asian banks' funding vulnerabilities is not readily available. As McCauley and Zukunft (2008) note, it is necessary to have data on maturing foreign currency obligations, hoarding of maturing interbank deposits, holdings of high-quality liquid securities such as US treasury bills, as well as measures of off-balance-sheet commitments in foreign currency. If Asian policy-makers are to play an active role in designing and shaping the 'macro-prudential' debate, they will need to ensure disclosures of financial sector balance sheets to enable such analyses to be carried out, and be willing to be candid about those findings. They will need to lead, and contribute to, international exercises that gather data on international and national inter-linkages of banks in a systematic fashion.

A key consideration for the developing economies of the region, such as India and China, relates to their need to realize the full benefits offered by financial integration. In this respect, a crucial concern relates to the evenness of the playing field between domestic-owned banks and branches of foreign banks. Viewed through a financial stability lens, if a host country judges a foreign branch to be systemic, it could reasonably expect to apply the same capital and liquidity requirements to the foreign branch as it would to its domestic banks, and the foreign branch may need to become a separately capitalized subsidiary. Policy-makers in the region will need to reflect carefully on the implications of such systemic issues since they imply a trade-off between the efficiency gains of cross-border banking and financial stability. Clear multilateral rules will need to be worked out between home and host country regulators to ensure that the trade-off is appropriately balanced. Multilateral burden-sharing between countries will also need to be considered in the event that crises arise. Asian policy-makers will, in particular, need to consider how lender/capital-provider/market-maker of last resort procedures that are devoid of the stigma associated with emergency (central bank) lending might best be constructed.

Finally, there is much for Asian policy-makers to do in order to bolster the self-confidence of the FSB to play the role of independent umpire. They can take a lead by actively encouraging the development of new systemic risk models and standing ready to implement their lessons by, for example, pioneering dynamic stress-test exercises in the main Asian financial centres. They can also insist that the FSB members from each G20 country be eminent experts in the field of financial stability, chosen on the basis of their stature and integrity, rather than being captive to the whims of finance ministries. By helping to give the FSB a clear, independent and respected voice in this manner, Asian policy-makers can help advance the cause of systemic risk management. The end result will be to limit the scope for countries to pursue their own self-interest, and provide important leverage to national authorities in their dealings with financial firms.

NOTES

1 This chapter draws on many fruitful conversations and joint research with colleagues at the Bank of England, notably Piergiorgio Alessandri, Andy Haldane and Sujit Kapadia. The views and opinions expressed herein are, however, strictly those of the author and not of the Bank of England.

2 Professor of Macroeconomics, University of Auckland, Auckland, New Zealand; p.gai@auckland.ac.nz.

3 See Gai *et al.* (2008) and Gai and Kapadia (2010) for formal arguments demonstrating how the financial system can both absorb and amplify risks.

4 See Gai and Haldane (2006) for an early account anticipating these issues; Haldane (2009) and Brunnermeier *et al.* (2009) provide more-recent assessments. Running alongside these financial frictions is, of course, the issue of macroeconomic imbalances. There is little doubt that the build-up of leverage during the Great Stability, neglect of financial stability mandates by central banks and persistent global imbalances have all mattered greatly to the crisis. A detailed analysis is beyond the scope of this chapter, however. Gai *et al.* (2008) and Lorenzoni (2008) provide formal models depicting the nexus between macroeconomic and financial stability.

5 See, for example, Oudiz and Sachs (1985) and the ensuing literature.

6 Or, in the modest language of a G20 (2009) working group, 'Risk management also needs to be enhanced to better evaluate vulnerabilities arising from low-frequency, system-wide risks'.

7 See, for example, the De Nederlandische Bank (2006) and Haldane (2009). Sheng (2009) also makes a forceful case for integrating 'top down' and 'bottom up' risk management to better capture interconnectivity and feedback mechanisms.

8 A fundamental by-product of Keynesian 'cross' analysis, for example, was the formation of a consistent set of national (and international) statistics for

macro-economic data, which is now routinely used for monetary policy. We are still some way from a similar situation on the financial stability front.

9 See, for example, Kida (2008) and Gauthier *et al.* (2009).

10 This tendency is especially strong in Asia. Sheng (2009) observes that Asian policy-makers frequently take the view that their best contribution to the global good is ensuring that their national house is in order.

11 See Remolona and Shim (2008) for a detailed analysis of credit risk markets and instruments in the Asia–Pacific region during the crisis.

12 The interbank market varies considerably across Asia. Interbank activity is significant in Hong Kong and Singapore, but lacks depth in many other countries, including mainland China and the Philippines.

13 For formal analyses of carry trades and their consequences, see Plantin and Shin (2008), Hattori and Shin (2009) and Gai and Trivedi (2009).

REFERENCES

Aikman, D., P. Alessandri, B. Eklund, P. Gai, S. Kapadia, E. Martin, N. Mora, G. Sterne and M. Willison (2010) 'Funding liquidity risk in a quantitative model of systemic stability', in R. Alfaro (ed.), *Financial Stability, Monetary Policy and Central Banking*, Proceedings of the 12th Annual Conference of the Central Bank of Chile, pp. 371–410, Santiago: Bank of Chile.

Alessandri, P., P. Gai, S. Kapadia, N. Mora and C. Puhr (2009) 'Towards a framework for quantifying systemic stability', *International Journal of Central Banking*, 5(3): 47–81.

Anand, K., S. Brennan, P. Gai, S. Kapadia and M. Willison (2013) 'A network model of financial system resistance', *Journal of Economic Behavior and Organization*, 85(1): 219–235.

Brunnermeier, M., A. Crockett, C. Goodhart, A. Persaud and H. Shin (2009) 'The fundamental principles of financial regulation', *ICMB–CEPR Geneva Reports on the World Economy*, No. 11, Geneva: International Center for Monetary and Banking Studies; and London: Centre for Economic Policy Research.

De Nederlandische Bank (2006) 'Financial stability: is the Dutch financial sector stress-resistant?', *Quarterly Bulletin*, November.

Gai, P. and A. Haldane (2006) 'Public policy in an era of super-systemic risk', paper presented at conference on *Financial Stability: Theory and Applications'*, 18–19 May 2006, London: London School of Economics.

Gai, P. and S. Kapadia (2010) 'Contagion in financial networks', *Proceedings of the Royal Society A*, 466(2120): 2401–2423

Gai, P., S. Kapadia, S. Millard and A. Perez (2008) 'Financial innovation, macroeconomic stability and systemic crises', *Economic Journal*, 118(March): 401–426.

Gai, P. and K. Trivedi (2009) 'Funding externalities, asset prices and investors' "search for yield"', *Bulletin of Economic Research*, 61(1): 73–82.

Gauthier, C., A. Lehar and M. Soussi (2009) 'Systemic risk in the Canadian banking system', Ottawa: Bank of Canada (mimeo).

G20 (Group of Twenty) (2009) *G20 Working Group 1: Enhancing Sound Regulation and Strengthening Transparency, Final Report*, available at <http://cdm16064.contentdm.oclc.org/cdm/singleitem/collection/p266901coll4/id/2932/rec/15>.

Haldane, A. (2009) 'Why banks failed the stress test', speech to the Marcus-Evans Conference on Stress Testing, 9–10 February, London.

Hattori, M. and H. Shin (2009) 'The yen carry trade and the sub-prime crisis', *IMF Staff Papers*, 56(2): 384–409.

Kida, M. (2008) 'A macro stress testing model with feedback effects', *Discussion Paper*, 08/2008, Wellington: Reserve Bank of New Zealand.

Krugman, P. (2008) 'The international finance multiplier', Princeton, NJ: Princeton University (mimeo).

Lorenzoni, G. (2008) 'Inefficient credit booms', *Review of Economic Studies*, 75(3), 809–833.

Loretan, M. and P. Wooldridge (2008) 'The development of money markets in Asia', *BIS Quarterly Review*, September, 39–51, Basel, Switzerland: Bank for International Settlements.

McCauley, R. and J. Zukunft (2008), 'Asian banks and the international interbank market', *BIS Quarterly Review*, June, 67–79, Basel, Switzerland: Bank for International Settlements.

Oudiz, G. and J. Sachs (1985) 'International policy coordination in dynamic macroeconomic models', in W. Buiter and R. Marston (eds) *International Economic Policy Coordination*, pp. 274–330, Cambridge, UK: Cambridge University Press.

Plantin, G. and H. Shin (2008) 'Carry trades and speculative dynamics', Princeton, NJ: Princeton University (mimeo).

Remolona, E. and I. Shim (2008) 'Credit derivatives and structured credit: the nascent markets of Asia and the Pacific', *BIS Quarterly Review*, June, 57–65, Basel, Switzerland: Bank for International Settlements.

Sheng, A. (2009) 'From Asian to global financial crisis', *Third Dr KB Lall Memorial Lecture*, Indian Council for Research on International Economic Relations (ICRIER), 7 February 2009, New Delhi.

5 Demographic changes and asset price bubbles

Lessons from Japan

Kazumasa Iwata[1]

INTRODUCTION

The current 'great recession' brought about a sharp decline in world trade in 2009. The decline in world trade volume was larger than that in the Great Depression of the 1930s. While the US recession was the deepest in the postwar period, the Asian economies, including Japan, saw a more sizeable decline in economic activity than the USA. Although the world economy seems to have passed through the worst phase, it is difficult to foresee the likely 'new normal' of the world economy after the financial crisis.

After the bubble burst in 1990, Japan faced a prolonged slump, although its real gross domestic product (GDP) has never dropped below the peak in 1990. During the 'lost decade' covering from 1992 to 2002, we observed two business cycles, followed by persistent deflation from 1998 to 2005. The stagnant activity coupled with deflation can be attributable not only to the legacy of the asset bubble burst, but also to the structural change to the labour market against the background of a rapidly ageing Japanese society.

In light of the experience of Japan and the USA, we put emphasis on the role of demographic changes as a contributing factor for emerging asset price bubbles. China moves out from the global recession as a frontrunner after seeing economic growth fall below 8 per cent in the fourth quarter of 2008 and the first half of 2009. Notwithstanding the sizeable decline of exports, China will show sound growth in the coming several years, reflecting the rising share of the working-age population,

Yet, the recent rapid expansion of money supply and bank lending may amplify the risk of bubbles on the stock and real estate markets. Furthermore, China will also encounter the difficult issues arising from a sharp decline of the working-age population after the mid 2010s.

This chapter is designed to draw lessons and policy implications from Japan's experience of the emergence of asset price bubbles and the 'lost decade' in the aftermath of the asset price bubble burst. At the same time, we evaluate policy measures to prevent a recurrence of financial crises in the future.

The next section compares the recent asset price bubbles in the USA with Japan's bubbles in the latter half of the 1980s. This is followed by a section discussing the causes of asset price bubbles and examining the alternative explanation about the 'conundrum of long-term interest rates' to the Asian 'excess saving' hypothesis. The third section of the chapter provides an assessment of policy response during the period of the 'lost decade' in Japan, as compared with current US policy measures. The final section evaluates the role of macro-prudential policy in relation to monetary policy management to pre-empt the financial imbalance.

SYNCHRONIZED BUBBLES VERSUS SEQUENTIAL BUBBLES

Let me start with the difference between emerging asset price bubbles in Japan and the USA. In Japan, the two synchronized bubbles in the equity and land market emerged almost at the same time and burst with a lag of only one year.

In contrast, four bubbles have emerged sequentially since the mid-1990s in the USA (Figure 5.1). When the signs of the first information technology (IT) bubble appeared, Mr Greenspan, the former Chairman of the Federal Reserve, sent a warning signal to the market as early as 1996, stating that an 'irrational exuberance' prevailed in the market.

The IT bubble collapsed in April 2000, while the housing price bubble continued to grow. This housing price bubble eventually burst in mid 2006, resulting in a more than 30 per cent decline in housing prices from the peak in mid 2009. However, this decline in prices is less than half of what Japan experienced. In Japan, the land price for commercial use in the major six cities fell by 87 per cent. It took 15 years to reach the bottom in 2006, four times longer than the case in the USA.

When I participated in the international conference at Jackson Hole organized by the Federal Reserve Bank of Kansas City in summer 2007, Professor Robert Schiller presented a chart that depicted the long-term historical development of US real housing prices since 1890. US real housing prices more than doubled from the low in 1997 to the peak in summer 2006. He argued that, this time around, the decrease in housing prices from mid 2006 would be the deepest since the Great Depression. It impressed me that he rejected any explanation based on economic theory about the cause of housing price bubbles, including the role of a low long-term interest rate.

Both the size of the increase and the decline of US housing prices are less than half those of Japan's land price developments. However, the US economy is more than double the size of the Japanese economy. My conjecture at that time was that the likely loss to US financial institutions would be about US$1 trillion, as Japan's earlier loss had amounted to about ¥100 trillion (US$1 trillion) (Table 5.1).

Further evidence to support this estimate was the ratio of outstanding US mortgage loans to nominal GDP, which increased sharply after 1997, from below 50 per cent to about 80 per cent in 2006. In contrast, the ratio of Japan's bank lending to nominal GDP increased from 100 per cent to 160 per cent from the early 1980s to 1990. This also suggests the size of

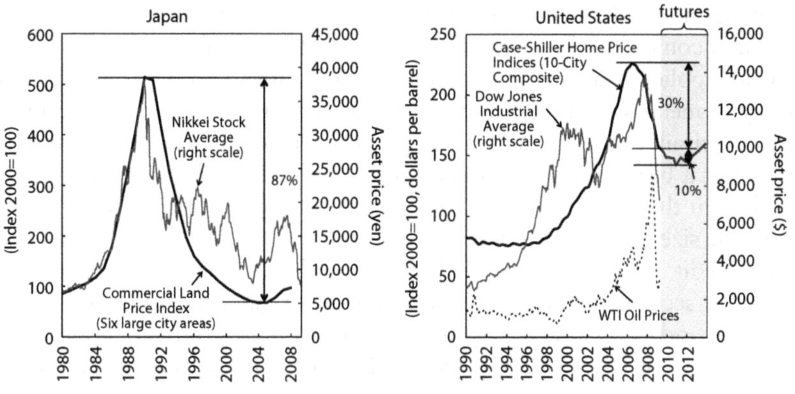

Figure 5.1 Asset price bubbles in Japan and the USA. Sources: Japan Real Estate Institute; Bloomberg; S&P.

Table 5.1 Non-performing loans in Japan in the 1990s compared with estimated toxic asset losses in the USA in the late 2000s

Japan in 1990s	*United States*
Non-performing loans (NPLs)	*Toxic asset losses (estimates)*
Total amount of NPLs at its peak (March 2002)	IMF estimates (US-originated)
¥43.2 trillion (8.5% of GDP) (US$0.44 trillion)	US$2.2 trillion (IMF, January 2009)
Total disposal of NPLs	BOE estimates (Bank of England, Financial Stability Report, October 2008)
¥99 trillion (1.0 trillion $)	US$1.6 trillion

Sources: Cabinet Office; IMF; Bank of England.

losses arising from the excessive mortgage loans was similar to that from Japan's excessive bank lending.

In reality, the loss that is likely to be incurred by the US financial institutions has exceeded Japan's loss by a wide margin. According to the International Monetary Fund (IMF) estimates in April 2009, the potential loss by US financial institutions during the period from 2007 to 2010 would amount to US$2.8 trillion. This was primarily due to another bubble burst, this time in the credit market.

Credit bubble

It is debatable when the credit bubble was initiated. In the early 1980s Professor Benjamin Friedman (Friedman *et al.* 1980) found a stable relationship between the total private credit outstanding and the nominal GDP, instead of the destabilized relationship between the monetary aggregates and the nominal income. Based on this observation he developed a 'credit view' of the monetary policy transmission mechanism, in contrast to a 'monetary view' held by monetarists. The ratio of private credit outstanding to nominal GDP was very similar to the ratio in the postwar era of the USA, until the mid 1980s. But it began to deviate significantly thereafter, and the deviation accelerated from the mid 1990s. By 2007 the total amount of private credit was double the size of nominal GDP.

The credit bubble was fuelled by an underestimation of risks in the process of securitization and repackaging of original mortgage loans, and consumer and other credit, against the background of 'great moderation'. The moderation was indicated by the diminishing volatility of the growth and inflation rates in the advanced economies since the mid 1980s. Japan seems to be the exception to the 'great moderation', because of the persistent slump and deflation during the 'lost decade'.

The credit bubble was further fuelled by the rapid expansion of the 'shadow banking system' in which the main players were the investment banks, hedge funds, private equity funds and structured investment vehicles/asset-backed commercial paper (ABCP) conduits.[2] The securitized, market-based financial system and the security broker–dealer sector developed rapidly after the mid 1980s. This brought about a long chain of financial intermediation financed by short-term repurchase agreements (repos) and ABCP transactions. Moreover, credit derivatives expanded vigorously, reflecting the advance of financial technologies. Both the credit derivatives and the transactions through structured investment vehicles are off-balance-sheet activities. They enabled financial firms to evade monitoring by the regulatory authorities.

The index of market liquidity, comprising the inverse of various spreads and premiums, has indicated that the excessive complacency by investors became prominent, notably after 2004, and continued to persist despite the collapsing US housing price bubble in mid 2006, even though it was preceded by the two global risk reductions in 2006 and 2007 that foreshadowed the financial tsunami (Figure 5.2). Market liquidity fell suddenly in August 2007 when the liquidity crisis took place, initially in Europe, then spreading widely to the USA and global economies. The liquidity shock has been accompanied by the freezing of securitized markets.

As market liquidity dried up, this immediately led to funding difficulty. Notably, the dollar liquidity shortage, or the liquidity hoarding, suddenly prevailed in the money market in Europe, due to the malfunctioning of the currency swap market. Then, the end of 2007 saw the conclusion of the dollar swap arrangements between central banks of the USA and major advanced economies. This remarkable event caused a paradigm shift such that the currency of the dollar is now provided by non-US central banks through a network of swap arrangements, violating the sovereignty of currency issue. Virtually, this implied the replacement of market transactions by cross-border trades between a number of central banks.

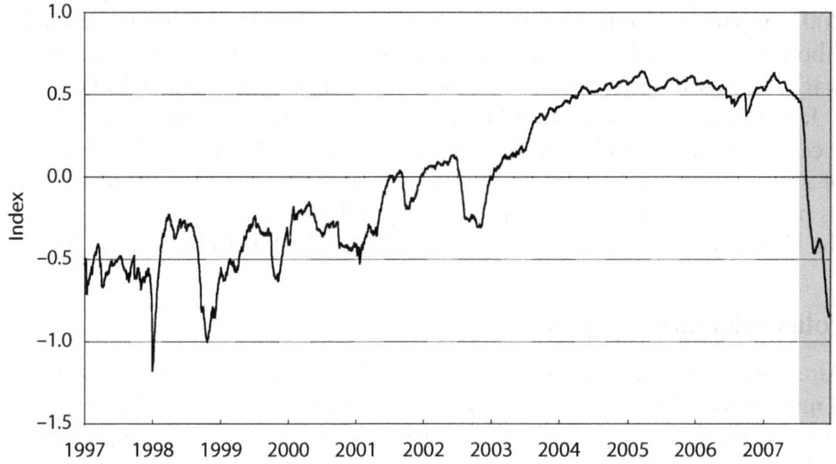

Figure 5.2 Index of market liquidity, 1997–2008. Source: Bank of Japan.

The oil price bubble and the recession

The burst of the credit bubble was not the end of the story. As the credit bubble collapsed, the oil price started to rise after the northern summer in 2007 (Figure 5.1). The increase in the price of oil had accelerated in mid 2004, although the price was fairly stagnant from mid 2006 to mid 2007. The sharp swing in the oil price complicated monetary management in major economies. The increased usage of derivatives and other financial instruments in the commodities market posed a serious challenge for central banks; they faced the trade-off between recession and the risk of inflation caused by the oil price hike.

There were three hypotheses to explain the oil price hike. The first was the peak oil hypothesis. The second was the fundamentals hypothesis, based on the longer-run supply shortage due to insufficient investment in oil exploration. The third was the speculative bubble hypothesis. Given the 70 per cent decline in the oil price from the peak of $147 per barrel in July 2008, the oil price hike meets the definition of bubbles given by Mr Greenspan. In his view it is difficult to identify the emergence of asset price bubbles, yet it is a bubble if it declines more than 20–30 per cent in a short period of time.

The oil price hike was not due to disruption of supply. It was due mainly to the strong demand for oil confronting stagnating world production. However, the terms of trade loss in Japan began to increase from early 2003 and accelerated after 2005. The size of the accumulated loss from 2004 to 2007 was almost comparable to that of the second oil price hike during the period from 1979 to 1980.

Since 2005, Japanese firms have faced a profit squeeze due to the sizeable terms of trade deterioration caused by the oil price hike. Moreover, nominal wages again began to register a negative rate of growth at the beginning of 2007, in part due to the massive retirement of the first baby boomers from the labour market. In the longest expansion phase, from 2002 to 2007, nominal wages increased over only a limited time period from late 2005 to 2006.

It is interesting to note that Hamilton (2009) attributed the US economic recession in the period from the fourth quarter of 2007 to the third quarter of 2008 to the oil price run-up of 2007–08. He argues that, in the absence of its negative impact on consumption and purchases of domestic automobiles, the USA would not have gone into recession in the fourth quarter of 2007.

Policy dilemma in Japan

After terminating the quantitative easing policy in March 2006, it took about 3 months to reduce the excess bank reserves to a normal level without causing any disruption to the market. The first policy rate increase was implemented in July 2006 under the circumstance of global expansion, although the base-year change in the consumer price index (CPI) in August created uncertainty as to whether the inflation rate would remain in positive territory (the effect of base-year change was more sizeable than the Bank of Japan (BOJ) expected). It reduced the rate of change of the core CPI by 0.5 per cent, thereby squeezing the positive margin to maintain the above-zero inflation rate in a stable manner.

The BOJ raised the policy rate from 0.25 per cent to 0.5 per cent in February 2007 for a second time. As a BOJ Board member, I voted against the second policy rate increase proposed at the monetary policy meeting in February 2007. I was concerned about the trend of weakening domestic demand and the risk of returning to deflation. I found it at least necessary to explain that the deflation was temporary by showing a forecast of consumer prices for fiscal year (FY) 2008. Never returning to deflation was one of the requirements to end the quantitative easing policy. But the forecast period covered by the BOJ at that moment was only FY2006 and FY2007. Moreover, in my view the depreciation of the yen helped to avoid the risk of a return to deflation.

What bothered me most in the decision-making of voting was the development of the yen rate. The yen carry-trade was borrowing a low interest rate currency to fund the purchase of a high interest rate currency; that is, the yen was being sold forward at a significant premium that was equal to the interest differential between Japan and abroad.

The players in yen carry-trades were not only individual traders, including housewives, but also the hedge funds and financial intermediaries. The trade gathered momentum at the end of 2006 and facilitated the leveraged bets through interlocking balance sheets of foreign financial intermediaries.[3] Hattori and Shin (2007) observed that the yen liabilities of foreign banks located in Japan grew when foreign overnight rates were high relative to the overnight rate in Japan. At the same time, this worked to maintain at a low level the yen rate vis-à-vis the US dollar, the euro and other currencies with high interest rates.

The carry-trades are a type of 'momentum trade' that is not necessarily rational, and contradicts interest rate parity. The parity doctrine predicts an expected yen appreciation if Japan's interest rate is lower than abroad. Insofar as there may be equilibrium on the foreign exchange market, one-way betting speculators will suffer losses eventually.

The European countries endeavoured to avoid the excessive appreciation of the euro and pointed to the importance of rectifying the global imbalance between the US and Asian economies including Japan. When I met with Mr Allan Bollard, Governor of the Reserve Bank of New Zealand, in summer 2006, he expressed his concern about the consequence of speculative carry-trades on excessive volatility in the exchange rate and government bonds. The low interest rates in Japan and Switzerland were deemed to be the main cause of carry-trades. On the other hand, the use of the intervention policy was not an option for the Japanese Ministry of Finance after implementing the 'great intervention' in 2003 and 2004.

Eventually, the second increase in policy rate was implemented based on the following recognition (Minutes of Monetary Policy Meeting, 20–21 February 2007):

> ... if expectation took hold, in such a situation, that interest rates would remain low for a long time regardless of economic activity and prices, there was a possibility that sustained economic growth would be hampered by misallocation of funds and resources through excess financial and economic activities.

Later developments were exactly in line with my prediction. The CPI excluding fresh foods fell into negative territory again, from February to October. Exactly in October, Japan entered into recession, preceding the US recession in December. Afterwards, the oil price rise pushed up the inflation rate, which reached a peak of 2.4 per cent in July and August 2008. The inflation was mainly sustained by oil and food price hikes. As it was accompanied by neither wage nor profit increases, nobody welcomed it.

This was the first serious challenge for me to encounter; the trade-off in monetary policy implementation between the macro-economic policy goal aimed at avoiding deflation and preventing greater financial imbalance. If we wanted to achieve the goal of minimization of deviations from the desired inflation rate and the output gap in a forward looking way (notably, the economic development one year ahead is the most important), it was right not to raise the policy rate. Yet, there remained the issue of likely distortions on the financial market.

Policy response by the US Federal Reserve and the European Central Bank

Facing the accelerating increase in the oil price led by the future market price, the Federal Reserve stopped cutting the policy rate in July 2008, at the level of 2 per cent. In fact, the economy had already fallen into recession at that time, due to the sharp rise in oil prices. The lower federal funds rate was perceived to encourage a decline in the dollar value and thus accelerate speculative investment on the commodity futures market. It is not clear whether an earlier stop in cutting the policy rate could have mitigated the adverse effect on domestic demand, thus avoiding the recession in December 2007.

On the other hand, the European Central Bank (ECB) reacted against the acceleration of oil price increases by raising the policy rate in early July 2008. However, the oil price bubble collapsed in mid July 2008. The increase in the policy rate intensified the risk of deeper recession in the euro area at a later stage. These episodes also pointed to the need for additional instruments to curb excessive risk-taking by financial intermediaries and investors, which compromises the achievement of macro-economic stability.

To sum up, the period from 1996 to mid 2008 in the USA can be described as the 'decade of sequential bubbles' during which, as bubbles collapsed, new bubbles emerged sequentially. The sequential bubbles are in sharp contrast to Japan's 'synchronized bubbles' in the latter half of the 1980s.[4]

The sequential bubbles resemble the 'bubble substitution' described by Jean Tirole (1985). According to his view, there is a random transfer of a bubble from one asset to another, while the 'deterministic aggregate bubble' persists under the condition that the bubble-free economy is dynamically inefficient. Yet, there is no firm evidence that the US economy was dynamically inefficient; i.e. that the rate of return on capital was lower than the economic growth rate.[5]

Monetary policy has two aspects: as a macro-economic instrument and as an instrument to maintain financial stability. The latter macro-prudential policy includes the task of pre-empting the emergence of financial imbalance. It has a global dimension through the interlocking balance sheets of financial intermediaries in a globalized financial market. A policy dilemma could emerge when there appears to be a trade-off involved in implementing the two policy tasks.

CAUSES OF THE SEQUENTIAL AND SYNCHRONIZED BUBBLES

Causes of bubbles in the USA and Japan

Behind the persistent tendency to produce new sequential bubbles in the USA, we observe that there was a trend towards heavy leveraging by financial institutions against the background of rapid securitization and financial innovations, while the household sector accumulated debt at a rapid pace above the historical trend. The amorphous 'shadow banking system' enhanced the excessive leveraging in the process of securitization. Under the information asymmetry, distorted incentives such as the problems of moral hazard (due to the lack of supervision on mortgage lenders) and adverse selection (due to the lemon problem on the collateral market), and an agency problem (as in the case of fund managers and the rating agencies), aggravated the mis-pricing of risks. Furthermore, there has been a tremendous increase in the proportion of short-term liabilities (such as in repos and the ABCPs) which, under the sustained low short-term interest rates, heightened the leveraging by investment banks and the maturity mismatches.

In the case of Japan in the latter half of the 1980s, the move towards securitization was underdeveloped and slow. The gradual and lopsided financial liberalization played an important role in creating the asset price bubbles. For instance, ABCP issue was initially allowed only for non-financial firms; it was not until 1998 that the banks were permitted to issue ABCPs. The large-lot time deposit rates were liberalized while the small-lot time deposits were regulated, resulting in cross-subsidization.

The gradual and partial deregulation both in interest rates and new security issues distorted the allocation of funds, as exemplified by the interest rate of the ABCP issued by non-financial firms being lower than the liberalized time-deposit rates. Banks provided real estate loans by collecting time deposits with high rates, while the non-financial firms engaged in the 'zaitech'[6] (notably, by employing the various investment trusts); they embarked on real estate investments by issuing commercial paper, warrant bonds and convertible bonds, on both the domestic and international markets. The money moved around the market from non-financial firms to financial institutions, and vice versa, leading to an acceleration of asset prices.

Moreover, the Jusens (the non-banks affiliated with major banks specializing in housing and real estate loans) expanded loans rapidly into the real estate sector, because of the shift of major banks' strategy to refocus on the housing loan business as their own.

In addition, the monitoring function through the capital market was not strong enough when the role of the main banks as a 'delegated monitor' was diminishing, reflecting the strengthening financial position of big non-financial firms. The weakening monitoring role by the main banks in the absence of effective market monitoring resulted in a moral hazard by bank and non-bank managers in financing the real estate investments. Land value as collateral was wrongly perceived to be immune from declining in postwar Japan.

One of the salient differences between Japan and the USA in the process of emerging bubbles was the movement of the leverage ratio. The leverage ratio, defined as the ratio of total assets to the sum of common stock and capital reserves held by banks, declined during the period of accelerating asset prices in the case of the Japanese banks. In contrast, it increased sharply in US investment banks and the European banks. Anticipating the likely introduction of the Bank for International Settlements' (BIS) capital ratio rules in 1988, the Japanese banks augmented capital and capital reserves by issuing equity under the circumstance of the stock market boom (Hattori *et al.* 2009). Despite the decreasing tendency in leverage ratio of the Japanese banks, the asset price bubbles persisted to grow. This story has some implications for implementing macro-prudential policy.

The conundrum of the long-term interest rate

On the emergence of sequential bubbles in the USA, many commentators mentioned the important role of low long-term interest rates, given the high nominal growth rate and the easy funding conditions. In the process of raising the Federal Fund rate from 2004 to 2005, after avoiding the risk falling into deflation in 2003, Mr Greenspan noticed the insensitivity of long-term interest rates to changes in short-term interest rates and named it the 'conundrum of the long-term interest rate'.

His successor, Chairman Bernanke, elucidated the puzzle in 2005 by pointing out that the world saving–investment balance shifted towards excess saving after the Asian currency crisis in 1997 and 1998. He insisted that this worked to maintain the real long-term interest rate at a low level, despite the booming world economy after the IT bubble burst. The high growth combined with the low real long-term interest rates created the macro-economic circumstances conducive to the emergence of bubbles.

This recognition gave rise to the controversy between the US and Chinese governments on the cause of sequential bubbles. Mr Paulson, then US Treasurer, pointed out that, to the extent that the capital inflow from China tended to lower the nominal long-term interest rate in the USA, China had joined the bubble-generating process. The Chinese Government blamed the USA, since it was responsible for allocating the flow of funds available for US investors.

Chairman Bernanke (2009) admitted that the USA should have used the capital flowing from abroad in a more productive way, by noting:

> The global imbalances were the joint responsibility of the United States and our trading partners, and although the topic was a perennial one at international conferences, we collectively did not do enough to reduce those imbalances. However, the responsibility to use the resulting capital inflows effectively fell primarily on the receiving countries, particularly the United States.

But, if we look at the longer-run movements in real long-term interest rates (the interest rate on 10-year government bonds minus the rate of changes in consumer prices), they had already peaked in the mid 1980s, and showed a scalar decline until 2008 (Figure 5.3). In addition, the excess saving itself could work not only to reduce the long-term real interest rate, but also to lower the growth rate. Furthermore, the world saving-ratio estimated by the World Bank has remained almost unchanged in recent decades, contradicting the excess saving hypothesis. We should seek a different explanation for the low long-term real interest rates in the USA, aside from the capital inflow from abroad.

The role of demographic change

As another background factor of sequential bubbles in the USA, we can mention changes in the population structure. The share of the US working-age population between 20 and 64 years old started to increase after the mid 1960s, and remained flat from the early 1980s to the mid 1990s. It started to increase again from the mid 1990s and reached a peak in 2007, a period that virtually coincided with the 'decade of sequential bubbles' (Figure 5.4).

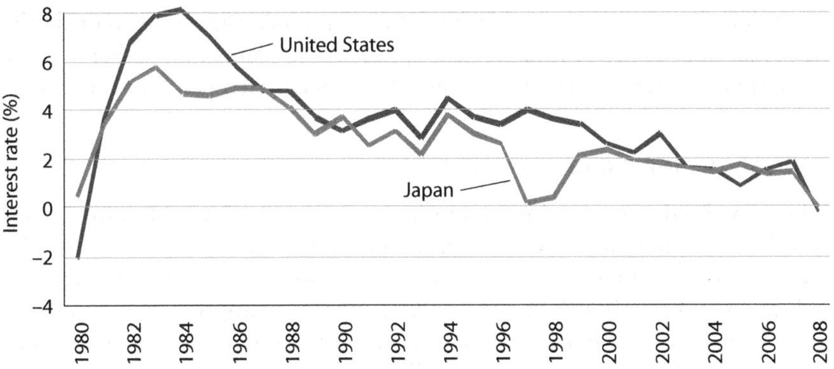

Figure 5.3 Long-term real interest rates in the USA and Japan. Source: IMF.

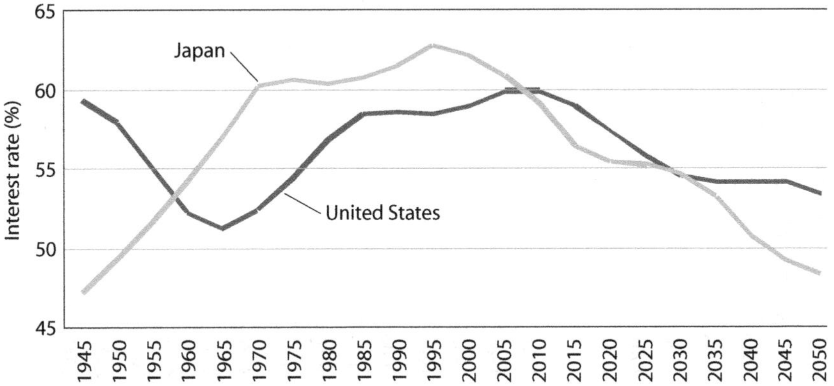

Figure 5.4 Proportion of the working-age population in the USA and Japan, 1945–2050. Source: United Nations.

Usually, we observe that the increase in the share of the working-age population is associated with a high growth rate in per-capita consumption, as the age profile of lifetime consumption reveals an inverted U shape with a peak at 40–50 years old. The economic miracles in the postwar era are often attributed to the increasing share of the working-age population. Indeed, the high growth era in Japan overlapped the period of very rapid increase in the share of working-age population, from 1945 to the early 1970s.

What is interesting is the fact that Japan's working-age population again began to increase in the early 1980s, peaking in the mid 1990s. We see about a 10-year difference between the USA and Japan in the re-acceleration of the share of working-age population (Figure 5.4).

Moreover, to the extent that market participants anticipate a sharp decline in the share of working-age population over the future, this will work to lower the long-term real interest rate. If we interpret the Euler equation of consumers as the 'pricing kernel of asset price determination', as is the case in the Lucas asset-pricing model, the future decline of per-capita consumption, namely the rise in marginal utility of future consumption, must bring about either a lower long-term real interest rate, or a higher rate of time preference (Martin 2005).[7]

Implications for Asian economies

If this view holds true, the bubbles in Japan and the USA could share a common demographic factor. Moreover, the place most likely to experience the next bubbles is China, where the share of the working-age population will peak in the mid 2010s (Figure 5.5). Per-capita consumption will accelerate until the mid 2010s, yet the real long-term interest rate will be maintained at a low level in the face of the financial liberalization process underway.

A similar risk also exists in other Asian economies. Japan is a frontrunner in the population ageing process. For Japan, the 'demographic opportunity', when the country enjoyed the 'demographic bonus' conducive to high

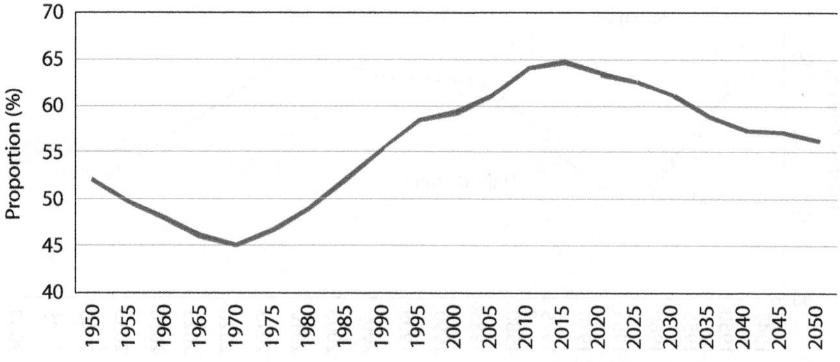

Figure 5.5 Proportion of the working-age population in China, 1950–2050. Source: United Nations.

growth due to the increasing labour force and the relatively low dependency ratio, ended exactly in 1990 at the time of bursting bubbles. This move is likely to be followed, in order, by Singapore, Thailand, China, Taiwan, Korea, Hong Kong, Malaysia, Indonesia and the Philippines over the period from 2010 to 2040.

Timing of bursting bubbles, and the 'mop-up-after' approach

On the role of demographic change, there remains a question with respect to the difference in the timing of asset price bubble burst, because the peak in the working-age population in Japan was in the mid rather than the early 1990s. The disparity between Japan and the USA in this timing can be explained at least partly by the difference in policy reaction.

Mr Greenspan might have drawn a lesson from the slump with deflation in the post-bubble-burst Japanese economy; it is extremely important to wipe out the demand-dampening and deflationary impact arising from a bubble burst as soon as possible. Another lesson learnt from Japan's experience could have been to prevent the crisis by containing, at an early stage of emerging bubbles, the excessive risk-taking by financial institutions and borrowers.

The 'mop-up-after' approach is to ignore emerging bubbles and just clean up the problem afterwards. The approach cherished by Mr Greenspan allowed the emergence of sequential bubbles by providing a 'Greenspan put' for excessive risk-taking by investors and financial institutions. This approach is based on the recognition of a number of difficulties to pre-empting the emergence of bubbles, such as the identification of bubbles, the cost involved in containing them, and the inability to burst bubbles by using only the interest rate in the presence of non-linearity of asset price developments.

Professor Frederic Mishkin (2007), a former Governor of the Federal Reserve, in a paper presented at the Jackson Hole conference in 2007, enumerated the reasons why it is so difficult to prevent asset price bubbles by the use of conventional monetary policy instruments. Moreover, if the bubbles are sequential, it is all the more difficult to contain a new bubble at the same time as engaging in cleaning-up the problems caused by an already burst bubble.

Japan, on the other hand, adopted a more determined and restrictive policy to contain the synchronized bubbles. The BOJ started to tighten monetary policy from May 1989 to August 1990, although belatedly. The stock price peaked in 1990, yet the land price continued to increase. The Ministry of Finance introduced a tough quantitative restriction on real estate lending in 1991. The quantitative measure implied a prohibitive lending rate to the real estate industry and thus brought about an abrupt end to the land price bubble. In addition, the restrictive tax measures on capital gains introduced in 1991 seemed to work to collapse the bubble.

Ultimately, these tough policy measures eradicated the mythos of a 'never-declining land price' in postwar Japan. They prevented the emergence of sequential bubbles, despite the increasing share of working-age population, until the mid 1990s. The other side of the coin was the delayed action to prevent the 'lost decade' being accompanied by price deflation.

Structural change in the labour market

Drastic demographic changes in Japan aggravated the damage inflicted by the bubble burst. The 'share economy', notably the employment system traditional in the postwar era, was shaken by the demographic changes. In addition, against the background of the globalization of the financial market, the increasing pressure from the foreign equity holders induced the corporate managers to raise the rate of return on equity.

Structural change in the labour market was accelerated by the financial turmoil. The bankruptcy of the Sanyo security company on the money market, coupled with the closedown of the Yamaichi security company in October 1997, brought the Japanese economy into the 'vicious circle' of deterioration of private banks' balance sheets and worsening economic prospects. Subsequently, the three major banks (the Hokkaido Takushoku Bank, the Long-Term Credit Bank of Japan, and the Securities and Credit Bank of Japan) collapsed or were nationalized in 1998. The non-performing assets in the banking sector increased sharply and resulted in the second loss arising from the recession under persistent deflation.

Given the rise in unemployment under the circumstance of the erosion of the traditional Japanese corporate system, the number of suicides jumped

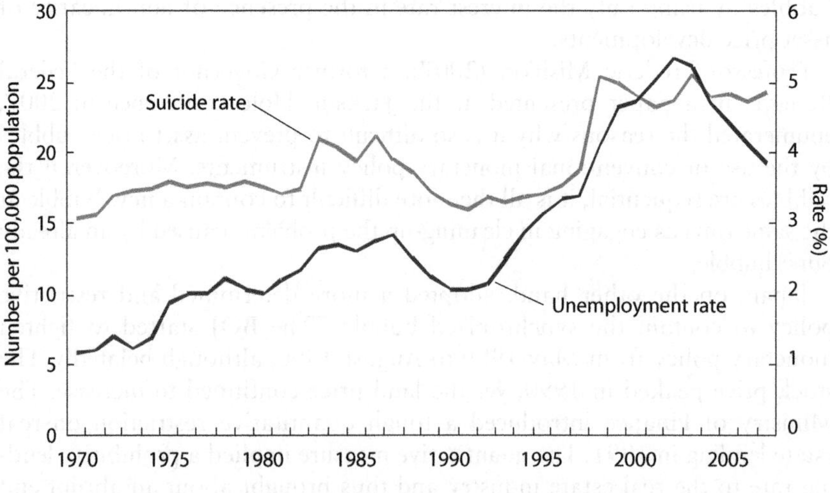

Figure 5.6 Unemployment and suicide rates in Japan, 1970–2006. Source: Ministry of Welfare and Labor.

from about 20,000 annually in the mid 1990s to more than 30,000 in 1998 (Figure 5.6). It has remained at a high level, with the number of young-worker suicides increasing in more recent times. Among high-income OECD countries, Japan's male (female) suicide rate ranked highest (second highest) in 2004 (Chen *et al.* 2009).

This symbolized a structural change in the labour market where the young workers found it difficult to secure jobs and have a lifetime plan. This diminishing 'hope' over the future among younger people worked to aggravate the damage inflicted by the bubble burst.

Moreover, nominal wages began to fall after 1998. This indicates the erosion of nominal wage rigidity against a background of the trend to an increasing share of non-standard workers. This tendency was reinforced by the IT bubble recession; its share reached 34 per cent of total employed workers in 2008.

It was more than coincidence that the CPI, excluding fresh foods, began to register a negative rate of change after September 1998.

POLICY RESPONSE IN THE 'LOST DECADE'

After the bubble burst, the Japanese economy entered into recession in February 1991. Given the remaining heat in the economy, the move towards expansionary monetary policy was delayed and non-aggressive. The first reduction in the discount rate, from 6.0 per cent to 5.5 per cent, was in July 1991. It subsequently fell to 0.5 per cent by September 1995. Not only the monetary base, but also the money supply (M2+CD), contracted sharply and registered a negative rate of increase in 1992.

When the stock price plummeted in summer 1992, Mr Miyazawa, the then Prime Minister, sensed the smell of crisis and urged the need for capital injection into the banks. But there was no political support. Notably, the non-financial business circle reacted to his proposal with benign neglect. Thanks to the fiscal stimulus measures from 1993 to 1995, coupled with the increase in exports, Japan moved out of recession in October 1993.

On the other hand, the yen appreciated sharply after the Plaza accord in 1985, and reached a record level of ¥80 per US$1.00 in April 1995. Yet, the turnaround of the US exchange-rate policy towards achieving a 'strong dollar' brought about the yen's depreciation after 1995. The Japanese economy saw a slowdown in 1995, yet it avoided a recession.

Fiscal policy response in the 'lost decade'

On the fiscal policy response during the period of the 'lost decade', Adam Posen (1998) found that the fiscal stimulus in 1995 was exceptionally significant and resulted in solid growth in 1996. Actually, the accumulated effect of stimulus measures adopted in the period from 1992 to 1995 was sizeable in terms of changes to the structural budget deficit (Figure 5.7). However, the economic expansion was interrupted by restrictive fiscal policy measures in FY1997 and the subsequent Asian currency crisis. Under the Fiscal Structure Reform Act, which prescribed a strict schedule of spending cuts and the tax increases, the Hashimoto administration implemented a consumption tax increase from 3 per cent to 5 per cent, coupled with an expenditure cut and an increase in social security contributions. The fiscal policy contraction, which totalled to ¥9 trillion in FY1997, was too much to bear for the Japanese economy; it suffered from the balance-sheet adjustments arising from the three excesses of debt, employment and capital equipment due to inefficient investments in the real estate, distribution and services sectors.

In hindsight, the cyclical expansion phase was already close to its end when the fiscal consolidation process started. The Act should have been equipped with a 'contingency clause' that allowed more-flexible implementation. As regards tax reform, the consumption tax increase could have been combined with an income or corporate tax cut to moderate the dampening effect.

In the period from 1992 to 2002, the economic package measures were implemented through supplementary budgets, which, with the exception of FY1996 and FY1997, were introduced almost every year, to counter the three recessions, in February 1991 – October 1993, May 1997 – January 1999 and October 2000 – January 2001.

The legislative process for single rather than multi-year budgets constrained the effective use of fiscal policy. The total mobilized expense amounted to ¥145 trillion, although the 'pure water' of fiscal expenditure financed by issuing government debt was much smaller, amounting to about ¥60 trillion. A tax cut was employed four times (in April 1993, February 1994, and April

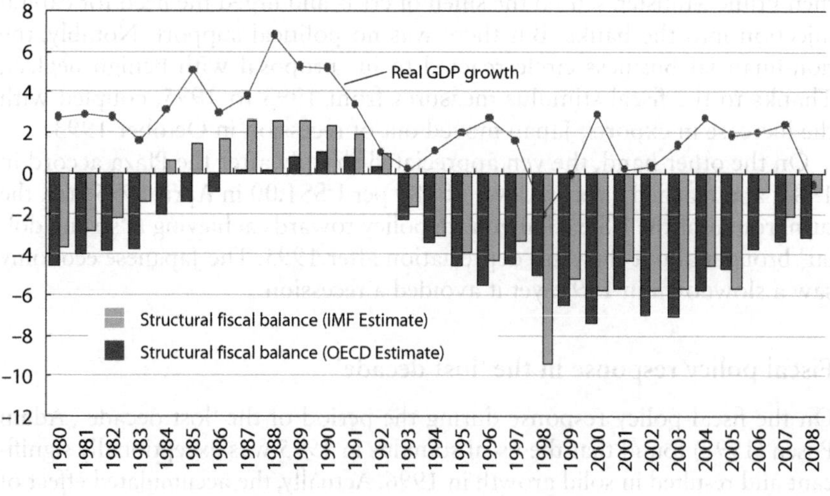

Figure 5.7 Fiscal measures taken in Japan during the 'lost decade'. Sources: OECD; IMF; Cabinet Office.

and November 1998), yet the total size of the cut was much smaller (¥17 trillion) than the substantial increase in public investment.

To conclude, the fiscal policy action succeeded in preventing a deep recession. As a result, real GDP has never dropped below its peak in 1990. Yet the heavy reliance on public investment in conducting fiscal policy did not bring about a private-domestic demand orientated growth. It did not succeed in preventing a secular decline in labour productivity, due to the lack of economic reforms to revitalize the economy. Moreover, the debt–nominal GDP ratio doubled from 73.9 per cent in 1993 to 158.0 per cent in 2003, and reached 175 per cent in 2008.

The US Government employed active fiscal stimulus measures of about 5 per cent in terms of nominal GDP in a timely, targeted way. China adopted a more sizeable fiscal stimulus than the USA, while fiscal measures similar in size to those in the USA were adopted in Japan. The concerted fiscal action among major economies succeeded in stopping the freefall of world economic activity. But there remains uncertainty whether the policy-sustained recovery can lead to private-demand orientated growth, thereby diminishing the size of external imbalance without destabilizing the value of the dollar.

Deflation and monetary policy action

In the mid 1990s the GDP deflator entered into the deflation phase, while the policy rate was already close to zero (0.5 per cent in September 1995). In September 1998, the CPI, excluding fresh foods, began to register a negative rate of increase. The BOJ employed a zero-interest-rate policy in February 1999 and expressed the intention to continue this policy until the fears about deflation were wiped out. However, the intention of the BOJ did not materialize. The exit from the zero interest rate in August 2000 failed, due to the IT bubble burst in April and the concomitant global recession since autumn 2000.

The BOJ moved to adopt a 'quantitative easing policy' in March 2001, one week after the announcement by the government that a 'mild deflation' prevailed in the Japanese economy; the CPI, excluding fresh foods, had then registered a negative rate of change for more than 2 years. The government adopted the definition of deflation employed by the IMF, namely a 'sustained price decline for more than two years'.

The quantitative easing policy was designed to calm financial instability by providing ample liquidity to the market and intensifying the effectiveness of monetary policy through the expectation channel (the 'policy duration effect') by announcing the conditions for the exit. The accumulation of bank reserves was accompanied by a lower interest rate for longer maturities. Against the background of the sizeable increase in the bank reserve target from ¥6 trillion to ¥30–35 trillion, the market interest rates of one year came close to zero.

'Great intervention' combined with quantitative easing policy

In order to overcome the deflation, Professor Lars Svensson (2001) recommended that the BOJ adopt an exchange rate targeting policy as a 'fool-proof way' of doing so. I sympathized with his proposal, because the effect of the quantitative easing policy would be reinforced by the direct purchase of foreign bonds by the BOJ, as compared with an operation using short-term government bonds; they are close substitutes for money. But the exchange rate policy is in the domain of the Ministry of Finance. In addition, it was considered to be difficult for a large economy like Japan to target the exchange rate at a significantly depreciated level.

The Ministry of Finance embarked on the 'great intervention' during the period from January 2003 to March 2004, with the implicit support of the US Treasury (Taylor 2006); the total amount of intervention was about ¥35 trillion. In the same period, the additional liquidity provision through the increase in the bank reserve target was about ¥13 trillion.

Usually, funds provided by the yen-selling intervention policy are automatically sterilized by the central bank, which works to prevent the policy rate from declining below a targeted positive level (the 'sterilized intervention'). Although there is some time lag (about 2 months) for the Ministry of Finance to issue the Financing Bill, the BOJ absorbs the funds of the yen-selling intervention by daily market operations, regardless of the sources of inflow of funds into the market. Yet, under the particular condition of the zero rate policy regime, there is no need for the BOJ to sterilize the yen funds, because there is a zero bound on the nominal interest rate. Even if the additional yen funds are provided on the market, the policy rate will not be below zero.

Watanabe and Yabu (2009) found that about 40 per cent of yen funds were not actually sterilized. This roughly corresponds to the amount of the increase in target bank reserves in the same period as the 'great intervention' policy. More interesting is their finding that the effect of the 40 per cent 'unsterilized intervention policy' on the exchange rate is stronger than the sterilized one, as long as market participants expect that the additional liquidity will remain in the market until the policy rate begins to depart from zero.

The additional provision of money matters, unless all the market interest rates are zero, regardless of the instruments of market operation, except for virtually zero-rate bills. From the general equilibrium perspective, the effect of an unsterilized intervention policy can be translated and measured by the changes in non-zero market interest rates of longer maturities. The main field of battle for the BOJ is the domestic money and bond market. In my view, the BOJ managed market expectations on the future course of monetary policy fairly well, thus bringing the market interest rate for 2–3 year maturity to a lower level. Furthermore, it initiated the unconventional policy measures to purchase longer-maturity private bills in October 2002 and ABCP in July 2003.

The quantitative easing policy consisted of three pillars. The first was the zero policy rate combined with the 'policy duration effect' through the commitment on the exit from the unconventional policy regime. The second was the 'bank reserve target policy', including the purchase of long-term government bonds when the market operation in terms of short-maturity instruments was not effective to achieve the target level of bank reserves. The third was the 'credit easing policy' to purchase the risky assets such as the ABCP.

In December 2002, the BOJ also engaged in the outright purchase of the stock held by private banks with a view to securing financial stability, because the mutual holding of stocks by banks aggravated the risk of destabilizing the banking system through sharp changes in stock prices. However, this move can be identified as implementing the 'macro-prudential policy'. Actually, the policy measure was decided at the Policy Board Meeting in September 2002, rather than at the Monetary Policy Meeting, based on the procedure prescribed in the Bank of Japan Law.

US monetary policy response

In the case of the USA, the Federal Reserve acted swiftly and decisively. The federal funds rate came close to zero within 16 months of September 2007, as compared with 9 years in the case of the Bank of Japan. The Federal Reserve embarked on a 'credit easing policy' by establishing a number of new facilities[8] and, since October 2008, the size of its balance sheet has expanded rapidly, offsetting the shrinking private credit supply.

One of the differences in policy response was that the BOJ's quantitative easing policy focused on the liability side of the central bank, namely the bank reserves and the provision of liquidity, whereas the Federal Reserve emphasized the asset side of the central bank to provide credit and take risks from private financial institutions (credit easing policy). In contrast, the Bank of England has continued the quantitative easing policy by increasing the target amount of long-term government bonds.

Another difference from the Japanese quantitative easing policy was that US interest rates were applied to required and excess reserves. The positive margin creates room to maintain market transactions. (The Swedish central bank, on the other hand, applied a negative interest rate on bank reserves in July 2009 with the intention of activating the idle balance.)

Furthermore, the interest attached to reserves enables the separation of the decision-making on liquidity provision from that on policy rate changes, though not completely, due to the existence of the government-sponsored enterprises such as Fannie Mae and Freddie Mac; they hold no deposit account at the Federal Reserve. In the process of the 'rolling exit' from a credit easing policy the increase in policy rate can be postponed to avoid the risk of significantly undershooting the target of price stability. But there remains uncertainty whether the excess liquidity could be dismantled without disrupting the market, by simply raising the interest rate attached to bank reserves.

The final difference was that, since January 2008, the Federal Reserve has expanded the network of swap arrangements with other central banks. This implied a regime shift of dollar provision in the world economy, which may also complicate the exit process.

Restoring financial stability

Turning to the measures to restore financial stability, the instability of the banking sector was already apparent in the mid 1990s with the closure of Kizu Credit and Hyogo Bank. However, it took 3 years to embark on the capital injection because the political debate on the use of public money with respect to the Jusens induced an attitude of forbearance in the regulatory authority. The stumbling block was how to allocate the burden between the main banks and the agriculture corporative credit unions that also provided credit to the Jusens. The voice of the taxpayers was strongly against the use of public money for the resolution of non-performing assets held by the non-banks. The regulatory authority failed to reconcile the interests of different lenders.

Capital injection

After the failure of Hokkaido Takushoku Bank in November 1997, a first capital injection was implemented. Three such were made (in 1998, 1999 and 2003), totalling ¥12 trillion. However, simple capital injection by the government failed to solve the problem. Capital injection in the absence of strict assessment on the asset side of banks' balance sheets failed to restore financial stability.

In April 1998, an early warning system was introduced. This enabled the regulatory authority to recommend, based on on-site examination, the adequacy of reserves for non-performing assets held by banks. It contributed to improving the business operations of financial institutions with capital lower than specified soundness criteria.

The Long-Term Credit Bank and the Nippon Credit Bank were put under special public management based on the Financial Revitalization Law in late 1998. One lesson learnt from the nationalization is that it is costly if it persists too long. The government was obviously not suited to the efficient management of banks.

Further, in May 2003, the Financial Crisis Management Council, with members from the Prime Minister's office, the Minister of Finance, the Minister in Charge of Financial Issues and the Governor of the Bank of Japan, was convened for the first time. It decided to make a capital injection into the Risona Bank based on the Deposit Insurance Law (Article 102-1 bearing on capital enhancement before bankruptcy), even though the bank's debt was likely to exceed its asset value. This capital injection resulted in more than 70 per cent of voting shares being owned by government, while the interests of equity-holders were protected. On the other hand, in November 2003 the Ashikaga Bank was nationalized (the purchase of the bank's equity at zero value by government) based on the Article 102-3 bearing on special crisis management.

The rescue operation for the Risona Bank signified the end of fears of bankruptcies by major banks and brought about a sharp rise of stock prices. It may be noted that the resolution procedures were different from one bank to another, but they were implemented based on the Laws.

Restoration of financial stability in the USA

In contrast, the absence of a regime for resolving systemically important non-depository financial institutions has been a serious deficiency in the USA. In the case of the US Bear Stearns takeover by J.P. Morgan, the Federal Reserve helped by buying $29 billion of risky assets, based on the recognition that it is too interconnected to be allowed to suddenly fail.[9] Lehman Brothers was allowed to suddenly fail, while the Treasury and the Federal Reserve prevented the bankruptcy of the American International Group (AIG), and the Federal Reserve provided credit up to $85 billion to AIG (the total amount later increased to $150 billion), because it too was judged to be too entangled to fail. The Treasury and the Federal Deposit Insurance Corporation (FDIC) provided Citibank with a guarantee of assets up to a maximum of $306 billion, because it was deemed to be 'too big to fail'.

It seems desirable to apply the FDIC resolution procedure to the systemically important financial institutions under an integrated supervision authority. The current US supervision system is fragmented and riddled with gaps and overlaps. It seems necessary for the USA to have a more consolidated supervision system.

Supervision authority

In Japan, the Financial Supervision Agency was established in June 1998. It was reorganized as the Financial Service Agency (FSA) in 2000 after serious debate on the appropriate separation between fiscal and financial policy, both of which had been under the control of the Ministry of Finance. The FSA supervised almost all the financial institutions, including the securities and insurance companies, and the hedge funds, and embarked on the more strict examination of non-performing assets after the first capital injection.

In April 2001, Mr Yanagisawa, the then Minister in charge of Financial Services, persuaded the banks to off-balance the non-performing assets in 2 years (for existing assets) or 3 years (for new assets). Then, in October 2002, Mr Takenaka, the successor to Mr Yanagisawa, announced a new Financial Revitalization Program which set a target to reduce the non-performing assets held by banks by half by March 2005. The BOJ proposed to employ the discounted cash flow method to assess the quality of non-performing assets; common standards were applied across different banks, because loans to the same company were often classified differently from one bank to another.

With a view to convincing the taxpayers about the need for public money injection, it is essential to form a 'common knowledge' among regulatory authorities and market participants on the likely loss incurred by financial institutions. The strict examination of assets held by financial institutions constitutes a precondition for the convergence on expectation.

The 'stress test' implemented by the US supervisory authorities in April served well to form a common knowledge by increasing the transparency on the asset side of financial institutions. But the incentive to off-balance the toxic assets for the US financial institutions is still weak, due to the lack of target-setting in the reduction of bad assets.

Off-balancing of non-performing assets

The Japanese Government attempted several times to separate the non-performing assets from banks' balance sheets. The first corporation funded by private money in 1992 received the funds under terms similar to those for the initial proposal for the 'Super-TARP' in the USA. However, the move served only as storage for the non-performing assets. After some trial and error, the Resolution and Collection Corporation (RCC) purchased bad assets from banks amounting to ¥10 trillion at transparent prices that were close to market prices. As a result, the eventual loss to taxpayers in purchasing bad assets was negligible. It is important that the purchase price be seen as fair in the eyes of taxpayers. An explicit and implicit subsidy on the purchase price would add to the difficulty of getting taxpayer approval for the use of public money.

Moreover, the RCC engaged not only in purchasing bad assets, but also in restructuring the indebted companies by employing debt-equity swaps and other measures. At a later stage, the Industrial Revitalization Corporation specialized in restructuring the indebted companies. It was, indeed, a long process to fully digest the non-performing assets.

In view of the experience in Japan, it was quite unfortunate that the Private–Public Partnership Investment Program by the US authorities to purchase the toxic assets was scaled down significantly in July 2009.

Fiscal costs

The disposal of non-performing assets in Japan amounted to 20 per cent of nominal GDP (about ¥100 trillion). The government contributed ¥70 trillion. The public money, amounting to ¥12 trillion, was injected into the banking sector with a view to strengthening the banks' capital. In addition, bad assets of about ¥7 trillion were purchased by the RCC. The ultimate fiscal costs incurred by the capital injection, the resolutions of banks and the purchase of non-performing assets were not so large, amounting to about ¥15 trillion (Table 5.2).

PREVENTION OF BUBBLES AND CRISES

Two-perspectives approach and macro-prudential policy

Given the massive provision of liquidity under the virtually zero-interest policy rates in the advanced economies, there is a risk of the emergence of new asset price bubbles. The exit process from the unconventional policy regime may require the employment of an adequate mix of monetary policy and macro-prudential supervision.

When the BOJ abandoned the quantitative easing policy, it announced the 'two-perspectives approach' coupled with the 'understanding of medium-term price stability' among the Board members; the price stability expressed in numerical form by Board members ranged from zero to 2 per cent.

On the first perspective, the BOJ carries out the task of smoothing-out economic fluctuations in a forward-looking way. Within the forecast periods of 6 months or 2 years, the Board members examine economic development in the light of their projections.

On the second perspective, the BOJ pays due attention to potential risks over a time horizon longer than the forecast period; namely the risks of harmful impact events with low probability. The second perspective may

Table 5.2 Use of public money and actual losses

	Amount	
	Total	*Recovered*
Deposit Insurance Corporation	47,060	31,818
Purchase of troubled assets	9,776	9,596
Capital injection	12,427	10,539
Cost related to bank failures (deposit insurance payout etc.)	18,868	6,824
Others (cost related to bank nationalization)	5,989	4,859
BOJ's purchase of shares held by banks	2,018	
Sub-total	49,078	31,818
Government guarantee for credit to SMEs	28,944	
Government guarantee for Industrial Revitalization Corporation of Japan (IRCJ)	10,000	
Total	88,022	

Sources: Deposit Insurance Corporation; Bank of Japan; Financial Service Agency.

Note: as of September 2008. Billion yen.

be a useful starting point for the macro-prudential policy as well as the maintenance of price stability over the longer run. The second perspective can incorporate the risk of asset price bubbles or the risk of deflation in a forward-looking way.

If we succeed in managing the economy from the first perspective, we cannot exclude the risk of harmful events with low probability. Macroeconomic stability may not automatically assure financial stability. Rather, the success of the first perspective could promote complacency and excessive risk-taking by investors.

The New Keynesian view versus the Hayekian view

This paradox led to the question raised by Mr William White (2006), former Director of Research Department at the BIS; namely 'Is price stability enough?'. This question recalled the article by Hayek (1975) titled 'Is full employment enough?'. According to the Austrian's view, relative prices are the key to future outcomes. Hayek observed that when inflation created in the pursuit of full employment collapsed, then a 'stabilization crisis' followed.

Today, the terms 'inflation' and 'full employment' can be replaced by 'asset price bubbles' and 'price stability'. Mr White argued that the 'deviations between the financial and natural interest rate lead the financial system to create credit which encourages investments that, in the end, fail to prove profitable' (White 2006:13). In his view, the relative price distortion created by a New Keynesian way of managing monetary policy could eventually lead to financial imbalance. For instance, a low interest rate that is sustained for too long will lead to a financial imbalance, including the emergence of bubbles. In other words, the success (the 'great moderation' realized in part by successful monetary policy) creates the failure (asset price bubbles).

I had occasion to talk with Professor Michael Woodford at the international conference organized by the ECB in December 2005. I posed the question whether it is possible to formulate the emergence and collapse of asset price bubbles in the New Keynesian model. The answer was negative. He pointed out that the bubbles can emerge for various reasons and thus it is difficult to incorporate them into a formal model.

Indeed, the bubbles can be modelled in several ways (Brunnermeier 2008). In one type of model, bubbles can be generated on an equilibrium growth path within the framework of an overlapping generation model with rational expectation (Tirole 1985). Tirole (2009) provided a different model in which asset bubbles replace liquidity under constrained borrowing by investors. In another type of model, Barsky (2009) argues that the heterogeneity of investors can easily lead to the emergence of bubbles, if there are constraints on short selling in a subset of investors. The combination of the heterogeneity and the incompleteness of markets allowed a subset of bullish investors to dominate asset price determination. Furthermore, the interaction between rational and behavioural traders can create bubbles due to the limited arbitrage by rational investors. Finally, in the absence of common knowledge of emergence of bubbles, some traders perceive gains from trade, even if there are no such gains. Matsushima (2009) presented the bubble–crash model; in that model there is a small probability that every arbitrageur behaves rationally and the bubbles can persist under this circumstance until such time as there is no common knowledge that any arbitrageur is behaving rationally.

Given the risk of emergence of asset price bubbles under more general conditions than the conventional wisdom tells us, there is a reason to be cautious about the emergence of financial imbalance in terms of quantity. As early as 2003, the BIS had sent a warning signal of the financial imbalance problem by pointing to the above-trend provision of liquidity, money supply and bank credit. Borio and Lowe (2002) observed that financial crises are likely to be preceded by some combination of sustained above-normal rates of credit growth, asset prices and investments. At the same time the USA enlarged the size of its current account deficit substantially. The financial imbalance grew together with the size of the global imbalance. The USA expanded the current account deficit from 1 per cent of nominal GDP in 1996 to 6 per cent in 2007.

Although I do not believe that the sheer size of a current account deficit will indicate the magnitude of the financial imbalance, there have been two financial distortions in the two economies. It seems obvious that US consumers relied excessively on borrowing to finance housing investment, while the investment banks expanded their balance sheets too rapidly by increasing the leverage ratio. Credit bubbles seem to have enabled the ratio of US consumers' debt to disposable income to deviate significantly from the historical trend. The ratio was stable at 45–50 per cent between the mid 1960s and the mid 1980s, but it increased sharply since the mid 1980s, reaching about 100 per cent in 2008.

While the savings ratio of Chinese consumers is, at about 18 per cent, not far from the level in other Asian countries, the national saving ratio increased sizeably due to the increase in corporate savings, notably that of state enterprises.

Fat-tail risks

Even if the BOJ adopts the two-perspectives approach, there remain several difficulties in the actual implementation of macro-prudential policy. First, it is extremely difficult to predict the emergence of low-probability harmful events. Second, there is a shortage of policy instruments. The interest rate policy is already used to attain the two goals of lessening the size of economic fluctuations and securing price stability.

What was remarkable was the role of the fat-tail risks in the birth–burst process of sequential bubbles.[10] One of the implications for monetary policy is that the non-linearity in the process of emerging bubbles will undermine the effect of the stepwise interest rate increases to contain bubbles. As the strategic behaviour by fund managers tended to concentrate on investments of higher yield with higher risks in the phase of asset price increases, the frequency and severity of catastrophic movements of asset prices are augmented.

Measurement of systemic risk

To identify catastrophic events, a reliable assessment of the systemic risk or a vulnerability indicator is needed. The IMF has already promoted the importance of a list of Financial Soundness indicators for individual countries. The early warning system in the working of the US Federal Deposit Insurance Corporation Improvement Act prescribes that the regulatory authorities be required to act if an indicator falls below certain benchmark levels. Yet these measures are not designed to provide an assessment of systemic risk.

Adrian and Brunnermeier (2009) propose the adoption of a measure called 'conditional value at risk (VaR)', (CoVaR), focusing on the externalities relating to fire sale, hoarding, runs and network externality. It is defined as the VaR conditional institution being in distress, which also affects other institutions. It captures both the exposure and the contribution of a financial institution to the systemic risk. This difference between CoVaR and VaR captures an institution's contribution to systemic risk. In order to oversee the systemically important financial institutions, it may serve as a useful indicator. However, it still seems difficult to predict the systemic risk accurately in advance, as is also the case of the prediction of large-scale earthquakes.

However, it is useful to carry out the 'stress test' on occasions where asset prices deviate from historical trends, and to provide an assessment on the adverse impact of sharp reversals on the real economy. It is worthwhile constructing a model that incorporates the feedback effects from financial stress to the real economy.

Three dimensions of macro-prudential policy

Macro-prudential policy aims at achieving the stability of the financial system as a whole, while micro-prudential policy attempts to secure the soundness of individual financial institutions. It seems appropriate that a new policy instrument should be introduced to achieve this policy goal, independently of the interest rate policy. Yet, this may entail attention to the subtle issue of the interaction between macro-prudential policy and monetary policy.

From the perspective of preventing systemic risk, we can identify three dimensions of macro-prudential policy. The first is to pre-empt the emergence of financial imbalance and to prick the asset price bubbles as they form. The second is to minimize the damage to financial institutions by preparing a sufficient buffer against unpredictable loss and liquidity shortage in the future. The third is the resolution procedure for systemically important financial institutions.

Prevention of financial imbalance

On the prevention of financial imbalance, the first candidate instrument relates to credit growth and asset prices. Traditionally, the BIS stressed the importance of establishing prudential norms of credit growth and asset prices. If the inflation risk is relevant over the future, then the trade-off between the monetary policy and the norm of credit growth and asset prices disappears. Yet, if deflation is a serious risk, solving the trade-off may become more complicated. The restraint on credit growth by higher interest rates may drive the inflation rate to an unacceptably low level. William White (2004) recommended resisting financial excesses first and securing price stability over a somewhat longer time horizon on the assumption of existing wage/price rigidities.

But the issue can become more serious in the case of diminishing nominal rigidities like Japan after 1997–98. If the pattern of export-investment-orientated growth is not accompanied by household income growth, there is a risk of simultaneous price deflation and bubbles. If the deflation persists over a longer run, it will undermine the credibility of the central bank on price stability. I find it appropriate to provide forecasts for a time horizon longer than 2 years, based on alternative optimal policy projections that incorporate the risk of financial distress.

Loose lending standards associated with excessive leveraging activity, instead of lower policy rate, can create an asset price bubble. Dampening bubbles can also be more targeted and surgical. In these cases we can separate the monetary policy from policies geared towards financial stability. Adrian and Shin (2008) argued that these two policies are two sides of the same coin (namely the size of balance sheets of financial firms) under the securitized, market-based financial system. Notwithstanding the financial system view, which emphasizes the effect of a low policy rate on the rise of the leverage ratio, we can separate the decision-making on monetary policy from macro-prudential supervision by introducing new instruments to contain the excessive expansion of firms' balance sheets.

As a second instrument, we can mention the leverage ratio, defined as the ratio of total value of assets to equity, given the fact that a sharply rising leverage ratio of investment banks fuelled asset price bubbles. Recently, Switzerland has introduced a cap on the leverage ratio. Alternatively, we can introduce counter-cyclical capital requirements that will contain the excessive risk-taking by managers of financial firms. Yet, they may not be sufficient to pre-empt the emergence of bubbles, as the case of Japan's bubbles demonstrated.

The third instrument is to change the incentive structure to seek short-term profit by introducing standards for compensation of managers. It seems wrong to impose a legal restriction on the manager's compensation, as the direct intervention on the determination of compensation may impede the efficient management of financial firms. However, it makes sense to enhance the voice of equity-holders (on 'say on pay', for instance) and promote the full disclosure and the explanation of a metric on management incentive, thereby shifting the focus to longer run profitability of financial intermediaries.

Buffer against likely loss, and liquidity management

With respect to preparing a buffer against likely loss, more and better quality capital is required. The current BIS capital requirements failed to pre-empt the financial crisis, because of pro-cyclicality and the inability to increase the equity issue under financial stress. In addition, the Basel II missed the important role of liquidity management. The funding shortage problem triggered the liquidity spirals, as the cases of Bear Stearns and AIG clearly demonstrated. Moreover, the precautionary hoarding by individual financial firms amplified the loss and the margin spirals.

One of the ways to remove the pro-cyclicality of capital ratio is 'dynamic provisioning'. The measure has already been adopted by Spain. It ensures the loan loss provision rises when new loans are made. It creates a buffer against the loss, but it cannot prevent excess provision of credit.

Another instrument is the use of the insurance scheme. Instead of a higher capital ratio in good times, the insurance policy (capital insurance) can provide a buffer of capital in the event of crisis. The insurers put the fund in Treasuries and receive the insurance premium and the interest payments (Kashyap *et al.* 2008).[11]

With respect to liquidity management, some commentators recommend introducing minimum liquidity requirements. Yet, the liquidity shortage arises basically from the asset–liability mismatch. It seems sensible to create an incentive for reducing the mismatch by adopting 'mark-to-funding' accounting (Brunnermeier *et al.* 2009); under this accounting rule, assets are valued according to the funding capacity of the holder. For regulatory purposes it is appropriate to publish the balance sheets based on the 'mark-to-funding', while fair-value accounting rules are required for securing transparency.

Resolution procedure for systemically important financial institutions

Finally, on the resolution procedure for systematically important financial institutions, it is extremely difficult to establish a cross-border resolution procedure that can avoid high transaction costs, given the lack of harmonized bankruptcy laws. The US Government decided that the Federal Reserve should become the overseer of systemically important financial institutions. This new task may entail fiscal outlays, as exemplified by the cases of Bear Stearns and AIG. While it is desirable to observe Bagehot's principles in establishing new facilities by the requirement on collateral and haircuts, it was difficult to observe them at a time of crisis. This implies the need of collaboration of the Federal Reserve not only with other financial supervisory authorities, but also the fiscal authority.

Moreover, the lawmakers at the Congress argue that strict auditing by the Government Auditing Office (GAO) is needed on the Federal Reserve actions, including monetary policy. In 1978 the Federal Reserve became subject to examination by the GAO, with respect to the functions such as payment system activities, regulation of derivatives and the institution's budget. However, the GAO is prohibited from examining monetary policy activities. A closer examination of the Federal Reserve activities would threaten its independence in monetary policy management. This issue will become more serious, as the general public's trust in central banks in major economies has been eroded since the start of the crisis.

International cooperation on macro-prudential policy

In accommodating the need to establish macro-prudential policy on the international front, the Financial Stability Board (FSB), successor to the Financial Stability Forum, is now in charge of the task of collaborating with the IMF on the early warning system, while the 'college of supervisors' monitors global financial institutions. The FSB might have a role to play in the event of crisis management or the resolution of global financial institutions. Although these institutions serve to improve the international exchange of information, they have no power. Ultimately, a new international organization should be established, under the charter of global international institutions, that prescribes the code of conduct as well as the resolution procedure. However, it will take a long time to reach a consensus on the construction of a new international financial architecture.

It seems more practical to encourage the bank managers' initiative on the resolution procedure. The US Government proposed that the Federal Reserve should request the big institutions to have a 'rapid resolution plan'. Similarly, Lord Turner, the Chairman of the FSA, maintained that the global regulatory drive should force the big financial institutions to pre-plan for their own demise and draw up 'living wills', i.e. wind-down plans in the event they fail. The preparation of wind-down plans subject to board and regulatory approval may serve to constrain the too-rapid growth of financial institutions that are too big or too interconnected to fail.

Market-based approach and information sharing

In implementing the macro-prudential policy, I find it more important to rely on the market mechanism and information-sharing rather than restructuring the international and domestic regulatory system.

First of all, it is worthwhile investigating an 'early-exit strategy' adopted by the successful financial institutions to evade catastrophic loss. Similarly, the Canadian financial system, which was virtually immune from the financial turmoil, can provide a good case study.

To mitigate the pro-cyclicality of capital ratio, we can employ the use of 'reverse convertible bonds' in capital regulation; these must be converted from bond to equity in the case of systemic risk events (Flannery 2005; Scholes 2009).

Another example is to change the incentive of creditors. The incentive should be aligned to make the net counter-party exposure subordinated to other creditors. This will enhance the shift of bilateral trading activity into clearing houses and exchanges.[12]

Finally, a precondition for successful macro-prudential policy is the availability and mutual sharing of information relevant to identifying the systemic risk. The Financial System Department of the BOJ continues to implement both on-site and off-site examination of financial institutions, based on the contract of deposit transactions. At the same time the Financial Market Department in charge of market operations provides daily information to the Financial System Department.

The integrated information flow derived both from the balance sheets of individual banks and the everyday market transactions and liquidity positions can serve as a base to implement macro-prudential policy to monitor the systemic risk. It is essential for the supervising body to have in-house expertise on the assessment of the financial firms' conditions and the quality of collaterals, in case of emergency.

Certainly, the establishment of a more formal coordination mechanism between the BOJ and the FSA seems desirable. In contrast, the UK had completely separated the supervision task from the Bank of England. When the 'tripartite system' was tested for the first time, it failed to manage the financial crisis.

CONCLUSION

In this chapter we have evaluated the role of demographic changes in the emergence of asset price bubbles. The role of demographic change is twofold. First, it works to maintain the long-term interest rate at a low level, if market participants anticipate a future decline in the working-age population. Second, the damage inflicted by the bubble burst will become more serious the larger is the size of the decline in the working-age population. The Asian economies, notably China, will face peaks in their working-age population share in the mid 2010s. It is therefore essential to strengthen the macro-prudential policy in exiting from the unconventional policy regime.

In moving out from the financial turmoil and an unconventional policy regime, several lessons can be drawn from Japan's experience.

First, transparency of financial markets and assets should take precedence, rather than re-regulation. In particular, it is important to carry out a strict assessment of the quality of assets held by financial institutions. In off-balancing the toxic assets, the purchase price must be transparent and fair in the eyes of taxpayers. Fair-value accounting is needed for transparency, while the 'mark-to-funding' may be useful for regulatory purposes. Lack of transparency can easily lead to forbearance by regulators.

Second, we should not delay in cleaning up the banks' balance sheets. Leaving toxic assets on the balance sheets of financial institutions works to delay the recovery.

Third, in injecting capital into banks, the following conditions must be satisfied:

- numerical targets should be set to reduce the amount of toxic assets by half within 2–3 years; and
- lending to smaller firms and the household sector should be secured, in order to prevent a credit crunch.

Fourth, we see the lack of an exit strategy in conducting the unconventional policy regime. In the last quantitative easing policy, the BOJ made a commitment to exit the policy when the core consumer price registered a positive rate of change in a stable manner. This time no such commitment has been made. Given the large expansion of the balance sheets of central banks and the sharp rise in the ratio of government debt to nominal GDP, it is desirable to provide a clear message on the exit process.[13]

Fifth, in order to mitigate the possible trade-off between the monetary policy and the macro-prudential policy it seems appropriate to provide forecasts with alternative optimal policy projections for a longer time horizon than 2 years, thereby incorporating the feedback from financial stress to the real economy.

Finally, in implementing the macro-prudential policy it is more practical to rely on the market mechanism and information-sharing between regulatory authorities and the central bank.

NOTES

1 Japan Center for Economic Research, President, 1-3-7 Otemachi Chiyodaku, Tokyo, Japan (email: iwata@jcer.or.jp).

2 The expansion of the shadow banking system facilitated the ample provision of credit and a narrowing of various risk spreads and risk premiums. Paul McCulley (2009) characterized the process of developing the 'shadow banking system' as Minsky's economic journey from financial stability to instability. The journey is now reversed, passing through the Minsky moment, where the liquidity shortage and the fire sales of assets seized the market.

3 In contrast, household and institutional investors such as pension funds and insurance companies, even though they engaged in the carry-trade for diversification of asset holdings, are not the major players determining global market liquidity conditions.

4 Professor Masaya Sakuragawa insists that bubble substitution exists also in Japan. The emergence of government and base money bubbles has replaced the land price and equity price bubbles, resulting in the lower interest rate for long-term government bonds, and deflation, despite the rapid accumulation of government bonds, and the implementation of quantitative easing policy.

5 In a standard model of rational bubbles, productive investment is crowded out, for the bubbles compete with the securities issued by corporations, as is the case of public debt. It is not obvious whether productive investment was crowded out in the period of US sequential bubbles. Yet, Tirole (2009) argues that in the presence of non-pledgeable income, or the asynchronicity between cash availability and cash needs by corporations, bubbles are consistent with dynamic efficiency.

6 The practice of companies investing money borrowed at low interest rates so as to show higher profits than they got from their business activities alone.

7 The ageing process may be accompanied by the rise of the rate of time preference because of the increasing probability of death, although Blanchard (1985) adopts the different assumption of constant probability of death common to babies and the elderly. It is also possible that the real equilibrium interest rate is adjusted downwards. Within the framework of the neoclassical growth model the steady-state rate of return on capital is lower if the growth rate of per-capita consumption is lower, because the equilibrium rate of return on capital (= the natural interest rate) is equal to the sum of the per-capita consumption growth and the rate of time preference in the steady-state equilibrium. As a result, the natural interest rate becomes lower if the share of working-age population is smaller. The real long-term market interest rate moves around the natural interest rate in the business cycle.

8 The Federal Reserve introduced new facilities such as the Term Discount Window and Term Auction Facility (TAF) in late 2007, the Primary Dealer Credit Facility and the Term Securities Lending Facility (TSLF) in March 2008, the Asset-Backed Commercial Paper Funding Facility (CPFF) in October 2008 and the Term Asset Lending Facility in March 2009.

9 The way of providing credit to Bear Stearns was similar to the case of close down of the Yamaichi Securities Company in Japan combined with the bad bank scheme in Sweden. The BOJ provided a special loan through the Fuji Bank to the Yamaichi, given the statement of the government's guarantee in the Diet by Mr Miyazawa, then Finance Minister. The Federal Reserve provided the loans to Maiden Lane (the bad bank to digest the toxic assets) through J.P. Morgan. Mr Paulson stated in the Congress that the amount of payment by the NY Fed to the Treasury would be cut if any costs were incurred.

10 The fundamental issue here is that the distribution of statistical returns of assets may not be log-normal at the edges. Instead, it may have a Pareto–Zipf distribution of power laws (Mandelbrot and Hudson 2004; Taleb 2007).

The assumption that price changes follow the proportions of the bell curve may not be tenable, although modern finance theory since the seminal work by Bachelier (1900) is based on the assumption of normal distribution. It is interesting to observe that the personal income distribution is well-known to be the Pareto distribution, although it is often approximated by the log-normal distribution. The financial income earned by super-rich investors can be the reflection of their attempt to exploit the upper fat-tail of asset returns.

In the recent decade, the tail risk could become much larger and more frequent than previously anticipated, due to the systemic risk arising from the network externality, the fire sales externality, the myopia and the misaligned incentives to financial managers. Apparently, the small probability, high-impact events were underestimated. The systemic risk can be generated internally from the complexity of financial instruments or the heterogeneous investors' behaviour. The event which is assumed to occur once in 143 years has actually happened more than once (1.4 times) in a year in the case of the USA. The standard deviation of equity returns jumped to about 10δ during the period of the Great Depression, but in October 1987 it jumped to 22δ on the futures market (Mandelbrot and Hudson 2004).

11 In the crisis period, not only the deposit insurance scheme or the blanket guarantee for deposits, but also the temporary guarantees for debt insurance and,

in some cases, for asset losses, are also offered to banks. It may be added that the traditional deposit insurance premium, however, does not incorporate the part of systemic risk. If we incorporate systemic risk into the deposit insurance scheme, the efficient premium should be above the actuarially fair premium, with the systemically important banks paying higher charges. A similar problem exists with respect to capital insurance and the insurance for asset-loss schemes.

12 The creation of CDS clearing house may not be an optimal solution if a number of clearing houses are established.

13 On the exit strategy of fiscal policy in Japan, see Iwata (2009).

REFERENCES

Adrian, Tobias and Markus Brunnermeier (2009) 'CoVaR', *Staff Report*, No. 348 (August), Federal Reserve Bank of New York.

Adrian, Tobias and Hyun Song Shin (2008) 'Financial intermediaries, financial stability and monetary policy', paper presented at the Jackson Hole international conference organized by the Federal Reserve Bank of Kansas City, August 2008.

Bachelier, Louis (1900) *Théorie de la Spéculation*, Paris: Gauthier-Villars.

Barsky, Robert B. (2009) 'The Japanese asset price bubble: a heterogeneous approach', *NBER Working Paper*, No. w15052, Cambridge, MA: National Bureau of Economic Research, available at http://www.nber.org/papers/w15052.

Bernanke, Ben (2009) 'Financial reform to address systemic risk', speech to the Council on Foreign Relations, 10 March 2009, available at http://www.federalreserve.gov/newsevents/speech/bernanke20090310a.htm.

Blanchard, Olivier J. (1985) 'Debts, deficits and finite horizons', *Journal of Political Economy*, 93(2), 223–247.

Borio, Claudio and Philip Lowe (2002) 'Asset prices, financial and monetary stability: exploring the nexus', *BIS Working Papers*, No. 114, Basel: Bank for International Settlements.

Brunnermeier, Markus (2008) 'Bubbles', in S. Durlauf and L. Blume (eds) *The New Palgrave Dictionary of Economics*, 2nd edition, London: Macmillan.

Brunnermeier, Markus, Andrew Crocket, Charles Goodhart, Ari Persaud and Hyn Song Shin (2009) 'The fundamental principles of financial regulation', *Geneva Reports on the World Economy*, No. 11, Geneva: International Center for Monetary and Banking Studies; London: Centre for Economic Policy Research, available at http://www.cepr.org/pubs/books/cepr/booklist.asp?cvno=P197.

Chen, Joe, Yun Jeon Choi and Yasuyuki Sawada (2009) 'How is suicide different in Japan?', *Japan and the World Economy*, 21(2): 140–150.

Flannery, Mark J. (2005) 'No pain, no gain? Effecting market discipline via reverse convertible debentures', chapter 5 in Hal S. Scott (ed.) *Capital Adequacy Beyond Basel: Banking Securities and Insurance*, Oxford: Oxford University Press.

Friedman, Benjamin M., Milton Friedman and A.W. Clausen (1980) 'Postwar changes in the American financial market', in M. Feldstein (ed.) *The American Economy in Transition*, pp. 9–100, Chicago: Chicago University Press.

Hamilton, James (2009) 'Causes and consequences of the oil shock of 2007–08', *Brookings Papers on Economic Activity*, Spring 2009: 215–261, Washington, DC: Brookings Institution.

Hattori, Masazumi and Hyun Song Shin (2007) 'The broad yen carry trade', Institute for Monetary and Economic Studies, Bank of Japan, *Discussion Paper Series*, No. 2007-E-19, available at http://www.imes.boj.or.jp/research/papers/english/07-E-19.pdf.

Hattori, Masazumi, Hyun Song Shin and Wataru Takahashi (2009) 'A financial system perspective on Japan's experience in the late 1980s', paper presented at the international conference organized by the Institute for Monetary and Economic Studies, Bank of Japan, 27–28 May 2009.

Hayek, Friedrich A. (1975) 'Full employment at any price?', *Occasional Paper*, No. 45, London: Institute of Economic Affairs.

Iwata, Kazumasa (2009) 'Fiscal stimulus and the exit strategy', keynote policy speech at the Japan Project meeting, National Bureau of Economic Research, Cambridge, MA, June 2009.

Kashyap, Anil, Raghuram Rajan and Jeremy Stein (2008) 'Rethinking capital regulation', paper presented at the Jackson Hole international conference organized by the Federal Reserve of Kansas City, August 2008.

McCulley, Paul (2009) 'The shadow banking system and Hyman Minsky's economic journey', *PIMCO Global Central Bank Focus*, May.

Mandelbrot, Benoit and Richard L. Hudson (2004) *The Misbehavior of Markets: a Fractal View of Financial Turbulence*, New York: Basic Books.

Martin, Robert F. (2005) 'The baby boom: the predictability in house prices and interest rates', *International Finance Discussion Paper*, No. 847.

Matsushima, Hitoshi (2009) 'Behavioral aspects of arbitrageurs in timing games of bubbles and crashes', *CARF F-Series*, No. CARF-F-144, Tokyo: Center for Advanced Research in Finance, Faculty of Economics, University of Tokyo.

Mishkin, Frederic (2007) 'Housing and the monetary policy transmission mechanism', paper presented at the Jackson Hole international conference organized by the Federal Reserve Bank of Kansas City, August 2007.

Posen, Adam (1998) *Restoring Japan's Economic Growth*, Washington, DC: Peterson Institute for International Economics.

Scholes, Myron S. (2009) 'Market-based mechanisms to reduce systemic risks', chapter 7 in John D. Ciorciari and John B. Taylor (eds) *The Road Ahead for the Fed*, Stanford, CA: Hoover Institution Press.

Svensson, Lars (2001) 'The zero bound in an open-economy: a foolproof way of escaping from a liquidity trap', *Monetary and Economic Studies*, 19(1): 277–312.

Taleb, Nassim Nicholas (2007) *The Black Swan: the Impact of the Highly Improbable*, Penguin Books UK.

Taylor, John (2006) 'Lessons from the recovery from the "lost decade" in Japan: the case of great intervention and money injection', background paper for the international conference of Economic and Social Research Institute, Cabinet Office, Government of Japan, 14 September 2006, available at http://esri.go.jp/en/workshop/060914/taylor.pdf.

Tirole, Jean (1985) 'Asset bubbles and overlapping generations', *Econometrica*, 53(6): 1499–1528.

—— (2009) 'Illiquidity and all its friends', *TSE Working Papers*, No. 09-083, Toulouse: Toulouse School of Economics.

Watanabe, Tsutomu and Tomoyoshi Yabu (2009) 'Intervention on the foreign exchange market during the period of quantitative easing policy', *Working Paper Series*, No. 45, Research Center for Price Dynamics, Institute of Economic Research, Tokyo: Hitotsubashi University, (in Japanese).

—— (2004) 'Making macro-prudential policy concerns operational', *BIS Review*, No. 71, Basel: Bank for International Settlements.

White, William (2006) 'Is price stability enough?', *BIS Working Papers*, No. 205, Basel: Bank for International Settlements.

6 China's responses to the global economic crisis

Yu Yongding[1]

INTRODUCTION

Economic growth is cyclical. Since the reform and opening up, the Chinese economy has experienced several economic cycles. In 1992, as a result of Deng Xiaoping's call for further reform and opening up, the economy was woken from its hibernation of the late 1980s and began to rebound rapidly. By 1993 the rebound had, to some extent, led to overheating. From 1993 to 1997, the government implemented tight monetary and fiscal policies to cool down the economy, the effects of which coincided with the breakout of the Asian financial crisis. As a result, the Chinese economy entered a period of relatively low growth and deflation. In response, in October 1997, the government changed policy direction and implemented expansionary monetary and fiscal policies. The economy began to recover in 2002. In September 2003, the People's Bank of China (PBOC) raised interest rates for the first time since October 1997, ushering in a new period of monetary tightening. In the same period, China's fiscal policy was more or less neutral. This policy matrix lasted until October 2008.

Since the onset of the American subprime crisis, it was expected that the growth of China's trade surplus would slow, retarding overall economic growth. In coastal areas, large numbers of exporting enterprises (especially those engaged in processing trade) were closing down from early 2008. However, in the first half of 2008, China's growth rate was still above the potential rate and inflation reached 8 per cent in February – the highest it had been since 1996. As a result, the Chinese Government did not change its policy until the global economic crisis worsened dramatically in October (soon after the collapse of Lehman Brothers). Following the freefall of the global economy, China's growth fell to 6 per cent in the fourth quarter of 2008, from 13 per cent in 2007, and inflationary pressure suddenly disappeared. This dramatic change of fortune was unexpected by most economists worldwide.

The dramatic change in the domestic economic situation since September–October 2008 ignited a rigorous debate on economic policy. Was the government's economic posture aimed at cooling the economy since 2003 appropriate, or did it leave the economy vulnerable to external collapse? Did the government change its policy direction enough? Should the PBOC have tightened monetary policy in 2007 and early 2008 in response to inflation in the consumer price index (CPI) and the rapid increase in real estate investment? Many economists criticize the government's approach and especially the policy of renminbi (RMB) appreciation as an act of self-destruction. Some are adamant that China should *never* allow the RMB to appreciate. Others ridicule the 4 per cent CPI target.

While finger-pointing in this situation is unhelpful, it is indeed necessary to re-examine the policies adopted since 2003, especially those implemented since the second half of 2007, after the American subprime crisis had surfaced. Furthermore, we need to know whether there were mistakes or deficiencies in the underlying theories that had been guiding Chinese Government policy. With the benefit of hindsight, we can, and should, learn the right lessons, so as to avoid past mistakes, if indeed there were any.

In November 2008, the Chinese Government acted quickly. A 4-trillion-yuan stimulus package was introduced and, in the following month, the PBOC cut both interest rates and the growth rate of loans, resulting in a rapid increase in the quantity of money from abroad. Signs of a bottoming out in the economy were apparent as early as the first quarter of 2009, owing largely to the implementation of the stimulus package. Whether the recovery will be lasting or temporary is, at the time of writing, unclear. More fundamentally, the central control required to implement the stimulus package unavoidably exacerbates some structural problems in China's economy. There is a risk that these structural problems will hamper the sustainability of economic growth.

Around the world, the urgency of the current environment has trumped the importance of long-term structural objectives. It seems that facing the danger of falling into a deep and prolonged recession the whole world has suddenly converted to Keynesianism. But is this conversion necessarily good for the future of the world economy?

The current global financial and economic crisis is the result of financial speculation run amok, which is, in turn, partially attributable to global imbalances. On the one hand, American households are living beyond their means. Strong and increasing consumption was supported by rising net housing and equity wealth, driven by large capital inflows and the country's expansionary monetary policy. On the other hand, together with oil exporting countries and Japan, China, the hundredth-poorest county in per-capita terms, has injected hundreds of billions of dollars into the USA year by year to fuel America's frothy capital markets and hence finance the unsustainable lifestyle of American households. In this cross-border circulation of goods, services and debt, China is able to maintain a growth rate higher than its potential growth rate. China ships goods to the USA and, in return, America provides China with greenbacks. China accumulates claims on the USA, and the USA accumulates obligations to China. China provides the USA with tangible resources and the USA provides China with promises.

The virtue of this arrangement for China is the absorption of its excess capacity, enabling the high growth rates China has enjoyed over recent years. The regretful characteristics of the arrangement for China are threefold. First, a poor country has been persistently transferring real resources to the USA, the richest country in the world, for more than one-and-a-half decades. Second, a large proportion of China's foreign-exchange reserves are borrowed foreign funds mainly in the form of foreign direct investment (FDI) inflows. The returns on China's holdings of US Treasuries (yields of US Government securities) are miserably low in comparison with those of foreign investment in China. Third, China has suffered, and may further suffer, greater capital losses to its dollar asset holdings. China's claims against the USA are denominated in the dollar. The value of China's foreign-exchange reserves depends on the stability of the US dollar, stability in the prices of US Treasuries and price stability in the US economy, over which China has no control whatsoever.

Many Chinese economists insist that to allow the RMB to appreciate is to bow to the pressure of America, and that an exchange rate that keeps Chinese export prices low is in China's best interests. In reality, decades of export-promoting policies have created an export-orientated economic structure in China. The exporting sector is very happy to continue to meet American consumers' unsatiated demand for Chinese goods. Without the current financial crisis, the Sino-American economic synergy characterized by imbalances may have been able to last for many more years to come. But, the American financial crisis exposed the ugly side of US financial markets, and the credibility of the USA has also been brought into question. Yet, for many Chinese economists, because the dollar is still strong and the prices of US Treasuries are still rising, why be concerned? Some others argue that China has already committed to this path, and has been left with no choice, and hence must stick to US Treasuries and continue to play the role of being their guardian angel.

The American financial crisis shows that current account imbalances are no longer sustainable and that unwinding the connection is inevitable. However, it seems that there are many contradictions in the current unwinding process. The USA must reduce its current account deficit, which is conditional on a fall in the growth rate of the US economy because of the necessity for households to repay their debts and both financial and nonfinancial enterprises to rebalance their books. In its most extreme form, this will mean recession. However, the US Government's policy is skewed towards preventing consumption and investment demand from falling further, which may conflict with the need for rebalancing. On the other hand, China is trying to stabilize its exports, afraid of the negative impact that a slowdown in exports may have on growth. However, to rebalance its economy, China must reduce the growth rate of its exports so as to reduce its trade surplus. Another contradiction is that, if China successfully reduces its trade surplus, as wished by the USA, China will have no more resources with which to buy the US Treasuries; which will cause serious problems for the stability of the US economy if the US Government fails to reduce its need for external finance.

Countries in the current crisis must strike a balance between crisis management and structural rebalancing. However, it seems that all countries, in their efforts to arrest the fall of the economy, have sidelined efforts focused on structural rebalancing. This situation is true of China as well as the USA. In other words, the current global financial and economic crisis is a result of excessive pursuit of profits and capital gains by the major players in the world economy. To redeem itself, the world must prepare to pay the costs in the form of recession, if not depression. The tendency of governments to desperately seek a quick fix may ultimately prolong the crisis. There can be no gain without the required pain.

This chapter seeks to analyze the causes of the abrupt change in fortune for the Chinese economy, and to assess China's policy responses to the global financial crisis. It is hoped that, by characterizing China's growth pattern, especially the pattern since 2002, we will have a clearer understanding of the pros and cons of China's policy since 2003, and therefore a better grasp of China's future growth trajectory. This may lead, furthermore, to a greater ability to predict the results of China's macro-economic policy since November 2008.

The chapter has six sections following this introduction. The next section is a short retrospection on China's growth since 1990, and its macro-economic policy since 2003. The third section analyses why the inflationary pressure in the Chinese economy disappeared so dramatically. This is followed by an assessment of the Chinese Government's expansionary policies in responding to the global crisis. The fifth section is devoted to a discussion of China's policy options with respect to reducing the risks associated with its foreign-exchange reserves. Section six discusses the need for reform of the current international monetary system, which has been exposed as one of the root causes of the current global financial crisis, and the options China has for expanding the role of the RMB in the international monetary system. The final section makes some concluding remarks.

CHINA'S GROWTH IN RESTROSPECT

Since the reform and opening up, China can only be described as an economic miracle. Its average annual growth rate of gross domestic product (GDP) over the past three decades since 1979 was 9.8 per cent. In the period between 2002 and 2007, China registered an average annual growth rate of 10.5 per cent (Figure 6.1), while the inflation rate was kept under 2 per cent. Furthermore, before the global financial crisis struck in the last quarter of 2008, China's growth momentum showed no sign of weakening. The unprecedented and sustained growth vastly improved the living standards of the Chinese people. An affluent middle class has emerged in China. However, as a digression, it should be pointed out that China's extraordinary growth performance has not been achieved without extremely high costs in terms of environmental damage, resource exhaustion, worsening social equality and falling ethical standards.

The factors contributing to China's extraordinarily high economic growth can be analyzed from different perspectives. Here, we confine ourselves to the traditional accounting framework, despite the fact that many important underlying micro and institutional contributing factors are omitted.

Fixed-asset investments (FAI) and exports were the two most important engines of China's growth during the period of 2002–07. During that period, the average annual growth rates in exports and in fixed-asset investments were 29 per cent and 24 per cent, respectively (Figure 6.2). In 2007, the combined contribution of fixed-asset investments and net exports to GDP growth was more than 60 per cent.

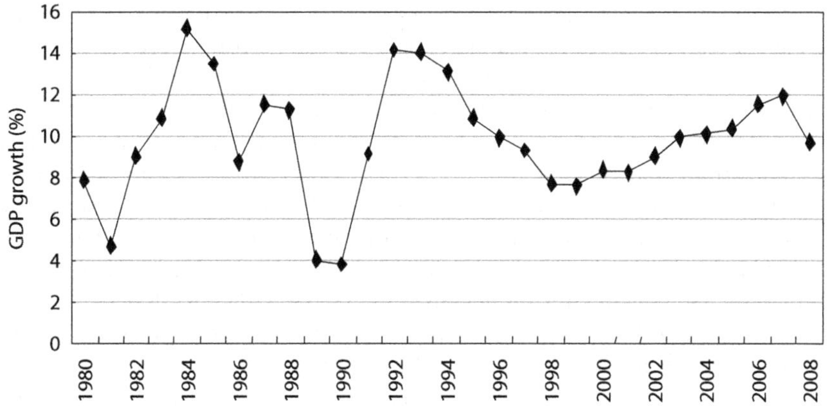

Figure 6.1 China's real GDP growth 1980–2008. Source: Statistical Year Book, various issues, Statistics Bureau of PRC.

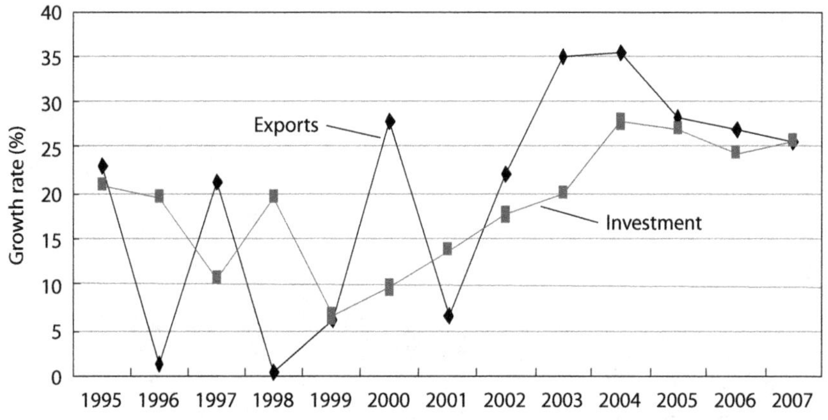

Figure 6.2 Growth rates (%) in exports and investment (current prices) in China, 1995–2007. Source: Statistical Year Book, various issues, Statistics Bureau of PRC.

FAI has long been the single most important factor contributing to China's economic growth. Also worth noting is the phenomenon that, in the past decade or so, the growth rate of FAI has been consistently higher than that of GDP[2] and hence, the investment rate has been steadily increasing (Figure 6.3).

The persistent increase in the investment rate means that the growth of the Chinese economy is in a non-steady state. Assuming, as initial conditions, that (1) aggregate demand is equal to aggregate supply (and so are their growth rates); (2) the growth rates of all components of aggregate demand are equal; (3) the growth rate of the economy is equal to the potential growth rate; and (4) the shares of all components of aggregate demand are constant, then the growth process can be said to be in the so-called steady state. By definition, such a growth process is sustainable.

Assuming that the steady state is disturbed by an external shock in the form of a sudden acceleration in the growth rate of FAI, then the growth process is no longer in the steady state. Because the growth rate of FAI is higher than that of GDP, the investment rate in the economy increases. Starting from the initial steady state and equilibrium, the increase in the growth rate of FAI will lead to overheating in the current period. However, provided that there is no change in the capital–output ratio, a higher investment rate, as a result of a higher growth rate of FAI than that of GDP in the current period, means a higher potential growth rate of the economy in the next period. If growth rates of other components of aggregate demand fail to increase so as to be equal to the higher growth rate of GDP in the next period, over-capacity will appear. Other things being equal, to absorb the over-capacity the growth rate of FAI must increase further. As a result, the investment rate will rise further and so will the potential growth rate.

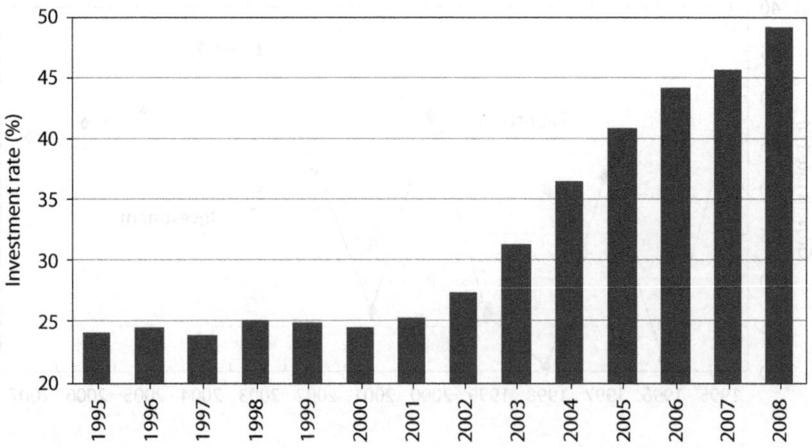

Figure 6.3 Investment rates in China. Source: Chinese Economics Online Database (中经网数据库).

If in the next period the increase in capital stock leads to extra production capacity, but the growth rates of all other components of aggregate demand stay unchanged, then, unless there is a second-round increase in FAI, over-capacity will surface and deflationary pressure will build up.

If the growth rate of FAI increases, and the increase in investment demand is large enough to absorb the extra capacity created by the first round increase in FAI, there should be neither overheating nor over-capacity in the second period. However, as a result of a further increase in the growth rate of FAI, the investment rate rises further, so there will be an even greater production capacity in the third period. If growth rates of all components of aggregate demand other than that of FAI remain what they were at the previous period, then, to absorb over-capacity, the growth rate of FAI must rise further, creating even larger over-capacity. Obviously, this is a vicious cycle and the process is unsustainable. Over the past three decades in China, overheating and over-capacity have happened in tandem. However, sooner or later, the growth rate of investment demand will hit an apex (or upper bound) imposed by social, environmental, ecological and other constraints. Under these circumstances, while the potential growth rate is very high because of the extremely high investment rate, the growth rate of FAI may suddenly falter. If the growth rates of other components fail to rise dramatically to offset the fall in the growth rate of investment, the gap between the potential growth rate and that of aggregate demand will be at its widest, and the economy will fall suddenly into deflation.

Such is the present situation in China. Since 2002, the growth rate of investment in China has been rising persistently. Over-capacity created by the ever-increasing investment rate was absorbed by a strong increase in investment demand. Faced with the pressures of over-capacity in the future, the government ushered in a restrictive macro-economic policy. Administrative methods were also used to clamp down on over-investment in various big projects, especially those in heavy industry. To curb overheating created by strong investment demand in the current period, policy was aimed at not only cooling down the economy but also preventing over-capacity from happening in the future. The Chinese Government's clampdown on investment in the steel industry was a case in point. In 2004, China's steel production capacity was about 400 million tonnes. Worrying about over-capacity, the government started to clamp down on building new steel mills. The government used administrative methods to ban unapproved construction of steel mills. Perpetrators even got jail terms. However, for various reasons that are dealt with in other studies, new steel mills were mushrooming exponentially anyway. China's steel production rose from less than 400 million tonnes to nearly 600 million tonnes between 2004 and 2007. It is worth mentioning that over-capacity is not confined to just a few industries, but rather it is prevalent across all major industries.

Despite the worry of over-capacity by the Chinese Government, before the onset of the American financial crisis, the Chinese economy has shown no prevalent sign of over-capacity. Rather, it suffered from overheating because of the investment fever as well as strong external demand. China's inflation began worsening rapidly in the middle of 2007. By February 2008, the growth rate of CPI was 8.7 per cent – the worst since 1996. The over-capacity in China was concealed by two factors. One was the high growth rate of FAI, and the other was the even higher growth rate of exports. The surge of exports due to global prosperity supported by the US asset bubbles postponed the final reckoning of China's over-capacity.

Since the turn of the century, the Chinese economy has become more and more reliant on external demand, and the share of the current account surplus (mainly trade surplus) in GDP has been rising rapidly. In 2007 the contribution of trade surplus to GDP growth was almost 10 per cent of GDP (Figure 6.4).

But exports cannot help to maintain the economic equilibrium forever, because export demand is highly unstable. More importantly, when the Chinese economy was relatively small, an increase in exports to absorb excess capacity was not a great issue. However, as a result of the expansion of the Chinese economy, it has become increasingly difficult for the global market to absorb China's excess capacity. Again, the steel industry is a case in point. China has already become the world's number one steel producer. In 2007, 37 per cent of global steel output was provided by China. It is easy to see that if external demand collapses, overheating will immediately turn into over-capacity, and inflation into deflation. In fact, in the second half of 2008, when growth of FAI was slowed by a contraction in monetary policy aimed at preventing over-capacity and worsening asset bubbles in China, export demand collapsed due to the global financial crisis. Over-capacity

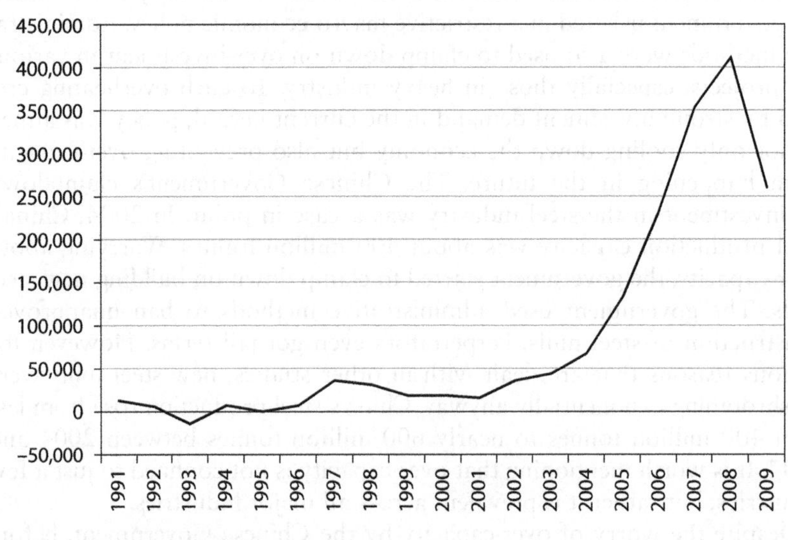

Figure 6.4 Share of current account surplus/GDP.

concealed by investment fever and strong export growth was suddenly exposed. The speed of the shift from overheating, and to inflation from deflation in the Chinese economy during September to October 2008 was stunning.

THE SUDDEN WORSENING OF THE ECONOMIC STITUATION IN THE THIRD QUARTER OF 2008

China's rapid growth came to a sudden halt in the third quarter of 2008, when:

- GDP growth dropped to 9 per cent, from a high of 13 per cent in 2007;
- the growth rate of industrial production fell to 8.2 per cent, about half of the rate in the same period of the previous year;
- growth rates of many important products fell from double digits to negative;
- the growth rate of exports fell from 20 per cent in October to –2.2 per cent in November;
- the share price index fell by 70 per cent;
- growth in real estate investment stagnated and house prices fell in some major cities; and
- inflationary pressures suddenly disappeared.

Statistics show that the most important cause for the collapse of China's growth in the third quarter of 2008 was the sudden collapse of the export market, which was, in turn, caused by the sudden worsening of the US financial crisis after the collapse of Lehman Brothers. Of all China's industries, the most dramatic fall in production happened in the steel industry. Analysis of the causes of the fall in steel production sheds a clear light on the cause of the fall in the Chinese economy generally (Table 6.1).

It can be seen that the drop in steel exports directly accounted for nearly 53 per cent of the total decrease in steel production in September 2008, which was, in turn, a direct result of the failing global economy.

Table 6.1 Direct impacts of fall in foreign demand on steel production (million tonnes) in 2008

Types	*Output, August*	*Output, September*	*Reduction in September*	*Percentage fall*
Exports	7.7	6.7	–1.0	12.9
Total output	47.8	45.9	–1.9	3.9
Exports/total output (%)	16.1	14.5	52.6	–

Source: Xue Qiyuan, based on various sources.

Besides the direct impact, the indirect impact of the fall in demand of steel-related exporting industries on steel production was also very large. On the whole, the fall in external demand can explain more than 60 per cent of the drop in steel production. We can conclude that the dramatic fall of export demand since the third quarter of 2008 is the single most important cause of China's economic slowdown.

The slowdown in FAI was the second important contributing factor. The effect of the fall of FAI on growth can, in turn, be attributed to the slowdown in real estate investment (as a result of monetary tightening over the past several years), the fall of export-related investment, the worsening of expectations and financial losses accrued in speculation on financial markets due to the burst of asset bubbles and the collapse of commodity prices.

The third important cause of the slowdown of the economy is the large inventory adjustment. Until the middle of 2008, many Chinese enterprises were still expecting further rises in prices, and thereby engaged in large-scale hoarding activities. The destocking of the inventory worsened, to a large extent, the fall of China's growth. Anecdotal evidence also suggests that the wealth-effect of the burst asset bubbles also played a certain role in lowering growth in consumption.

It is worth mentioning that supply-side factors have also played a certain role in the slowdown of the Chinese economy. Since the middle of this decade, labour costs have risen due to a tightening of the standards of labour protection and a shortage of labour supply in some areas and industries. More-stringent environmental standards also contributed to pushing production costs higher.

CHINA'S POLICY RESPONSES TO THE GLOBAL SLOWDOWN

When the global slowdown became apparent, the government shifted its policy direction quickly and forcefully. While the authorities tightened macro-economic policies during the first half of 2008 in order to control overheating, the central bank began to cut interest rates from September, and the State Council introduced a very large stimulus package in early November.

Fiscal policy

The 4 trillion yuan (US$580 billion) stimulus package announced in late 2008 for 2009 and 2010 was equivalent to 14 per cent of 2008 GDP. In addition, the government also considered possible tax reductions, which included value-added tax reform, business tax cuts and raising the threshold at which individual income tax becomes payable. Furthermore, on top of the central government's stimulus policy, provincial governments were encouraged to raise money to launch their own complementary stimulus packages. The total amount of planned stimulus packages announced by local governments totalled 18 trillion yuan (US$2,610 billion). The majority of the stimulus spending has been on investment, especially infrastructure projects and post-Sichuan earthquake reconstruction (Figure 6.5).

The finance for the stimulus package was structured as follows:

- the central government would directly finance a quarter of the package;
- government bonds would be issued to cover the budget deficit;
- the central government would issue bonds on behalf of local governments to fill the shortfall in financing local projects; and
- bank loans would be important sources of funds, especially for local governments.

The National People's Congress approved the government's new budget for 2009 in March. According to this budget, the total government (central plus local) revenue would be 6.623 trillion yuan, up 8.0 per cent from 2008. Total government expenditure (central plus local) would be 7.635 trillion yuan, up 22.1 per cent. The total budget deficit would be 950 billion yuan (US$139 billion), the highest in six decades, compared with 111 billion yuan in 2008. The central government's deficit will be at 750 billion yuan, and the State Council will allow local governments to issue 200 billion yuan worth of government bonds through the Ministry of Finance. The expected budget deficit will total approximately 3 per cent of GDP, compared with 0.4 per cent in 2008.

The single most important element in the stimulus plan is public works. This is likely to be effective in lifting growth but could also hurt ongoing efforts geared towards structural adjustment. The growth rate of urban FAI

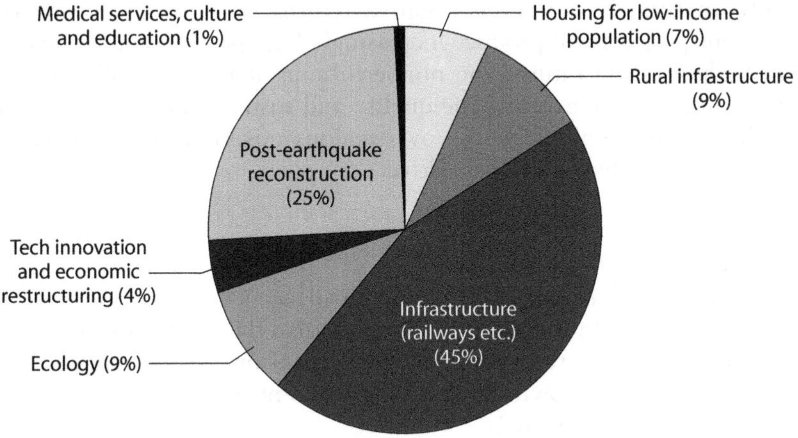

Figure 6.5 The structure of China's stimulus package. Source: National Development and Reform Commission.

already reached close to 33 per cent during the first 7 months of 2009, and this will lead to an even higher investment share of GDP. In turn, the excessively high investment rate will lead, in the long-run, to either more-serious over-capacity or lower efficiency reflected in an even higher capital–output ratio, which is already very high in China.

The government is aware of the over-capacity problem. This is exactly why government-financed investment is concentrated on infrastructure rather than manufacturing. However, this policy approach still poses three problems. First, China's infrastructure is far ahead of other developing countries. Therefore, waste is unavoidable and the future returns to current investment are uncertain. Second, ideally, more resources should be devoted to providing public goods and building decent social security networks. However, this is easier said than done. Lack of incentives for the local governments to support this endeavour is one of the most important constraints. Third, public spending should be conducive to private investment and thereby aid the development of small and middle-size enterprises. Nonetheless, the reality is that many local governments are squeezing small and middle-size enterprises that are finding it increasingly hard to compensate for the reduction in their fiscal revenues resulting from the slowdown in economic growth.

Compared with many other developing countries, China has the ability to carry out expansionary fiscal policies for an extended period. China's government budget has been in a very sound position for the past decade. Its debt/GDP ratio was only 18 per cent at the end of 2008. There is plenty of room for the government to use fiscal instruments to support economic growth.

However, complacency is dangerous. If self-sustained demand cannot be created or revived in a few years' time, the policy space can be expended quickly. In turn, low or even negative returns on government-financed investment projects will produce increasingly high pressure on the government budget in the future. The nonperforming loan ratio will definitely increase in the coming years. The quality and sustainability of the growth have been compromised by the over-zealous government-led, especially local-government-led, investment drive.

Monetary policy

During the first half of 2009, commercial banks' new loans reached 7.47 trillion yuan, almost 50 per cent higher than the 5 trillion yuan official target for 2009. Such credit and monetary expansion is astonishing. Indeed, the gap between the growth rate of M2 and nominal GDP broke a historical record recently (Table 6.2).

The most important cause of the rapid increase in credit and money supply was PBOC's expansionary monetary policy. Previously, in response to the rapid increase in liquidity caused by PBOC intervention in the exchange

Table 6.2 Credit and monetary expansion (%) in China, 2009

Billion Yuan	*January*	*February*	*March*	*April*	*May*
Growth of M1 (%)	6.7	10.9	17.0	17.5	18.7
Growth of M2 (%)	18.8	20.5	25.5	26.0	25.7
Credit (billion yuan)	1620.0	1070.0	1890.0	591.8	664.5
Growth of credit (%)	21.3	24.2	29.8	29.7	30.6

Source: People's Bank of China.

market, which was aimed at offsetting the appreciation pressure on the RMB created by a persistent trade (and capital account) surplus, the PBOC sold a large amount of central bank bills to mop up the excess liquidity. Since the fourth quarter of 2008, the PBOC has almost stopped selling more bills. As a result, the liquidity has inundated the inter-bank money market, and even once made the interest rates in the inter-bank market lower than interest on deposits with commercial banks with same terms of maturity. This was described in China's banking circles as 'flour being more expensive than bread'.

China's financial conditions have been very different from those in America and Europe during the global financial crisis. China just completed an overhaul of its banking system by large-scale capital injection and writing off non-performing loans. Its banking system was relatively safe when the Western banking system was on the edge. As a result, there was no credit crunch, and the monetary multiplier in China has not fallen as dramatically as in the USA. Therefore, the dramatic increase in liquidity in the inter-bank money market has been duly translated into a rapid increase in bank credit and broad money.

While the monetary policy should become accommodating in the current environment, the degree to which monetary policy was loosened during the first quarter was probably too great. Rapid expansion in credit and money supply was, to a certain extent, the result of non-market interference. There are no sound economic rationales supporting such a dramatic expansion. The unusual pace of monetary expansion has given rise to concerns about the rising non-performing loan ratio, the worsening of economic structure and, ultimately, a resurgence of asset bubbles in the future. In fact, anecdotal evidence suggests that a large chunk of excess liquidity has entered stock markets and real estate markets. The huge gap between the growth rate of M2 and nominal GDP implies very large inflationary pressure in prospect.

I never doubted China's ability to achieve 8 per cent growth in 2009. The confidence is based on (1) China's strong fiscal position, (2) the vast domestic market and (3) China's strong external position. As a result, the government's scope for using stimulus packages is huge. Because of this, the economy turned the corner as early as the beginning of 2009. Recent economic data confirmed continuous recovery of economic activities (renewed growth of power generation, re-acceleration of industrial production and an unusually high pace of investment growth).

Despite this strong showing, worries about sustainability of the recovery are still lingering. The Chinese Government is faced with the dual task of crisis management and structural adjustment. While we can say that the crisis management has been successful, it is difficult to say the same about structural adjustment. To achieve sustainable growth and improve the welfare of the nation, growth should not be achieved at the expense of structural adjustment. China's structural problems include:

- high external dependency;
- a high investment rate;
- pollution;
- energy inefficiency;
- the income disparity between different social groups and between rural and urban areas; and
- insufficiency in the provision of social goods (social safety net, Medicare, education etc.).

If China fails to tackle these structural problems, growth is likely to 'double-dip' and adopt a graphically represented 'W' shape. In order to deal with its structural problems, China should push for more reforms. In fact, the current crisis offers a good opportunity for accelerating these reforms. Some key areas for reform include:

- sanitation, education, finance, communication, transportation and liberalizing restrictions on the entry into Medicare. Fair competition rules should be applied to these areas. Anti-monopoly laws should be formulated and enforced in natural monopoly industries;
- liberalizing price controls over energy, water, electricity and allowing market demand and supply to determine the prices of these products;
- further liberalizing control on interest rates and establishing a more flexible exchange-rate regime, and further liberalization of capital controls side-by-side with internationalization of the RMB;
- allowing inefficient and polluting enterprises to go bankrupt, while simultaneously taking more responsibility for providing compensation to employees of these enterprises;
- taking strong measures to narrow the income gap between rich and poor, between urban and rural areas, and between regions; and
- accelerating the implementation of social support such as Medicare and free education.

Unfortunately, when the government responded to the global financial crisis, sometimes it was undoing what it had already achieved in rebalancing the economy. For example, as a result of the fiscal stimulus package,

China's investment rate has risen further, meaning that, in the future, China will face even more serious over-capacity. In the pre-crisis period, growth in exports absorbed a large proportion of over-capacity. In the future, if the growth rate of household consumption fails to increase significantly, investment will have to bear an even greater burden to absorb the over-capacity. Otherwise the capital–output ratio must increase dramatically. If more serious concerns for over-capacity eventuate, then the growth miracle of China will come to a sudden end.

In short, while China will be able to achieve a growth rate of 8 per cent for 2009, its structural problems are worsening on the whole. Anecdotal evidence suggests that low efficiency and wasteful behaviour are prevalent in investment projects that are part of the stimulus package. Asset bubbles aided by excess liquidity have begun to resurge. This development is very worrisome indeed.

SAFEGUARDING CHINA'S FOREIGN-EXCHANGE RESERVES

Besides the crisis management and structural adjustment, the Chinese Government has to deal with a third challenge: safeguarding the value of China's foreign-exchange reserves. As a result of the so-called twin surpluses for one and a half decades, China has accumulated more than 2 trillion US dollars worth of foreign-exchange reserves. The global financial crisis and the US Government's responses to the crisis have added a new dimension to the long-debated issue of rebalancing the Chinese economy. China's twin surpluses are no longer just a matter of misallocation of resources but also a matter of capital losses. As pointed out by some observers, all policy options available to the PBOC for safeguarding reserves are unattractive. If the PBOC does nothing and simply holds on to the dollars, the losses will increase. If it buys more to prop up the dollar, it will have only a bigger version of the same problem in the future. If, on the contrary, the PBOC diversifies into other currencies, it will drive down the dollar and create immediate losses.

What can China do to safeguard the value of its hard-earned foreign-exchange reserves? To correct the misallocation of resources embedded in the persistent twin surpluses and to reduce the possible capital losses of China's foreign-exchange reserves, China should explore all available channels to rebalance its international payments. The rebalancing problems facing China can be categorized into a flow problem and a stock problem. Putting aside the problem of safeguarding the value of its existing foreign-exchange reserves (stock) for the time being, an important fact is that China's foreign-exchange reserves are still increasing at an annual rate of around US$200 billion (compared with US$400 billion in the pre-crisis period). Therefore, the more urgent task for the Chinese Government is to reduce the increase in foreign-exchange reserves. Only after China's foreign-exchange reserves stop increasing can China shift its attention to the existing stock of reserves. To achieve this objective, the most obvious channel is to run a more-or-less balanced current account, or even a current account deficit which, in turn, will require a deepening of structural adjustment to eliminate the savings/consumption gap, reform of the exchange-rate formation regime to minimize government intervention in the foreign-exchange market and the elimination of an export promotion policy that creates price distortion.

With the flow problem, on the other hand, there are two things China should do. First, China should reduce its twin surpluses by earnestly implementing the policy measures that have been already agreed upon on paper by government officials and the public. Among these policies, the key, of course, is to stimulate domestic demand, especially domestic consumption. The global financial crisis may already have contributed to a reduction in the twin surpluses. Because the twin surpluses have become structural, China may not be able to reduce them, especially the trade surplus, in the short term.[3] Therefore, a key problem China must tackle head-on is the translation of its twin surpluses into assets other than US Treasuries. There are many avenues available for this objective.

- First, China should continue to promote outbound FDI in developing countries. China has a powerful ability in infrastructure construction. For many developing countries, lack of infrastructure is the most important bottleneck for economic development. The potential returns on investment in roads, railways and so on in developing countries in Africa, Latin America and some parts of Asia should be relatively high.
- Second, China should continue to acquire more strategic resources and gradually increase its reserves of strategic materials.
- Third, China should be more actively engaged in merger and acquisition activities in the developed world.
- Fourth, China can make bolder portfolio investment decisions. Besides the US Treasuries, holdings of other types of assets and assets denominated in currencies other than the US dollar should be increased.
- Fifth, China should increase lending to international organizations such as the IMF. However, China's claims should be denominated in special drawing rights (SDR) or RMB. Similarly, China should seek to increase its contributions to the regional financial architecture based on the Chiang Mai Initiative.
- Sixth, China should encourage foreign governments and corporations to issue RMB-denominated bonds (Panda bonds). China can also encourage commercial banks to extend RMB-denominated loans to foreign borrowers. RMD funds thus raised by foreign entities can be used to buy dollars from Chinese entities.
- Seventh, the PBOC should try to increase its currency swaps with foreign central banks.
- Eighth, China should increase its aid to the poorest developing countries in the world.

What can China do about its foreign-exchange reserve stock? In the next 4 years, the Obama administration is going to sell US$3.8 trillion worth of bonds. China cannot help but wonder if there is enough demand for these bonds. In fact, sale of these bonds is contingent on a very optimistic assumption about the US recovery from the recession. The true figure could turn out to be much larger. On the other hand, in the current climate of recession, whether US households will have the ability to digest the huge bond issuance is questionable. Currently, the Federal Reserve is implementing a very expansive monetary policy, and the excess reserve has increased from US$3 billion to close to US$800 billion. The quality of the asset side of the balance sheet of the Federal Reserve is akin to junk bond funds. At this moment of crisis, perhaps the policy is acceptable, but when the US economy turns around, risk appetite increases, and people stop hoarding money. Inflation can be very serious in the USA. China knows neither what the balance of demand for and supply of the US Government securities is, nor what the Federal Reserve's exit strategy will be. The US Government tries to assure China that its foreign exchange reserve is safe and that the US dollar will remain strong. But the US Government and the Federal Reserve fail to provide China with any details of how US policy responses to the global financial crisis will not lead to serious capital losses to China's foreign-exchange reserves. Nobody knows whether the US Government, when desperate, can resist the temptation to inflate away its debt burden. The devil is in the detail. Empty words of goodwill will not soothe China's nerves. China is worried, and its concern is legitimate. The US Government must earnestly respond to China's concerns.

The basic principle should be diversification. This action should have been taken a long time ago. Recall that, after 2004, Japan stopped further accumulation of foreign-exchange reserves by ceasing intervention in the foreign-exchange market. In contrast, over roughly the same period, China more than doubled its foreign-exchange reserves and surpassed Japan, shouldering the unenviable burden of being the largest holder of US Government securities. Even in the second half of 2008, when prices of US securities were rising, China failed to utilize the opportunity to diversify. If China had diversified at the time, it could have done so without dragging down the price of US Government securities. Instead China increased its holding of US Treasuries. However, despite this missed opportunity, China still can do something about the stock of its holdings of foreign-exchange reserves:

- First, China can buy more TIPS (Treasury Inflation-Protected Securities). Furthermore, the US Government should take the initiative to provide more TIPS, like financial instruments, and allow China to convert some of its holdings of US Government securities into similar but safer assets.
- Second, China should be allowed to convert part of its foreign-exchange reserves into SDR denominated assets. For example, the possibility of reintroducing substitution accounts should be considered.

- Third, China should not rule out the possibility of selling its holdings of US securities to make the composition of its foreign-exchange reserves mimic that of SDR. The US Government must realize that this is China's legitimate right. In order to avoid bigger losses, China may have to bear some losses due to the sale of the securities. Of course, China should do so with the utmost care, and with close cooperation with US authorities.
- Fourth, if the US Government cannot safeguard the value of China's holding of US Government securities, it should compensate China in some way or other. The US should not use the pretext that nothing can be done to interfere with the market mechanism. The US Government was not hesitant when it decided to protect the fund market when the funds were facing the danger of 'breaking the buck'. Some economists have proposed a so-called 'grand bargain'. This is a proposal worth exploration by the two governments.

THE REFORM OF THE INTERNATIONAL MONETARY SYSTEM AND THE FUTURE ROLE OF THE RENMINBI

One of the fundamental reasons why America was able to accumulate a huge amount of foreign debt is the dollar's unique position as the international reserve currency. The dual position of the US dollar as the international reserve currency as well as a national currency is a contributing factor to the instability of the current international monetary system. The world community is calling for reform of the current international monetary system. As the United Nations (UN) Commission of Experts on the Reform of the International Monetary and Financial System (UN 2009) has said:

> The increases in the U.S. national debt and the balance sheet of the U.S. Federal Reserve have led to concerns in some quarters about the stability of the dollar as a store of value. The low (near zero) return on dollar holdings means that they are receiving virtually no return in exchange for the foreign exchange rate risk which they bear. These are among the reasons to adopt a truly global reserve currency. Such a global reserve system can also reduce global risks since confidence in and stability of the reserve currency would not depend on the vagaries of the economy and politics of a single country. The current crisis provides, in turn, an ideal opportunity to overcome the political resistance to a new global monetary system. It has brought home problems posed by global imbalances, international instability, and the current insufficiency of global aggregate demand. A global reserve system is a critical step in addressing these problems, in ensuring that as the global economy recovers, it moves onto a path of strong growth without setting the stage for another crisis in the future.[4]

The following are some specific policy suggestions on the creation of a global reserve currency.

Ahead of the G20 Summit in April, Zhou Xiaochuan, Governor of the POBC, released an essay titled 'Reform of the international monetary system'.[5] Zhou called for the 're-establishment of a new and widely accepted reserve currency with a stable valuation' to replace the US dollar, which is a credit-based national currency. The central bank governor noted that the IMF's SDRs should be given special consideration. In its 2009 financial-stability report, the PBOC reiterated its call for the creation of a new international reserve currency based on SDRs.

At the end of 2008, as a result of an initiative of the President of the UN Assembly, the aforementioned UN Commission of Experts on the Reform of the International Monetary and Financial System was established. Indeed, the commission shares much common ground with the proposal by Governor Zhou Xiaochuan of the PBOC. According to the UN commission's suggestion (UN 2009),

> [o]ne institutional way of establishing a new global reserve system is simply a broadening of existing SDR arrangements, making their issuance automatic and regular. Doing so could be viewed simply as completing the process that was begun in the 1960s, when SDRs were created. The simplest version ... is an annual issuance equivalent to the estimated additional demand for foreign exchange reserves due to the growth of the world economy. But they could be issued in a counter-cyclical fashion, therefore concentrating the issuance during crisis periods.

The UN Commission specifically suggests a few possible approaches. One approach is that countries would agree to exchange their own currencies for the new currency – called, say, International Currency Certificates (ICC), which could be SDRs – and vice-versa, in much the same way as IMF quotas are made up today (except that developing countries would contribute only their own national currencies). This proposal would be equivalent to a system of worldwide 'swaps' among central banks. The global currency would thus be fully backed by a basket of the currencies of all members.

On 10 July 2009, the IMF Executive Board backed the allocation of SDRs equivalent to US$250 billion, as was requested in the US$1.1 trillion package agreed at the G20 London Summit. According to news reports, the SDRs allocated will count towards members' reserve assets, acting as a low-cost liquidity buffer for low-income countries and emerging markets. This will reduce developing countries' needs for accumulation of US Government securities for the purposes of self-protection and liquidity. Some members may choose to sell part or all of their allocation to other members in exchange for hard currency, while other members may choose to buy more SDRs as a means of reallocating their reserves.

The IMF decision has actually suggested a direction for the enhancement of the role of SDR in the reform of the international monetary system, which shows the use of SDRs to replace the US dollar as a global reserve currency. The system suggested should not be simply dismissed as utopian, it is feasible. The obstacles come from political rather than economic and financial spheres. If China wishes to push the reform, a more detailed road map still needs to be worked out.

The dissatisfaction felt by Asian countries about the IMF's insensitivity towards Asian countries' suffering found its initial expression in Japan's proposal for establishing an Asian Monetary Fund (AMF). The primary function of the proposed AMF is to provide emergency financial support to crisis-affected countries. Ideally, the emergency financial support provided by the AMF will be more accessible and the conditions for providing such support will be less harsh and more in line with the 'Asian way'.

The Chiang Mai Initiative (CMI) was the most important milestone of the Asian financial crisis. According to the Joint Ministerial Statement of the ASEAN+3 Finance Ministers Meeting at Chiang Mai, Thailand, published on 6 May 2000, the ASEAN+3 agreed to strengthen policy dialogues and regional cooperation activities in the areas of capital-flow monitoring, self-help and support mechanisms, and international financial reform. The finance ministers recognized the need to establish a regional financing arrangement to supplement the existing international facilities. They agreed to establish a network of research and training institutions to conduct activities of mutual interest in these areas. Besides these general statements, the statement declared that the CMI involves an expanded 'ASEAN Swap Arrangement' that would include Association of Southeast Asian Nations (ASEAN) countries, and a network of bilateral swap and repurchase agreement facilities among China, Japan and the Republic of Korea. The swap arrangement marked an important turning point in the history of Asian financial cooperation. In recent years, the swap arrangements have developed from bilateral to multilateral agreements, and a prototype AMF is taking shape. However, currently, the problems faced by East Asia as a whole and by individual countries in the region are very different from those during the Asian financial crisis.

On the whole, during the current global financial crisis, the performance of the East Asian governments in terms of financial cooperation and coordination is rather disappointing. The only result so far is a number of China–Japan–Korea currency swap agreements. It is frustrating that cooperation is practically nonexistent when it is most needed. If, at such a critical juncture as the current one, the ASEAN+3 are unable to coordinate, then future prospects for cooperation and coordination for this group do not seem bright. The 13 countries must get together and make concerted efforts to demand that the US Government safeguard the future value of their hard-earned foreign-exchange reserves, which are mostly in the form of US Government securities. Are the governments in the East Asian region so confident that the US Government will not get rid of its huge debt burden by inflation, devaluation of the US dollar and defaults? The East Asian region was swindled during the Asian financial crisis. This time around East Asia seems ready to accept the same fate without doing anything to try and guard against such an eventuality.

Over the past decade since the Asian financial crisis, discussions among economists have been concentrated on exchange-rate coordination. However, no significant result has been achieved. And now, when the global financial crisis has worsened rapidly, the issue of exchange-rate coordination seems as irrelevant as ever. The Euro countries' performance seems rather disappointing. Maybe regional financial cooperation needs to find another rallying point. The urgency of exchange rate coordination may have, for now, faded to secondary importance.

China's situation under the current financial crisis is paradoxical. On the one hand, as a captive lender to the US, it is facing the danger of making big losses. In the words of some financial observers, China has lost a lot already without knowing it clearly, if at all. On the other hand, due to China's huge foreign-exchange reserves and the appreciation of the RMB, China's currency is in a very favourable position. Hence, China is facing a historical opportunity for the internationalization of the RMB. The pros and cons of internationalizing the RMB are obvious. I will not dwell on them. Here, I just wish to mention a few possible measures that China may take to promote the internationalization of the RMB while minimizing the losses it would face as the biggest holder of US Treasury securities.

Currency swaps

In Asia, liquidity shortage and credit crunch have not been, on the whole, as serious as in the US and European countries. However, for various reasons, in many East Asian countries commercial banks are becoming more and more reluctant to lend, which has affected the real economy significantly. How to provide liquidity for foreign firms in domestic markets has become a serious issue. For example, a Japanese firm operating in China may need RMB loans. In this case, government currency swaps would help. Due to changes in circumstances since the Asian financial crisis, the money pooled together in line with the CMI may find a better use for stabilizing the regional financial system.

In early May 2008, finance ministers from China, Japan, South Korea and ASEAN agreed to expand their system of bilateral currency swaps under the CMI to a more multilateral system. Under the currency swaps, an Asian country hit by a foreign-exchange crisis could borrow US dollars from another country to bolster its reserves until the crisis had passed. Finance ministers from 13 Asian nations, including South Korea, Japan and China, agreed to make a pool of at least $80 billion in foreign-exchange reserves available to protect their currencies.

On 12 December 2008, China and Japan agreed with South Korea on bilateral currency swap accords in an effort to ensure financial stability in Asia. China and South Korea would sign an accord worth 38 trillion won ($28 billion yuan). Under the terms of the agreement, China would give South Korea access to 38 trillion won worth of yuan at any time for the following 3 years. The central banks of China, South Korea and Japan were to meet again in 2009, starting regular consultations to ensure currency stability in Asia.

On 19 December 2008, China's central government announced that 14 measures would be undertaken in seven areas to support Hong Kong's financial stability and economic development, including agreeing to a currency swap agreement between the PBOC and the Hong Kong Monetary Authority.

With the establishment of a currency swap arrangement, short-term liquidity support can be provided to the mainland operations of Hong Kong banks and the Hong Kong operations of mainland banks if required. This would bolster confidence in Hong Kong's financial stability, and would also help to promote financial stability in the region and the development of RMB-denominated trade transactions between Hong Kong and Mainland China. The currency swap agreement has a term of 3 years, which can be extended upon agreement by both parties. It can provide liquidity support up to RMB200 billion (HK$227 billion).

Settlement in RMB

In December 2008, China announced that it would allow the settlement of trade in RMB with Hong Kong, Macau and ASEAN nations on a trial basis. The pilot RMB trade settlement programme would be tested in Guangdong province, the Yangtze River Delta, Hong Kong and Macau. The RMB trial would also be implemented between Guangxi and Yunnan provinces and the neighbouring countries of the ASEAN trade group.

Panda bonds

There are countries in the region that need dollars, while there are others that wish to divest them. China has a huge volume of foreign-exchange reserves that it has no intention of accumulating further. But for China to provide dollar loans directly to foreign borrowers seems too risky, due to exchange rate and default hazards. Furthermore, China lacks the necessary expertise to lend dollars to foreign borrowers. There are many ways China can help its neighbours, including consortium loans, Panda bonds and so on. Countries that need dollars can borrow from China by selling Panda bonds. The Asian Development Bank (ADB) and some private international financial firms could be involved in issuing, underwriting, credit rating, legal service and so on. Governments and the ADB could get together to discuss the possibility of issuing Asian bonds. By doing so, the health of the regional financial system can be promoted and the role of US dollars could be gradually taken over by local currencies.

Loans to foreign banks

Of the world's commercial enterprises, three Chinese banks currently rank second, third and fourth in terms of cash richness. So, while at the moment no international bank has any meaningful liquidity available, Chinese banks are awash with excess liquidity. It is possible for those Chinese banks to lend RMB-denominated loans to qualified foreign banks. Borrowers can buy dollars with the RMB borrowed from the Chinese banks and repay the RMB over a specified period.

Wider use of local currencies

The credibility of US dollars has fallen significantly. Efforts should be made by countries in the region to reduce the use of the US dollar for international transactions. And efforts should be made by countries with strong currencies and advanced capital markets to encourage the use of their currencies as reserve currencies.

CONCLUDING REMARKS

Over the past three decades, owing to its gradual reform and opening up to the outside, the Chinese economy has maintained an average annual growth rate in GDP as high as 9.8%. Now China has become the third-largest economy, the second-largest trading nation and the largest holder of foreign-exchange reserves in the world. China's growth is truly an epoch-defining miracle.

Now, as the global financial and economic crisis is still unfolding, the growth strategy and economic policy of the Chinese Government are being put to the test. It seems that the government has been very successful in responding to the global slowdown in a very swift and determined fashion. As a result, the Chinese economy has already bottomed out. However, the seriousness of the impact of the global crisis on the economy shows that China needs to speed up its structural reform and adjust its once very successful strategy and policies in a timely way. Otherwise, the Chinese economy may lose its growth momentum in the near future.

To deal with one of the root causes of the global financial crisis, reform of the international monetary system should sit high on the agenda. While actively engaging on this front, China should also show further initiative in the areas of regional financial cooperation and the internationalization of the RMB.

NOTES

1 Institute of World Economics and Politics, Chinese Academy of Social Sciences, Beijing.
2 There have been controversies about the statistics of the growth rate of FAI in real terms. However, despite the inaccuracy, it is difficult to deny the fact that the growth rate of FAI in real terms has been consistently higher than that of real GDP.
3 Due to space constraints, this chapter will not discuss the issue of how to reduce the capital-account surplus.
4 UN (2009: 115).
5 Zhou Xiaochuan, Reform of the International Monetary System, website of the PBOC, accessed 23 March 2009.

REFERENCE

UN (United Nations) (2009) *Report of the Commission of Experts of the President of the UN General Assembly on Reforms of the International Monetary and Financial System*, New York: United Nations, available at http://www.un.org/ga/president.63/PDFs/reportofexperts.pdf.

FURTHER READING

Akyuz, Yilmaz (2009) 'Policy response to the global financial crisis: key issues for developing countries', Geneva: South Centre, available at http://www.awid.org/content/62595/697454/file/PolicyResponsetoGlobalFinancialCrisis_Yilmaz%20Akyüz.pdf.

Corden, W. Max (2007) 'The international current account imbalances: a skeptical view', *Economic Affairs*, 27(2): 44–48.

Dooley, Michael P., David Folkerts-Landau and Peter Garber (2003) 'An essay on the revived Bretton Woods System', *NBER Working Paper*, No. 9971, Cambridge, MA: National Bureau of Economic Research.

Perkins, Dwight H. (2006) 'China's recent economic performance and future prospects', *Asian Economic Policy Review*, 1(1): 15–40.

Stiglitz, Joseph (2006) *Making Globalization Work*, New York: W.W. Norton & Company.

Yu, Yongding (2005) 'China's rise twin surplus and the change of China's development strategy', paper prepared for Namura Tokyo Club Conference, Kyoto, 21 November 2005, available at http://nomurafoundation.or.jp/data/20051121_Yu_Yonding.pdf.

—— (2007) 'Comments on China's economic situation', Martin Wolf's Economists' forum, 16 October 2007, available at http://www.youtube.com/watch?v=tphFVI-WY4w.

—— (2007) 'Global imbalances and China', *Australian Economic Review*, 40: 3–23.

—— (2008) 'The management of cross-border capital flows and macroeconomic stability in China', *TWN Global Economy Series*, No. 14, available at http://www.twnside.org.sg/publications_ge.htm.

—— (2008) 'The new challenges of inflation and external imbalances facing China', *Asian Economic Journal*, 7(2): 34–50.

7 China's financial reform and financial integration in East Asia

Chai Yu and Weijiang Feng[1]

INTRODUCTION

The global financial turmoil triggered by the US subprime crisis in 2007 seems to have belied the conventional wisdom that China's financial system is weak, poor and inefficient. Few would deny that China's financial system has weathered the global financial turmoil fairly well. In fact, China's banking industry reported an after-tax profit of 583.4 billion yuan (US$85.79 billion) in 2008, soaring 30.6 per cent year on year; the rate of return on capital also went up to 17.1 per cent, significantly higher than the global average of 10 per cent. Industry-wide total profit, profit growth, return on capital and many other indicators of China's banking industry ranked first in the world in the late 2000s. In addition, a total of 978.4 billion yuan (US$143 billion) in premiums was collected, a jump of 39.1 per cent from a year ago. The exchange rate of Chinese currency (renminbi, RMB) has basically remained stable at a reasonable and balanced level, without volatile fluctuations during the crisis. This optimistic picture, however, may change if we consider the extremely high domestic saving ratio, the relative shortage of financial products, the financing difficulties of small- and medium-size enterprises, and the official control over transactions and currency exchanges on the capital account.

First, for a long time, China has been keeping a high national saving rate compared with other major countries (Figure 7.1). For an average 40 per cent domestic investment to gross national income (fully financed by domestic saving), growth between 8 and 10 per cent is not such a high return on investment. This situation implies that there must be some misallocation of resources contributing to the ineffectiveness of the financial system (see García-Herrero *et al.* 2006).

Second, the range of Chinese financial products is limited mostly to savings deposits and stocks, with few other financial products for investment (Figure 7.2). Although the China Financial Futures Exchange (CFFEX) was founded with the approval of the State Council and the China Securities Regulatory Commission on 8 September 2006 in Shanghai, China's Stock Index Futures was not launched until 16 April 2010 (the China Shanghai Shenzhen Stock Index Futures, often abbreviated to 'Hushen 300 Index', was introduced by the CFFEX on that day).

Third, most small- and medium-size enterprises (SMEs) raise funds externally through bank credit, but it is difficult for them to obtain loans from big state-owned commercial banks (CBs), because of the small size of the loans they seek, the asymmetric information and the absence of mortgages (Lin and Li 2005: 926). Moreover, most banking resources in China are held or controlled by the policy banks and the big state-owned CBs (Figure 7.3), and hence the SMEs are finding it hard to borrow from China's banking system.

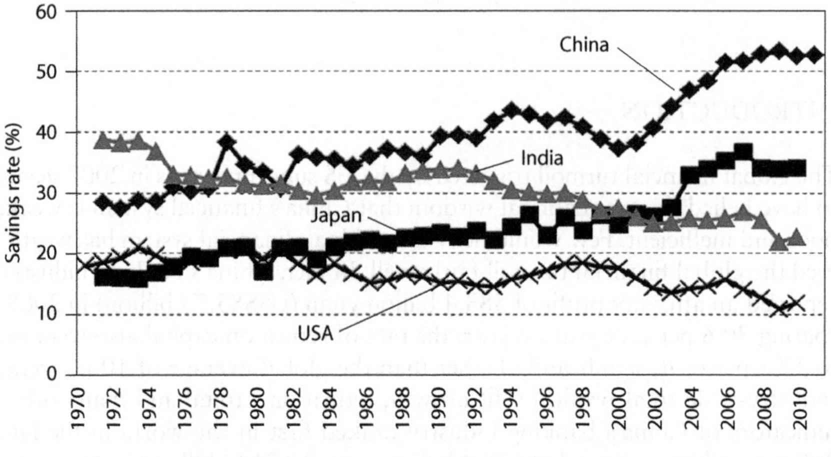

Figure 7.1 National saving rates (gross savings, per cent of gross national income) in China, India, Japan and the USA. Source: Development Data Group, World Bank. 2012, *2012 World Development Indicators Online*, Washington, DC: World Bank, available at: http://go.worldbank.org/U0FSM7AQ40.

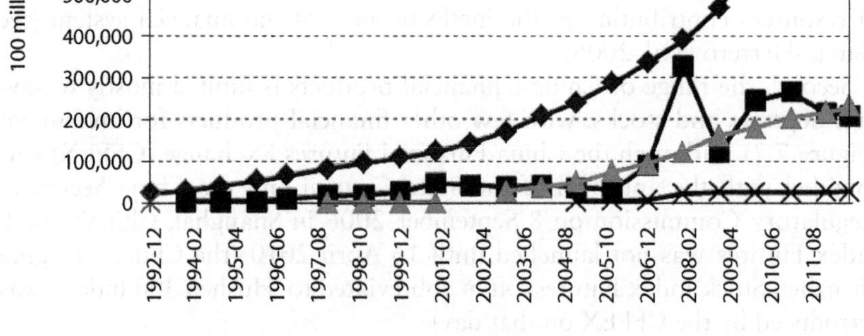

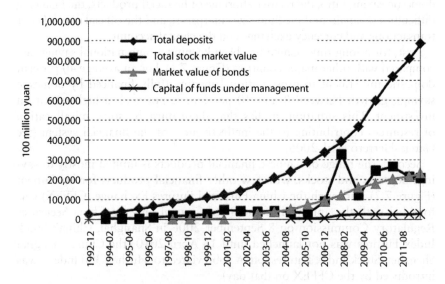

Figure 7.2 Structure of China's financial system. Source: Wind Information Co. Ltd.

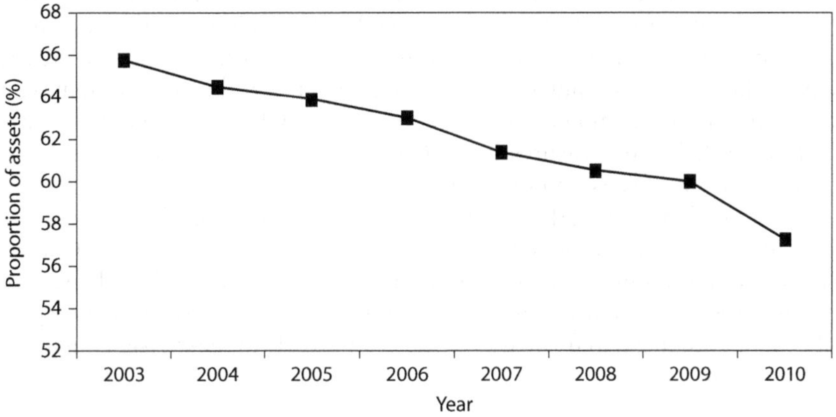

Figure 7.3 Proportions of China's policy banks' and state-owned commercial banks' assets to the whole banking system's assets. Source: China Banking Society (2008, 2011).

Fourth, although China has made progress in transforming its foreign-exchange control regime into a more market-orientated arrangement, it continues to maintain some control over transactions and currency exchanges on the capital account, including restrictions on cross-border capital flows as well as quantitative and regulatory controls on exchange between the renminbi (RMB) and foreign currencies (Zhang 2003). The 1997–98 Asian financial crisis prompted a rethinking of the issues related to capital-account liberalization, and the resultant cautious approach rendered China's banking sector largely immune from the worst effects of the global financial crisis. However, this isolationism resulted in China's reluctance to engage with the international monetary system, which has greatly delayed the process to internationalize the RMB.

On the whole, it seems that China's financial system always faces a difficult choice between, on the one hand, market-orientated reforms that would likely contribute to better efficiency and, on the other, the security of a more cautious approach to its opening-up policy. If this is so, it will be interesting to watch what steps the Chinese financial regulatory authority will undertake to resolve this dilemma.

It seems nothing short of miraculous that China has found a new way to prosperity without an effective traditional Western financial system. According to Laurenceson and Chai (2003), much important literature since Schumpeter (1912) has proved that the functioning of financial systems affects economic development (Gurley and Shaw 1955; Goldsmith 1969; Levine 1997), and many economists have argued that financial reform has a particularly important role to play in economies undergoing the transition to a market economy (Griffith-Jones 1995; World Bank 1996; Hermes and Lensink 2000). However, there is an academic consensus that China's financial sector, in contrast to most other areas of the economy, remains 'essentially unreformed' (Cheng *et al.* 1997: 204), although the economic performance of China has continued to improve during the past 30 years. Given the relatively stagnant pace of reform in the financial system, can China maintain the momentum of economic growth over the next 30 years and beyond? What measures is the Chinese Government going to take to ensure a sustainable economic growth in the future?

To tackle these issues, this chapter reviews the history of Chinese financial reforms and explores the source of, and the financial reasons for, China's economic development, then discusses the overall trends and challenges of the evolution of China's financial system. Finally, we deal with the prospect of China's financial reform under the framework of East Asian financial cooperation.

A REVIEW OF CHINA'S FINANCIAL REFORMS

Banking reform

The banking sector is the most important player in the Chinese financial system. Before the initiation of China's reform and opening-up, the government had incrementally closed down the commercial banks and replaced them with a single People's Bank of China (PBOC). From then on, the PBOC played the dual role of being both a central and a commercial bank. It wielded monopoly power over the banking system, disbursing investment and operating funds to state-owned enterprises (SOEs) according to government fiat (Barth *et al.* 2004). On the one hand, PBOC was a department of the government; it undertook financial business as an agent of the state, conducted the management and use of credit funds, and supervised the business activities of industrial and commercial enterprises. On the other hand, it was an economic organization and ran a credit business with its own capital and sought profits. Although the PBOC had complex functions at that time, its power was limited. The PBOC was only a subordinate agency of the Ministry of Finance. It could neither perform completely the duties of a central bank, nor could it completely fulfil the business of a commercial bank. Financial repression existed widely in China's financial system at that time.

In the first stage of reforms, the single-bank system was abolished, and specialized state-owned banks (SOBs) appeared. In 1979, Deng Xiaoping promoted the first stage of banking reforms. 'We must truly operate our banks on a commercial basis', Deng Xiaoping[2] said in *Some Comments on Economic Work*. Based on the relevant plans set by the central government, the Agricultural Bank was re-established as a separate entity from the PBOC in 1979.[3] The Bank of China was then created by carving out the PBOC's foreign-exchange division. Within a matter of years the State Council firmly decided to reconstitute the PBOC to serve solely as the nation's central bank, and launched a process of gradual reorganization. Its first major initiative along these lines was to transfer the bank's remaining commercial banking functions and certain other banking functions from the Ministry of Finance to two special-purpose banks: the China Construction Bank (formed in 1983) and the Industrial and Commercial Bank of China (formed in 1984). This dramatic reform led to the re-establishment of the PBOC as a true central bank without commercial banking arms (Barth *et al.* 2004).

On 10 May 1995, the National People's Congress (NPC) Standing Committee passed the Law of Commercial Banks of the People's Republic of China, which sped up the process of transforming state-owned specialized banks into commercial ones. The greatest contribution of this round of reform legislation was to promote a more market-driven banking system and generally advance the rule of law, both crucial components for effectively liberalizing China's economy (Barth *et al.* 2004).

On 30 December 2003, the government-owned Central Huijin Investment Company injected US$45 billion into the Bank of China and the China Construction Bank, and this initiated the transformation and consolidation of shareholding systems of the state-owned commercial banks. Since then, one after another, the China Construction Bank, the Bank of China and the Commercial Bank of China have introduced foreign strategic investors, and have successfully listed on the Shanghai Securities Exchange and the Hong Kong Stock Exchange. In this round of reform, commercial banks in China started to adapt to the new rules of the banking game, including competition and international management

In the past 30 years, the banking system of China has undergone drastic change. Many financial institutions have appeared and grown rapidly (Figure 7.4). However, by its very nature, centralization and monopolistic control are still essential features of China's banking system (Figure 7.5).

The reform measures from 1978 to 2005 have not brought about the results that were expected. Most financial resources are still in the hands of the SOBs, and their inclination to lend to inefficient and frequently unprofitable SOEs remains firmly in place. As a result, with a non-performing loans (NPLs) ratio of 20 per cent, major state-owned commercial banks had accumulated RMB2,100 billion (US$254 billion) worth of NPLs at the beginning of 2004. Foreign experts estimated the figure to be much higher, at around US$500 billion, equivalent to about half of China's total GDP (Nolan 2004; Zhang 2004).

The financial distress is 'likely to become systemic when the NPL share reaches 15 per cent' (Sheng 1996: 10). Throughout the years 2004 and 2005, despite strict measures to cut down NPLs, the average NPL ratio of the four state banks still hovered above 10 per cent in 2005, compared with 5 per cent for other Chinese joint-stock banks and 1 per cent for foreign banks in China (Peng 2007: 2). Even in 2007, the SOBs' rate of NPLs stood at 6.7 per cent while for the foreign banks it was only 0.5 per cent.

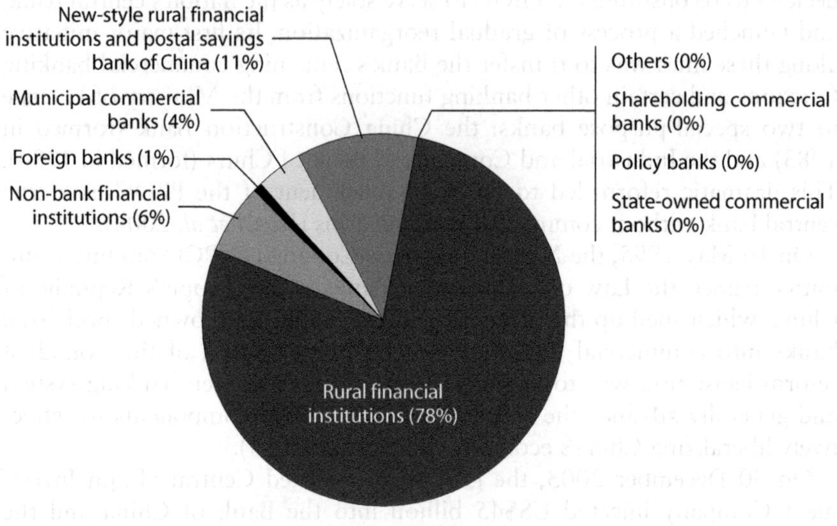

Figure 7.4 Proportions (total number 3,769) and types of banking institutions in China, 2010. Source: China Banking Society (2011).

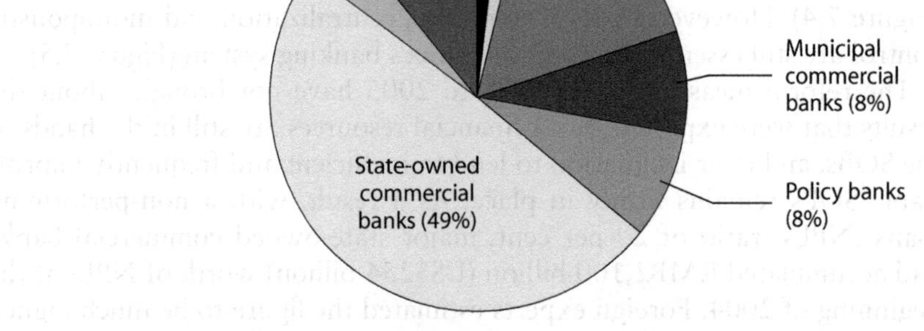

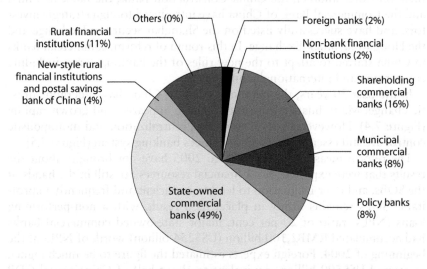

Figure 7.5 Proportions and composition of bank assets (total assets 95,305.3 billion yuan) in China, 2010. Source: China Banking Society (2011).

Financial market reforms

In July 1981, the government issued national treasury bonds for financing key infrastructure projects, such as in the energy and transportation sectors. However, the secondary market of debt was nonexistent at the time and stayed so until 1986, when the sale of securities on the public market was permitted.

Substantial progress of China's capital market was made after the establishment of two stock markets in 1990. From March 1990, the securities business suddenly thrived, mainly because the public discovered that the earlier investors had made a fortune overnight. From 1991 to 2000, the securities market soared. The number of new issues lagged far behind the investment demand. The government introduced new procedures, including an application process, casting lots and a method of quota allocation for distributing newly issued shares. Quota control was an important strategy for keeping the capital market in check. By having this control in place, the government firmly took into its own hands the power of deciding which companies' stocks should be admitted onto the market. Theoretically, quota control would ensure the quality of listed companies. However, because of policy preference, quota control was in fact exercised to safeguard the interests of state-dominated companies. Consequently, state-dominated companies were given priority in obtaining quotas. During this period, various types of shares including A, B, H, and N shares were introduced. A regulatory framework was built up. The market generally exhibited a booming trend, but it also fluctuated violently from time to time (Wei 2007: 337).

The split-share structural reform was one of the most important reforms of China's stock market. When China's stock market was in its early stages of development, in order to keep the public sector as the dominant force on the market, state-dominated companies held large numbers of non-tradable shares when they were listed. At the end of 2004, 1,377 companies were listed on the Shanghai and Shenzhen stock markets. These companies issued a total of 714.9 billion shares, but 457.1 billion of them were non-tradable shares, which comprised over 60 per cent of the total issue (Wang 2008: 170). The presence of so many non-exchangeable state-owned shares on the market created an illusion of prosperity and hampered the efficient functioning of the securities market. In 2003, China's stock market was on the brink of collapse. There was a great clamour to solve the problem of non-exchangeable state-owned shares. In 2004, the State Council unveiled guidelines 'promoting reform and stable development of capital markets'. These new guidelines included policy measures to ensure the protection of the interests of investors, to regulate the transfer of non-tradable shares of listed companies, and to promote the steady and healthy development of capital markets. However, declines in the stock market continued. With the approval of the State Council, in April 2005 the China Securities Regulatory Commission announced the commencement of split-share structure reform (Wang 2008: 171). One year later, the Chinese capital market had made significant progress with the split-share reform, the improvement of the quality of listed companies, the comprehensive management of securities firms, the development and growth of institutional investors, as well as the improvement of legal procedures. Up to 4 January 2007, 1,303 listed companies had either completed the share reform or were in the process of implementation.

Reform of the foreign-exchange administration system in China

China's foreign-exchange regulations were first promulgated in 1996 and focused on the control of foreign currency outflows; they have not been revised since 1997. After the reform and development in the past decade, China has undergone fundamental changes in its currency. To keep up with the rapid pace of international flows of funds, and to relieve the increasing pressure from the state's significant build-up of foreign currency reserves (Figure 7.6), on 5 August 2008 China promulgated the revised Regulations on the Administration of Foreign Exchange, which became effective on the same date (Chan and Pickrell 2008).

According to KPMG (2008), four major overhauls were introduced in the new regulations.

First, the amended regulations required that foreign currency receipts and remittances under current account transactions be based on actual and legitimate transactions, and that financial institutions processing foreign currency transactions verify the authenticity of the relevant transaction documents and their consistency with the foreign currency receipts or remittances under the particular transaction. The previous requirements of mandatory repatriation and settlement of foreign currency income were removed. Under the current account transactions, businesses with valid business documentation could remit payments overseas with foreign currency of their own or purchased from designated banks.

Second, the control of foreign exchange under capital account transactions was the focus of the amendment, with improvements made in three major aspects: the regulatory approval process for outbound direct

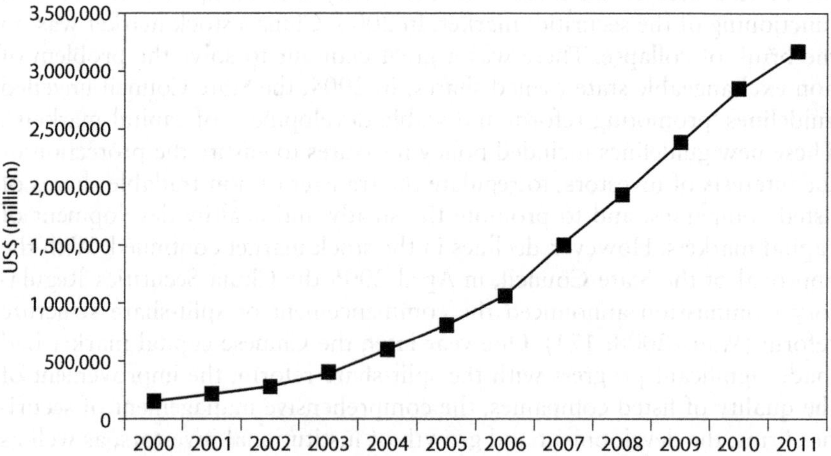

Figure 7.6 China's foreign currency reserves, 2010–11. Source: International Monetary Fund.

investments was simplified; measures controlling foreign exchange under capital account transactions were reformed; and the administration of incoming capital was tightened, requiring that foreign currency receipts under capital account transactions be utilized only for pre-approved purposes.

Third, improvements were made to the measures taken by foreign exchange administration institutions to monitor foreign currency flows, and the related authority and implementation processes.

Fourth, in preparation for potential turbulence in the international financial market, the amended regulations set out principles for establishing administrative mechanisms to deal with emergencies regarding severe imbalances in international payments.

As Hu Xiaolian, the Deputy Governor of the PBOC and Administrator of the State Administration of Foreign Exchange, mentioned in 2007:

> Reform of the foreign exchange management system has been accelerated with a view to gradually promoting RMB convertibility under the capital account. Steps have been taken to facilitate the holding and use of foreign exchange by enterprises and individuals. A system of qualified institutional investors has been established, and efforts have been made to liberalize domestic financial and capital markets in an orderly way. Various means have been explored to facilitate capital outflows, and enterprises have been encouraged to invest abroad. The monitoring of cross-border capital flows has been strengthened to pave the way for further opening-up.

CHARACTERISTICS, OVERALL TRENDS AND CHALLENGES

Preliminary analysis of the financial system in China and other countries shows three characteristics.

First, China's formal stock markets have remained small, in contrast to the capital held in the banking system. In 2011, the total market value of equities in China was $3,392.7 billion, or 45.4 per cent of GDP. However, the total value of bank assets in China was $15,056.1 billion, or 201.5 per cent of GDP.

Second, compared with the major regions and countries, the scale of the total financial system of China is relatively small. Considering the value of the financial sector (including bonds, equities, and bank assets) relative to GDP, it is 381.6 per cent in China, compared with 445 per cent in the USA, 580 per cent in the European Union and 547 per cent in Japan. Even in the emerging market countries of Asia, it is 389 per cent.

Third, China's debt securities market is rudimentary, relative to other regions and countries. The value of the bond market relative to GDP is 36.4 per cent in China, compared with 219.6 per cent in the USA, 210.1 per cent in Japan, 179.2 per cent in the European Union, 58.2 per cent in Asian emerging market countries and 45.1 per cent on average in all emerging market countries. Moreover, in most major industrialized countries, the value of private debt securities is greater than that of public debt securities; but, in China, the value of private debt securities in 2007 was only $149.7 billion while the value of public debt securities was up to $1,034.6 billion (Table 7.1)

In response to the features above, the following assessments can be made. First, China must vigorously develop its financial sector, including the financial market and banking system. The practices and experiences of developed countries show that a developed and effective financial sector is a powerful contributor to long-term economic growth. Obviously, China's financial sector has a long road to travel to reach that position.

Second, in the short term, reforms in the banking system should focus on the optimization of industrial structure and breaking the monopoly of SOBs, while reforms in the financial market should go further by expanding the market size and increasing the variety of securities.

Third, in the longer term, China may transform its bank-based financial system into a market-based financial system, but the process must be promoted with caution. From 1978 to the present, China has transformed itself from being an emerging economy into the second most powerful economy in the world, but its traditional enterprise system and bank-orientated financial system have undergone relatively little change. However, China has to encourage further growth by innovation in the future, which means it must develop a large, mature and open financial market. According to Lin and Li (2005), when a country is still at an elementary stage of development, the scale of most enterprises in the country tends to be small, the market often suffers from a lack of sound procedures, including standardized operations and good service, and enterprise has no direct access to funds. In this situation, indirect financing becomes the main form of raising funds. A rising level of economic activity results in direct financing methods rapidly gaining importance for enterprise promotion.

From the history of its financial reforms, we know that China has been trying its best to develop and improve its financial markets, although it has, until now, retained a bank-orientated financial system. The changes and reforms in this process are likely to be significant, difficult and risky. Even with the same reform content, a wrong sequence can lead to serious setbacks. They also argue that technology-based SMEs need a developed financial market to disperse uncertainty, while traditional enterprises need a strong banking system to support their production. If the types of enterprises do not change from the traditional ones to technology-based ones, changing the financial system from being bank-orientated to market-orientated without necessary regulatory reform would lead to an economic bubble. Capital would flow from productive industries and the bank system to the financial market. If there are not enough technology-based SMEs to absorb the funds and produce income through innovation, the industrial capital of society would become speculative, high-risk capital.

In the process of implementing financial reforms, especially the transformation from a bank-orientated financial system to the more effective market-orientated financial system, China faces tremendous risks and complex challenges.

First, the operational and credit risks will rise rapidly. Under the old banking system, the SOBs loaned mainly to SOEs with a simple and firmly established procedure. Even if there was something wrong with the operation, the government could act as a coordinator between the SOBs and the SOEs. In contrast to a favourable relationship with the government, the SOBs do not yet see professional ability as a useful attribute. However, with increased competition in the banking system, many banks will face even more enterprises demanding loans. Under the new, reformed banking system, most of the enterprises would not be SOEs, which means these inefficient banks may face greater operational and credit risks when they have to do business with more-complex partners.

Second, the reforms will lead to a sharp increase in market risk. Under the current system, the banks often get sound rewards from traditional industrial enterprises. Along with the deepening of reforms, in a market-orientated financial system the earnings yield of financial resources is highly susceptible to interest rates, exchange rates and asset prices, which always fluctuate widely in a fully functioning market.

Third, the government will face more-serious challenges in maintaining the stability of the financial system if the capital account is completely liberalized in the future. The establishment of a technology innovation system with private enterprise as the main player in China needs support from global capital providers. That is to say, in the longer term, China must make its capital account convertible, or the RMB will not be able to act as an international currency and an effective tool for allocating global resources. However, if China liberalizes its capital account, its financial system may suffer a shock from the huge inflow and outflow of capital, which increases the difficulty of regulatory monitoring.

To deal with these challenges, international financial cooperation, especially between East Asian countries, is an attractive choice for China. In the light of the formidable volume of international hot money (Figure 7.7), no country can effectively deal with the great onslaught of speculative hot money by itself. Although China's foreign-exchange reserves rose 16 per cent year-on-year to US$1.95 trillion by the end of March 2009, this sum is still insufficient to provide an effective buffer against international hot money, including hedge funds. Since China has the world's largest foreign-exchange reserves, if China is not immune from the risk arising from international hot money, no other country can hope to be immune from the influx.

Table 7.1 Selected indicators on the size of the capital markets, 2007. Values are in US$ billion unless noted otherwise.

	GDP	*Total reserves minus gold*	*Stock market capital-ization*	*Debt securities*			*Bank assets*	*Bonds, equities, and bank assets*	*Equities (as percen-tage of GDP)*	*Bonds (as percen-tage of GDP)*	*Bank assets (as percen-tage of GDP)*	*Bonds, equities, and bank assets (as percentage of GDP)*
				Public	*Private*	*Total*						
World	54,840.9	6,449.1	65,105.6	28,629.3	51,585.8	80,215.1	95,768.5	241,089.3	118.7	146.3	174.6	439.6
European Union	1,5741.1	279.7	14,730.9	8,778.3	19,432.3	28,210.5	48,462.0	91,403.5	93.6	179.2	307.9	580.7
Euro area	12,220.6	172.1	10,040.1	7,606.4	15,397.8	23,004.2	35,097.1	68,141.5	82.2	188.2	287.2	557.6
North America	15,243.6	100.5	22,108.8	7,419.2	24,491.9	31,911.1	13,851.9	67,871.8	145.0	209.3	90.9	445.2
Canada	1,436.1	41.0	2,186.6	823.3	763.6	1,586.9	2,657.8	6,431.3	152.3	110.5	185.1	447.8
USA	13,807.6	59.5	19,922.3	6,595.9	23,728.3	30,324.2	11,194.1	61,440.6	144.3	219.6	81.1	445.0
China	3,250.8	1,528.3	4,302.2	10,34.6	149.7	1,184.3	6,917.2	12,403.7	132.3	36.4	212.8	381.6
Japan	4,384.4	952.8	4,663.8	7,147.7	2,066.0	9,213.7	10,086.9	23,964.3	106.4	210.1	230.1	546.6
Memorandum items:												
EU countries												
Austria	371.2	10.7	236.4	217.3	438.4	655.6	615.9	1,508.0	63.7	176.6	165.9	406.2
Belgium	459.0	10.4	404.4	506.7	547.5	1,054.2	2,324.4	3,783.0	88.1	229.7	506.4	824.1
Denmark	310.5	32.5	290.9	93.3	613.9	707.2	1,082.4	2,080.6	93.7	227.8	348.6	670.1
Finland	246.2	7.1	359.1	130.1	121.7	251.8	303.4	914.3	145.9	102.3	123.2	371.3
France	2,593.8	45.7	2,737.1	1,447.2	2,923.8	4,370.9	10,230.4	17,338.4	105.5	168.5	394.4	668.5
Germany	3,320.9	44.3	2,105.2	1,700.3	3,902.3	5,602.7	6,600.1	14,308.0	63.4	168.7	198.7	430.8
Greece	312.8	0.6	265.0	453.8	134.0	587.8	513.0	1,365.7	84.7	187.9	164.0	436.7
Ireland	261.2	0.8	143.9	58.9	518.6	577.5	1630.7	2352.1	55.1	221.1	624.3	900.4
Italy	2,117.5	28.4	1,072.5	2,019.0	2,183.9	4,202.9	4,336.0	9,611.5	50.6	198.5	204.8	453.9
Luxembourg	49.7	0.1	166.1	0.0	94.6	94.6	1,347.6	1,608.3	334.2	190.3	2,711.5	3,234.4

Table 7.1 (continued)

	GDP	*Total reserves minus gold*	*Stock market capital-ization*	*Debt securities*			*Bank assets*	*Bonds, equities, and bank assets*	*Equities (as percen-tage of GDP)*	*Bonds (as percen-tage of GDP)*	*Bank assets (as percen-tage of GDP)*	*Bonds, equities, and bank assets (as percentage of GDP)*
				Public	*Private*	*Total*						
Netherlands	777.2	10.3	574.5	315.6	1,698.4	2,014.0	3,869.0	6,457.6	73.9	259.1	497.8	830.8
Portugal	223.7	1.3	147.2	174.0	269.9	443.9	280.4	871.5	65.8	198.4	125.3	389.5
Spain	1,440.0	11.5	1,799.8	580.0	2,564.1	3,144.2	2,979.4	7,923.4	125.0	218.3	206.9	550.2
Sweden	453.8	27.0	576.9	168.6	493.1	661.6	694.3	1,932.8	127.1	145.8	153.0	425.9
United Kingdom	2,803.4	49.0	3,851.7	913.5	2,928.0	3,841.5	11,655.0	19,348.2	137.4	137.0	415.7	690.2
Emerging countries	17,270.8	4,034.7	20,950.2	5,001.3	2,795.6	7,796.9	18,258.1	47,005.2	121.3	45.1	105.7	272.2
Of which:												
Asia	7,680.4	2,138.8	13,782.7	2,645.8	1,826.9	4,472.7	11,620.2	29,875.6	179.5	58.2	151.3	389.0
Latin America	3,641.0	445.2	2,292.2	1,456.5	628.6	2,085.1	2,260.8	6,638.1	63.0	57.3	62.1	182.3
Middle East	1,557.8	312.6	1,275.9	39.5	84.3	123.8	1,335.6	2,735.3	81.9	7.9	85.7	175.6
Africa	1,101.7	289.5	1,181.7	89.0	78.9	168.0	864.5	2,214.2	107.3	15.2	78.5	201.0
Europe	3,289.9	848.6	2,417.6	770.4	176.9	947.3	2,177.0	5,541.9	73.5	28.8	66.2	168.5

Sources: China Banking Society (2008) and IMF (2009).

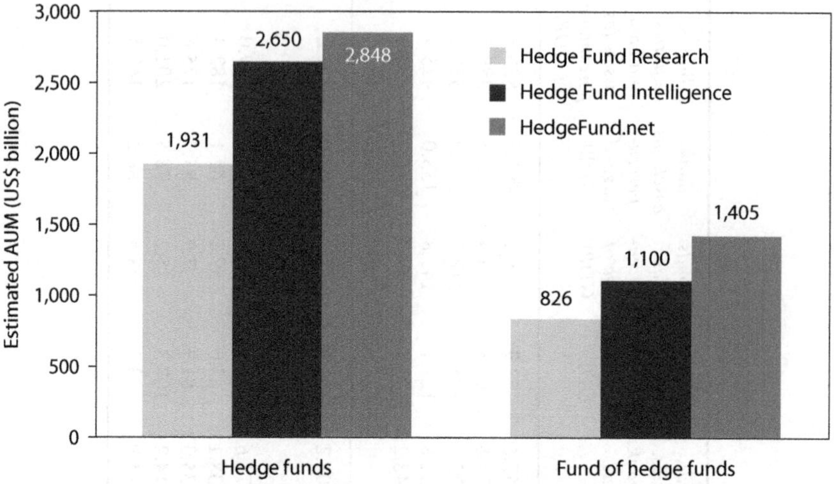

Figure 7.7 Assets under management (AUM) in global hedge fund industry. Source: *Aima's Roadmap to Hedge Funds*, November 2008, Alternative Investment Management Association, available at http://www.aima.org/en/education/aimas-roadmap-to-hedge-funds.cfm.

EAST ASIAN FINANCIAL COOPERATION AND THE PROSPECT FOR CHINA'S FINANCIAL REFORM

In light of the circumstances and the above analysis, China's participation in the ASEAN+3 (ASEAN plus China, Japan and the Republic of Korea) bilateral money exchange and other financial operations has two goals. First, it should aim to construct a regional financing network to support the development of a technology-based enterprise system. Second, it needs a huge regional financial market network to diversify financing risk arising during the reform. Most of the institutional arrangements, including the Chiang Mai Initiative (see below) and the Asian Bond Markets Initiative, should be compatible with these goals.

The Chiang Mai Initiative and China's bilateral swap arrangements

History indicates that East Asian regional cooperation is always driven and promoted by crisis. Since the 1997–98 Asian financial crisis, East Asia has pursued greater regional cooperation. Henning (2002) argues that the financial crisis of 1997–98 provided, among other things, a strong impetus for East Asian regionalism. In an effort to avoid repeating that painful episode, East Asian governments, their officials and academic commentators have proposed numerous enhancements to monetary and financial cooperation.

These proposals have ranged from suggestions to create new exchange-rate regimes and common currencies, to initiatives to build regional financial facilities and an Asian Monetary Fund. The movement to create a set of currency swap agreements among countries in the region, that could contribute to greater stability in the face of another financial shock, is the most advanced of these proposals. This movement, which was launched at a meeting of the finance ministers of ASEAN+3 in Chiang Mai, Thailand, in May 2000, is commonly referred to as the Chiang Mai Initiative (CMI).

The CMI is not, per se, about financial integration. It is about creating a fund that can help countries in the region to overcome, through swap arrangements, extreme volatility in currency values (Pasadilla 2008). It is designed to provide liquidity support for member countries that experience short-run balance-of-payment deficits, with the purpose of preventing an extreme crisis or systemic failure in a country and subsequent regional contagion, such as the kind that occurred in the 1997–98 Asian financial crisis (Sohn 2007). As of February 2009, US$90 billion had been committed by the ASEAN+3 for 16 bilateral swap arrangements (BSAs) (Figure 7.8).

To the extent that, through the CMI, monetary and fiscal authorities in the region are coordinating and agreeing to a regional monitoring system and gaining each other's trust, the CMI can be considered a precursor to further financial integration (Pasadilla 2008). On 5 May 2007, at the 10th ASEAN+3 Finance Ministers' Meeting in Kyoto, participants reached an agreement on the basic direction of the CMI multilateralization (CMIM). First, countries should establish a self-managed reserve pooling arrangement. Second, countries should reach a single contractual agreement. Third, countries should maintain the two core objectives of the CMI: to address short-term liquidity difficulties in the region; and to supplement the existing international financial arrangements. On 4 May 2008, major progress was made on the CMIM at the 11th ASEAN+3 Finance Ministers' Meeting in Madrid. Participants reached a consensus on the key elements, including basic modality, the size and amount of contributions, borrowing accessibility, the mechanism of activation, surveillance and future work. For example, the member countries have agreed that the total size of the CMIM Reserve Pool should be at least US$80 billion. They have also agreed that the proportion of the amount of contribution between the ASEAN and the Plus Three countries would be 20:80 (Yoshida 2009). At the Special ASEAN+3 Finance Ministers Meeting held in Phuket on 22 February 2009, ASEAN+3 members agreed to pursue the CMIM framework, increased the size of the CMIM by 50 per cent from US$80 billion to US$120 billion, and agreed to develop a more robust and effective surveillance mechanism to support the operations of the CMIM. It is important to note that the establishment of the CMIM was not intended to diminish the role of the IMF in East Asia, but rather to complement the Fund's work in the region by providing additional surveillance and liquidity support in times of need (see the ASEAN Priorities for the London Summit 2009[4]).

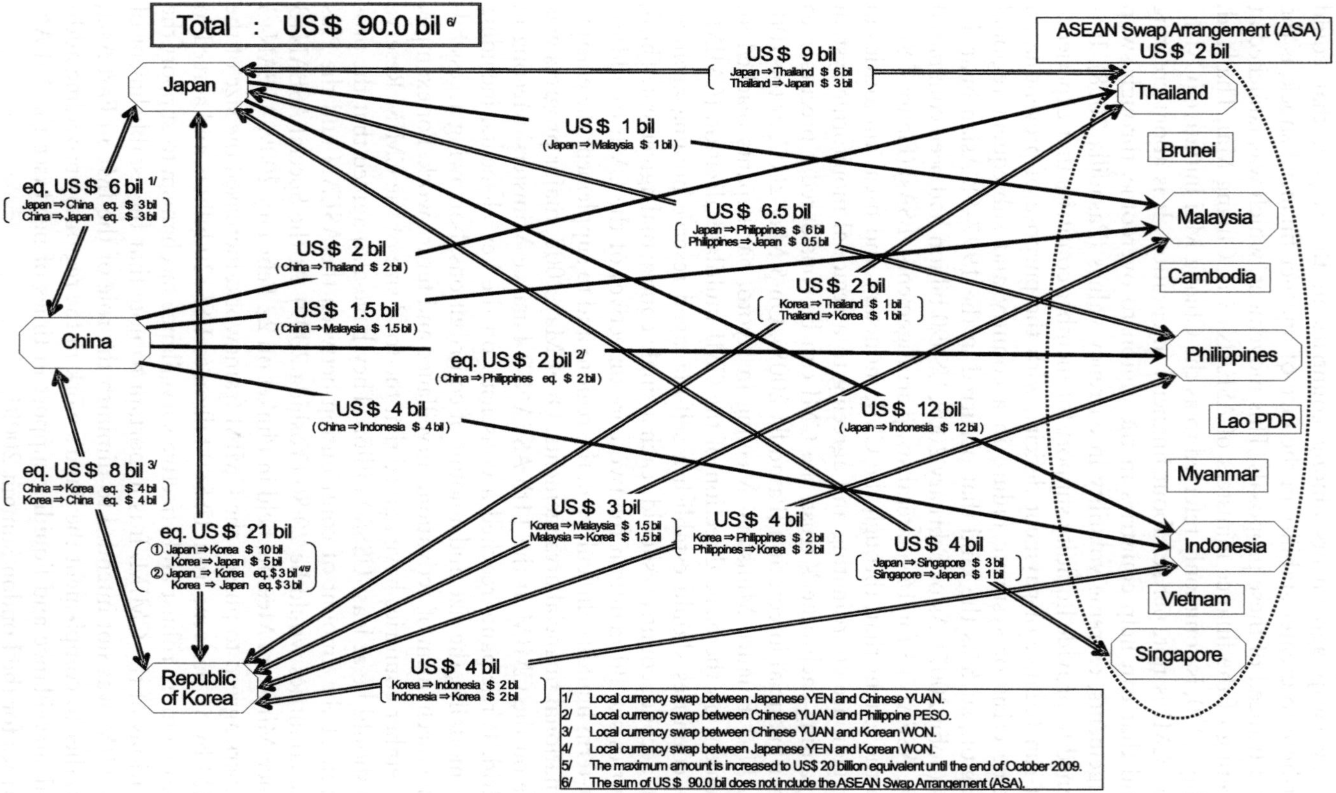

Figure 7.8 Networks of bilateral swap arrangements under the Chiang Mai Initiative. Source: http://www.mof.go.jp/.

Since the US subprime crisis, adapting to the changes of the CMI, China's BSAs have some new features. First, China expanded the swap size and number of participating countries. As of July 2012, the PBOC had signed bilateral currency swap agreements worth 1856.2 billion yuan (US$293.2 billion) with monetary authorities of the Republic of Korea, Malaysia, Belarus, Indonesia and other adjacent economies.[5] Second, these arrangements allowed for currency swapping between RMB and foreign currency. Before this, the BSAs, except for the China–Japan BSA, generally swapped US dollars for local currency (Henning 2002: 19) (Table 7.2).

Third, the new BSA's aim is to promote bilateral trade and the internationalization of the RMB. Crisis can only drive regional cooperation during turbulent times and in the short term, whereas institutional arrangements are necessary in the long term. Crisis-driven cooperation must be replaced by prosperity-driven cooperation in East Asia. China can act as one of the most important pivots of Asian prosperity. To achieve this target, China should be one of the most important providers of regional public goods, including consumer goods and the investment goods market, currency of settlement, standards of production and transaction, capital augmenting technologies and alternative development models.

Table 7.2 China's bilateral swap arrangements

Countries	*Process*	*Amount and currency*
Iceland	Signed 9 June 2010	3.5 billion yuan–66 billion Iceland krona
Singapore	Signed 23 July 2010	150 billion yuan–30 billion Singapore dollar
New Zealand	Signed 18 April 2011	25 billion yuan–5 billion New Zealand dollar
Uzbekistan	Signed 19 April 2011	0.7 billion yuan–167 billion som
Mongolia	Signed 6 May 2011	5 billion yuan–1 trillion tugrik
Kazakhstan	Signed 13 June 2011	7 billion yuan–150 billion tenge
South Korea	Renewed 26 October 2011	360 billion yuan–64 trillion won
Hong Kong	Renewed 22 November 2011	400 billion yuan–490 billion Hong Kong dollar
Thailand	Signed 22 December 2011	70 billion yuan–320 billion baht
Pakistan	Signed 23 December 2011	10 billion yuan–140 billion rupee
United Arab Emirates	Signed 17 January 2012	35 billion yuan–20 billion dirham
Malaysia	Renewed 8 February 2012	180 billion yuan–90 billion ringgit
Turkey	Signed 21 February 2012	10 billion yuan–3 billion lira
Mongolia	Revised 20 March 2012	10 billion yuan–2 trillion tugrik
Australia	Signed 22 March 2012	200 billion yuan–30 billion Australian dollar
Ukraine	Signed 26 June 2012	15 billion yuan–19 billion hryvnia
Brazil	Signed July 2012	190 billion yuan–60 billion real

Source: People's Bank of China.

The Asian bond markets

Asian bond markets are growing rapidly as Asian borrowers switch away from short-term bank loans towards longer term debt financing.

Kawai (2006) argues that the development of local currency bond markets in East Asia is required as a result of past crisis experience and the new reality. He gives four reasons. First, Asian bond markets can provide alternative sources of financing for public and private investment, and alternative modes of wealth-holding for Asian households. Second, Asian bond markets can improve financial resilience by putting in place the two, balanced wheels of the financial system – sound banking sectors and well-developed capital markets. Third, Asian bond market development can reduce the 'double mismatch' problem (currency and maturity mismatches) by mobilizing Asian savings for Asian long-term investment in local currencies. Fourth, mobilization of Asian savings for Asian investment can help reduce global payment imbalances.

Similarly, Pasadilla (2008) emphasizes the function of Asian bond markets in developing a liquid and efficient bond market in the region, to better utilize huge Asian surpluses for investments in Asia, and to provide an avenue for recycling huge Asian savings. By 2008, although affected by the international financial crisis, developing Asia[6] had a net lending (savings minus investment) position of 5.4 per cent of GDP (US$390.9 billion), whereas the Euro area had a net borrowing (investment minus savings) of 0.8 per cent of GDP (US$109.1 billion), and the USA had a much larger net borrowing of 4.7 per cent of GDP (US$670.5 billion) (Figure 7.9 shows the long-range situation).

According to Pasadilla (2008), this is largely because a major portion of gross savings in Asia finds its way into debt instruments of governmental and quasi-governmental issuers in industrialized economies, thanks to the

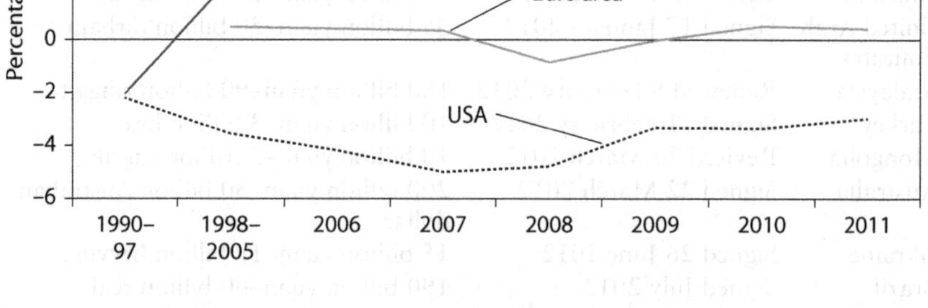

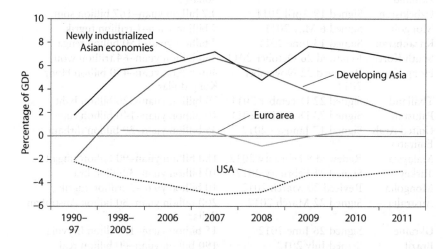

Figure 7.9 Net lending as a proportion of GDP in developing Asia, the Euro area and the USA, 1990–97 to 2011. Source: International Monetary Fund.

intermediation efforts of the USA and European investment banks, hedge funds and private equity funds. Meanwhile, Asian investments are financed, to a significant degree, by capital from those same countries, making countries in the region vulnerable to the 'sudden stop' phenomenon, as the Asian economic crisis in 1997 showed. That is to say, as Devlin and Brummitt (2007) argued, East Asian countries, fearing becoming victims of a new financial crisis, have accumulated a great deal of dollar reserves after the Asian financial crisis (Figure 7.10). But the security of these reserves did not primarily depend on the regional internal market itself.

In August 2003, the ASEAN+3 finance ministers, meeting in Manila in response to the Asian currency crisis, agreed that measures should be taken to develop local-currency-denominated bond markets in order to allow regional private savings to be used for regional development, by facilitating essential investment. Under this initiative, the Asian Development Bank and other international institutions, along with the Japan Bank for International Cooperation and government financial bodies, issued local-currency-denominated bonds, while financial institutions issued securitized instruments of loan receivables. This has contributed to the diversification of, and expanded the scale of, regional bond markets. In May 2008, at the ASEAN+3 Finance Ministers Meeting in Madrid, a new Asian Bond Markets Initiative (ABMI) Roadmap was agreed, aimed at the further development of Asian bond markets. The new ABMI Roadmap focuses on four key areas: (1) promoting issuance of local-currency-denominated bonds, (2) facilitating the demand for local-currency-denominated bonds, (3) improving the regulatory framework and (4) improving related infrastructure for the bond markets (Yoshida 2009).

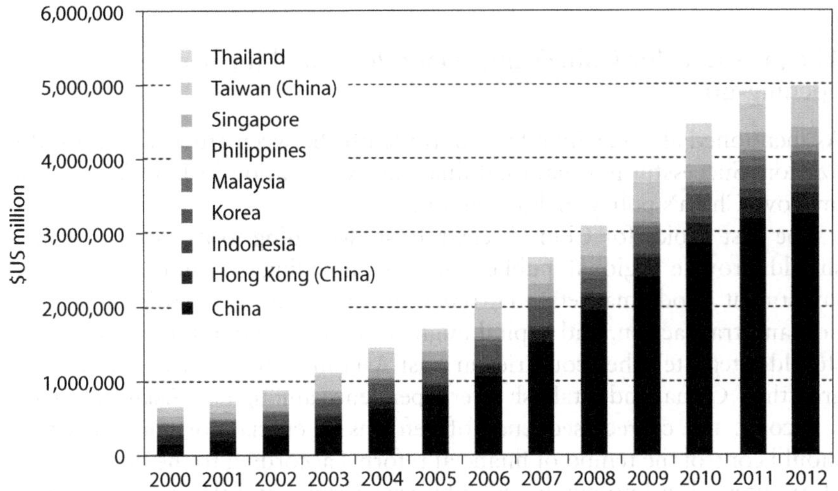

Figure 7.10 Foreign reserves of selected East Asian economies· Data for 2007 are calculated as an average over the 8 months to August. Source: International Monetary Fund International Financial Statistics.

Since the end of the East Asian financial crisis, the size of local-currency-denominated bond markets in ASEAN+3 countries has expanded significantly (Figure 7.11). Figure 7.11 also shows that government bond issuance continues to dominate the market, probably driven by deficit financing and monetary sterilization, while corporate bond market activity slowed as borrowing costs increased and credit dried up. Hence, major efforts should be devoted to developing the corporate bond market, which is consistent with China's strategy for developing technology-based enterprises with market-based financing instruments.

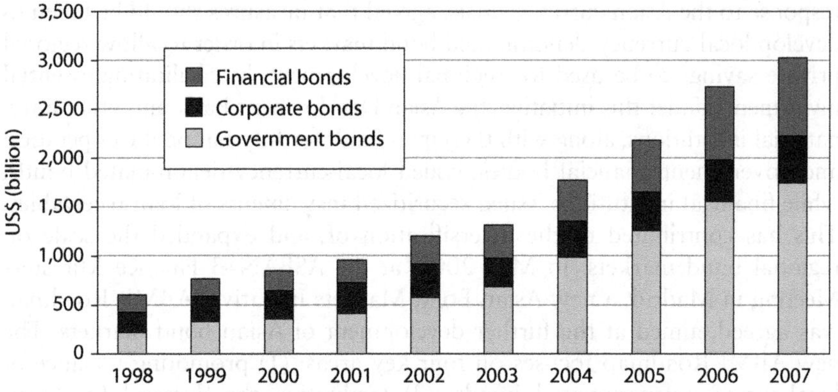

Figure 7.11 Size of local currency-denominated bond markets in ASEAN+3 countries. Source: http://asianbondsonline.adb.org/asiabondindicators/default.php, quoted by Zheng (2008: 36).

The prospects for China's financial reform and further opening-up

As mentioned above, China faces a 'trade off' between efficiency and stabilization. Successful international financial cooperation in East Asia would improve China's policy-making environment.

The best choice for China is clear. First, according to its capacity, China should provide regional public goods – including consumer goods and investment goods markets – currency of settlement, standards of production and transaction, and capital-augmenting technologies. Furthermore, it should integrate other countries in East Asia into the process of long-term growth of China, and establish interdependence among East Asian countries.

Second, the correct sequence of reforms is crucial for success. China should control the tempo of financial reforms according to the development of an internal technology-based enterprise system and the level of international financial cooperation.

Last but not least, reform must be artfully implemented in light of the experience of the region, to substantially promote regional cooperation and, at the same time, to obtain the endorsement, or at least the understanding, of the major powers outside the region. For China, it is obviously a difficult but worthwhile task to learn that art. But if China successfully masters the art, not only will it have a more prosperous future, so too will the whole of East Asia.

NOTES

1 Institute of Asia–Pacific Studies, Chinese Academy of Social Sciences, Beijing.
2 Selected works of Deng Xiaoping, 1975–82, Volume 2 (Beijing: Foreign Languages Press, 1984).
3 It previously had operated independently but had been merged with the PBOC in 1957.
4 Available at http://www.aseansummit.mfa.go.th/14/pdf/ASEAN_London_Summit_2009.pdf.
5 Alan Wheatley (2009) 'Watch China's FX swaps, not just super-currency plan', 30 March 2009, available at http://www.reuters.com/article/newsOne/idUSTRE52T1FB20090330?sp=true.
6 Developing Asia is composed of 23 countries: Bangladesh, Bhutan, Cambodia, China, Fiji, India, Indonesia, Kiribati, Lao People's Democratic Republic, Malaysia, Maldives, Myanmar, Nepal, Pakistan, Papua New Guinea, Philippines, Samoa, Solomon Islands, Sri Lanka, Thailand, Tonga, Vanuatu and Vietnam.

REFERENCES

Barth, J.R., R. Koepp and Zhongfei Zhou (2004) 'Banking reform in China: catalyzing the nation's financial future', available at http//:papers.ssrn.com/sol3/papers.cfm?abstract-id=548405.

Chan, J.W.K. and G.L. Pickrell (2008) 'China revises foreign exchange regulations', *Client Alert*, Volume 0804, No. 8069, Pillsbury Winthrop Shaw Pittman law company.

Cheng, H., H. Fong and T. Mayer (1997) 'China's financial reform and monetary policy: issues and strategies', in Joint Economic Committee, Congress of the United States, *China's Economic Future*, pp. 203–220, New York: M.E. Sharpe.

China Banking Society (2008 and 2011) *Almanac of China's Finance and Banking*, Beijing: China Financial Publishing House.

Devlin, W. and W. Brummitt (2007) 'A few sovereigns more: the rise of sovereign wealth funds', *Economic Round-up*, Spring 2007, 119–136, available at http://www.treasury.gov.au/.

García-Herrero, A., S. Gavilá and D. Santabárbara (2006) 'China's banking reform: an assessment of its evolution and possible impact', *CESifo Economic Studies*, 52(2): 304–363.

Goldsmith, R. (1969) *Financial Structure and Development*, New Haven, CT: Yale University Press.

Griffith-Jones, S. (1995) 'Introductory framework', in S. Griffith-Jones and Z. Drabek (eds) *Financial Reform in Central and Eastern Europe*, pp. 3–16, New York: St Martin's Press.

Gurley, J. and E. Shaw (1955) 'Financial aspects of economic development', *American Economic Review*, 45(4): 515–538.

Henning, C.R. (2002) 'East Asian financial cooperation', *Policy Analyses in International Economics*, No. 68, Washington, DC: Institute for International Economics.

Hermes, N. and R. Lensink (2000) 'Financial system development in transition economies', *Journal of Banking and Finance*, 24(4): 507–524.

IMF (International Monetary Fund) (2009) *Global Financial Stability Report: Responding to the Financial Crisis and Measuring Systemic Risks*, Washington, DC: IMF, available at http//:www.imf.org/external/pubs/ft/gfsr/2009/01/pdf/text.pdf.

Kawai, M. (2006) 'Asian bond market development: progress, opportunities and challenges', luncheon speech at the Asian Bond Market Summit, 14 November.

KPMG (2008) 'Major overhaul of PRC foreign exchange regulations', available at http://www.kpmg.com/cn/en/issuesandinsights/articlespublications/newsletters/chinaalerts/pages/china-alert-0808-27.aspx.

Laurenceson, J. and J.C.H. Chai (2003) *Financial Reform and Economic Development in China*, Cheltenham, UK: Edward Elgar Publishing.

Levine, R. (1997) 'Financial development and economic growth: views and agenda', *Journal of Economic Literature*, 35(2): 688–726.

Lin, J.Y. and Zhiyun Li (2005) 'China's SOE and financial system reforms', *China Economic Quarterly*, 4(4): 913–936.

Nolan, P. (2004) *China at the Crossroads*, Cambridge, UK: Polity Press.

Pasadilla, G.O. (2008) 'Financial services integration in East Asia: lessons from the European Union', *Asia–Pacific Research and Training Network on Trade Working Paper Series*, No. 53.

Peng, Yuanyuan (2007) *The Chinese Banking Industry: Lessons from History for Today's Challenges*, New York and London: Routledge.

Schumpeter, J. (1912) *Theorie der Wirtschaftlichen Entwicklung* [*The Theory of Economic Development*], Leipzig: Dunker & Humblot, translated by R. Opie (1934), Cambridge, MA: Harvard University Press.

Sheng, A. (1996) *Bank Restructuring: Lessons from the 1980s*, Washington, DC: World Bank.

Sohn, I. (2007) 'East Asia's counterweight strategy: Asian financial cooperation in an era of economic globalization', paper presented at the annual meeting of the *International Studies Association 48th Annual Convention*, 28 February, Hilton Chicago, Chicago, IL.

Wang Guangqian (2008) *Zhong Guo Jing Ji Gai Ge San Shi Nian: Jin Rong Gai Ge Juan* [*30 Years of Reforms in China's Economy: Volume of Financial Reforms*], Chongqing: Chongqing University Press.

Wei, Yuwa (2007) 'China's capital market and corporate governance: the promotion of the external governance mechanism', *Macquarie Journal of Business Law*, 4: 325–344.

World Bank (1996) *World Development Report 1996: from Plan to Market*, Washington, DC: World Bank.

Yoshida, M. (2009) 'Capital flows in Asia and recent developments in regional financial cooperation', available at http://www.fsa.go.jp/frtc/kenkyu/event/20090331/14-4.pdf.

Zhang, A. (2004) 'China's leadership rolls out reform agenda', available at http://www.pwc.com.

Zhang, Xiaopu (2003) 'Capital account management and its outlook in China', BIS Papers, No. 15: 19–24, Basel: Bank of International Settlements.

Zheng, Wenli (2008) 'A research on the development of Asian bond market', Ph.D. dissertation, University of Jilin.

8 Capital account liberalization in India

A post-crisis evaluation

D.M. Nachane[1]

INTRODUCTION

The three decades following the conclusion of the Second World War and the establishment of the Bretton Woods system were an era of heavily regulated capital flows in almost all the major economies of the world. Indeed, Keynes, the inspiring spirit behind this system, describes proposals 'to stabilize exchange rates and promote free trade without limiting international capital mobility' as 'exercises in squaring the circle' (see Felix 1995). In line with the Keynesian orthodoxy then prevalent, the International Monetary Fund (IMF) Executive Board in 1956 reaffirmed the right of member countries to impose capital controls. With the breakdown of the Bretton Woods system in the 1970s, and under the powerful impact of Milton Friedman's writings (and later the emergence of the new classical economics school), the intellectual climate became less propitious towards capital controls, with the general policy sentiment veering to the view (Boughton 1997) that

> ... no country can share in the benefits of international trade unless it allows capital to move freely enough to finance that trade, and modern financial markets are sophisticated and open enough that capital transactions can no longer be compartmentalized as trade-related or speculative.

Reflecting the new thinking, the IMF's Internal Committee in April 1997 unanimously voted in favour of amending the Articles of the Fund to allow capital controls only as emergency measures in exceptional situations.

As a consequence of this shift in thinking, in recent years emerging market economies (EMEs) are facing increasing pressures from the IMF and other multilateral institutions, as well as from developed countries, to liberalize their capital accounts. Capital account liberalization (CAL) refers to the process of dismantling restrictions on international transactions involving the movement of financial capital, both into and out of a country. The most common forms of restrictions are: (i) limits on foreign borrowings by domestic entities (banks, financial institutions and corporate entities); (ii) controls on foreign capital entering an economy; (iii) sectoral caps on foreign investment; and (iv) restrictions on repatriation of foreigners' earnings from their investments in the domestic economy.

MACRO-ECONOMIC EFFECTS OF CAPITAL ACCOUNT LIBERALIZATION

The case for opening up the capital account is essentially predicated on the following five claims:

(i) CAL achieves the optimum allocation of global financial resources, letting capital flow to those regions where its marginal productivity is highest. It thus helps EMEs to raise the rate of capital formation above their domestic savings rate and thereby contributes to higher growth (see, for example, Summers (2000), Fischer (1998), and Kaminsky and Schmukler (2002)).
(ii) Capital inflows promote long-term growth in EMEs by conferring several *collateral benefits* on host countries, such as transfer of technology, financial know-how and management skills.
(iii) Capital inflows have a disciplining effect on fiscal and monetary policies of the host country.
(iv) Capital inflows dampen the effects of exogenous shocks on the domestic economy.
(v) Free mobility of financial capital is essential for stimulating global trade.

The intellectual underpinnings of this advocacy of CAL may be traced to 'efficient markets hypothesis' (EMH) of new classical economics. As a matter of fact, this view not only overstates the supposed benefits of CAL, it does not recognize the several pitfalls and dangers (especially for less-developed countries (LDCs) and EMEs) of embarking on hasty CAL programmes.

CAL and economic growth

The relationship between CAL and economic growth has been debated at great length, both theoretically and empirically. The IMF view ignores several key features of the ground reality in a majority of LDCs and EMEs. In these countries, security markets are not the major source of long-term industrial finance. Instead, firms are bank-dependent for their working capital funds, whereas their long-term funding comes from either internal funds (i.e. retained funds) or external borrowing (including foreign borrowing). Because equity markets are narrow and shallow, they exhibit wide fluctuations in response to changes in foreign flows. Such fluctuations in turn affect the availability of bank credit (unless fully sterilized), real exchange-rate movements and interest rates (via monetary policy responses). As shown in Fitzgerald and Mavrotas (1997), such oscillations tend to magnify the effects on the domestic economy of financial frictions originating abroad, without having any compensatory positive effect on private-sector fixed capital formation. Aghion *et al.* (2000) qualify such conclusions by noting that CAL is deleterious only when it is premature (i.e. when undertaken without adequate financial development).

Given the conflicting theoretical picture, it is of interest to turn to the empirical evidence. Most of the studies designed to explain the growth implications of CAL, have employed panel data on sets of countries in the post-Bretton-Woods era. By and large, the picture that emerges from such empirical studies is that the case for capital account openness being growth-enhancing is far from convincing (see, in this regard, the detailed survey by Edison *et al.* (2004)). Several contingent effects also seem to be in operation. Rodrik (1998), Klein (2005) and Honig (2008) reveal the critical role played by institutional quality,[2] while Arteta *et al.* (2003) show that proper sequencing of reforms is an important factor determining the success of CAL.

Recently, several analysts have also brought into focus the issue of collateral *benefits* attached to CAL, such as better governance, more competition, institutional development, and correction of macro-economic imbalances (Kose *et al.* 2009). However, attempts to establish a causal nexus from CAL to total factor productivity growth have met with little success (see BIS 2009).

Proponents of CAL also brush aside the difficulties posed by capital flows to the conduct of monetary policy and the dangers they pose for financial stability. I discuss each of these briefly in turn.

CAL and financial stability

In stark contrast to the assumed rational behaviour of investors by the EMH, actual trading strategies of foreign exchange (forex) traders can often be in systematic violation of such behaviour.[3] Economists are increasingly realizing that the 1930s Keynesian description of financial markets as being 'casinos' guided by 'herd instincts' is nearer the mark (than the EMH) as a description of how real world forex markets operate today (see, for example, Russel and Torbey (2002) and Huberman and Regev (2001)). In the Keynesian view, volatile capital flows can produce violent swings in important asset prices such as real estate, equities and, of course, the exchange rate itself, especially if they (i.e. capital flows) are pro-cyclical as noted by Williamson and Drabek (1999) and Singh (2002) among others. The fragility of the financial system is also enhanced by freer capital mobility. Recent studies such as those of Calvo (2008) and Reinhart and Reinhart (2008) stress the link between financial liberalization, and exchange-rate and banking crises. In a regime of CAL, with adequate prudential banking norms not in place, currency crises can easily translate into more general financial crises (see Demirguc-Kunt and Detragiache 1998).

CAL and monetary policy

Capital inflows create several special problems for the conduct of monetary policy, as well. As a matter of fact, the famous 'trilemma' (see Bernanke 2005) succinctly sums up the various issues involved. The trilemma refers to the impossibility of maintaining in simultaneous operation (for a given country) all three of the following policy regimes: (i) an open capital account, (ii) a fixed exchange rate and (iii) an independent domestic monetary policy. Typically, for reasons of national sovereignty and pride, countries would be reluctant to sacrifice monetary policy autonomy, and the effective choice thus narrows down to that between capital mobility and a fixed-exchange-rate regime.

For the LDCs and EMEs, the choice is far from clear. One view (see Vegh 1992; Dornbusch and Warner 1994; Bernanke 2005) maintains that the best course for such economies is to let the exchange rate float freely and adopt 'inflation targeting' as an explicit and sole monetary policy objective, to provide the much needed 'nominal anchor' for the macro-economic system. There are two major arguments against a 'free float' for such economies. First, as Sargent (1982) has noted, a fixed (or heavily managed) exchange rate can be a suitable guard against high inflation, and can even act as a strong brake on persistent hyperinflations.[4] Secondly, Calvo and Reinhart (2000) have drawn attention to the low credibility of policy-makers in several LDCs, which could mean that a flexible exchange rate could exhibit excessive volatility (in both the short and long term).

Until 2005 or so, the substantial excess capacity in EMEs and the growing manufacturing capacity in tradable goods allowed several EMEs greater capacity to conduct sterilization operations. As Vargas and Varela (2008) put it 'a negative output gap made it possible for the central bank to engage in forex intervention at the same time that it was easing monetary policy'. However, this zone of comfort for sterilized interventions seems to have shrunk since 2005 (BIS 2009).

CAL: other important distortions

Capital account liberalization introduces several other potential sources of distortion, of which we note the following:

(i) Capital flows can have pronounced impacts on the fiscal budget, principally on its capital investment component. The most direct route through which CAL reduces the overall fiscal space available to governments in LDCs and EMEs is via the costs of managing capital inflows.[5] The classical tenets of public finance that the revenue budget should be in balance and that there should be a cap on the gross fiscal deficit (tenets that are a prominent component of India's *Fiscal Responsibility and Budget Management Act,* enacted by Parliament in 2003 to bring in fiscal discipline) usually serve to put the axe to capital expenditures (especially in categories such as health and education), given that revenue expenditures involving transfer payments are, for political reasons, often difficult to downsize.

(ii) Another important distortion is the steep rise in asset prices as foreign capital pours into important asset markets such as equities and real estate. The resultant bubbles, especially in real estate, can have disastrous implications for the well-being of the poor and middle-income groups in LDCs and EMEs.
(iii) A real exchange-rate appreciation could result from an upward pressure on asset prices. This could act as an important retardant of exports and undermine the progress of trade reforms.
(iv) As discussed in Fernandez-Arias and Montiel (2009), distortions to the perceived cost of foreign capital may arise because of externalities associated with aggregate country risk and credit rationing arising from limited cross-border contract enforceability.
(v) Distortions in the financial sector could give rise to improper financial intermediation (Calvo *et al.* 1993) and result in excessive foreign borrowing.

Several further instances of macro- and micro-economic distortions that can result from capital flows are discussed in Corbo and Hernandez (1996).

CAPITAL ACCOUNT LIBERALIZATION IN INDIA: A STATUS REPORT

First FCAC Committee (Tarapore I)

One of the major planks of the reforms process initiated in India in 1991 was a high level of trade and financial integration with the rest of the world. To that end, subscription to Article VIII of the IMF was taken as the first priority, and effective current account convertibility was achieved in August 1994. The government then directed its attention to the attainment of full capital account convertibility (FCAC). It is to be noted that India has remained firmly committed to the attainment of this ideal throughout the ongoing process of reforms. Capital inflows into India have been increasing since 1995, but there has been a marked acceleration in theses inflows – both of the FDI (foreign direct investment) and FPI (foreign portfolio investment) variety – in recent years. Shortly before the onset of the Asian financial crisis in June 1997, a committee to lay down a roadmap for moving to FCAC was appointed under the Chairmanship of S.S. Tarapore. I will refer to this committee as Tarapore I.

Tarapore I adopted a threefold approach (RBI 1997). First, it enumerated the major kinds of restrictions that were in force in India for capital account transactions.[6] Second, it laid down a framework for the progressive dismantling of each of these restrictions over a short span of 3 years (i.e. by April 2000). Third, it laid down a series of macro-economic conditions that needed to be fulfilled before FCAC was finally attained.

Second FCAC Committee (Tarapore II)

The Asian financial crisis cast the entire issue of CAL in a fresh perspective. As Goldstein (1998), Singh (2002) and Bhalla and Nachane (2001) have noted, the extent of CAL made a big difference to the severity of the effects of the crisis on individual countries. Mainly because their capital accounts still had a number of restrictions in place, countries such as India and China managed to avoid the worst consequences of the event. Nevertheless, the sobering effects of the crisis meant that the recommendations of Tarapore I had to be shelved for a few years after it.

Following the high-growth phase of the last few years, however, Indian policy-makers were emboldened to revive the CAC idea. A new committee was set up in 2006 (once again under the chairmanship of S.S. Tarapore) to re-examine the issue afresh. I will refer to this committee as Tarapore II (RBI 2006). It adopted an approach very much similar in spirit to that of the earlier committee. It began by reviewing the extent to which the earlier committee's recommendations had been implemented. It then laid down a detailed time frame for achieving full convertibility and drew up a new set of safety guidelines. I will deal briefly with each of these aspects in turn.

Since several of the key Tarapore I recommendations have been implemented (or in some cases even exceeded), one may say that, since 1997, there has already been in progress a creeping movement in the direction of FCAC. However, Tarapore II is far more ambitious in the scope of its recommendations, and intends to take India quite a bit further along the road to full (or almost full) CAC. This it proposes to do progressively in three phases: Phase I (2006–07), Phase II (2007–09) and Phase III (2009–11). The major recommendations of Tarapore II were as follows:

1. Remove the overall annual external commercial borrowings (ECB) ceiling of US$22 billion and remove restrictions on end use of ECBs.
2. Double the limit on corporate investments abroad from the current limit of 200 per cent of net worth (of a corporate).
3. Allow banks to borrow overseas up to 50 per cent of paid-up capital and reserves in Phase I, up to 75 per cent in Phase II and 100 per cent in Phase III.
4. Allow individuals to remit abroad (annually) up to US$50,000 in Phase I, US$100,000 in Phase II and US$200,000 in Phase III, as against the current limit of US$25,000.
5. Extend to all non-residents (through SEBI registered entities such as mutual funds and other portfolio management schemes) the facility to invest in companies listed on Indian stock exchanges. Currently, only non-resident Indians are allowed to do so.
6. *Prohibit* foreign institutional investors (FIIs) from raising money through Participatory Notes (PNs).

Most of the above recommendations have been taken on board by the Reserve Bank of India (RBI). Taking the implementation of the recommendations in chronological order, the foreign investment guidelines published by the RBI on 1 April 2007 clearly laid down that all non-residents can invest in shares (including preference shares) of both listed and non-listed companies (see recommendation 5). Next, in October 2008, the overall annual ECB ceiling was raised to US$35 billion and several restrictions on end use of ECBs were substantially modified (as per recommendation 1 above). Additionally, Authorized Dealers Category-I Banks were allowed to borrow funds from their head office, overseas branches and correspondents, up to a limit of 50 per cent of their unimpaired Tier-I capital or US$10 million (whichever was higher) – see recommendation 3 above. Further, in March 2009, the RBI relaxed the norms for overseas investment by individuals under the Liberalized Remittance Scheme, with residents now allowed to remit up to US$200,000 per year for acquiring property, investing in financial assets or maintaining a foreign currency bank account (as per recommendation 4 above). Simultaneously, under the revised rules (of March 2009), Indian companies are now permitted to invest up to 400 per cent of their net worth in overseas joint ventures or wholly owned subsidiaries under the automatic route (see recommendation 2 above). The RBI has also increased the overseas portfolio investment limit by domestic companies to 50 per cent of their net worth, as against 35 per cent permitted earlier, while doing away with the reciprocal investment requirement under the overseas portfolio investment scheme. The aggregate ceiling of overseas investment by mutual funds has also been raised from US$4 billion to US$5 billion. The only major recommendation of Tarapore II that has not been taken into consideration is recommendation 6, pertaining to Participatory Notes (which are discussed later in this chapter).

The problems raised (in the Indian context) regarding the conduct of monetary policy and the stresses on the financial system in the wake of capital inflows (and financial liberalization generally) have been discussed extensively by, for example, Reddy (2005), Mohan (2007), Nachane and Raje (2007) and Nayyar (2008). Keeping the capital account reasonably open has implied a general movement away from the heavily managed exchange rate system of the 1980s and early 1990s towards a more flexible policy of letting the exchange rate gravitate towards its equilibrium value (as determined by market fundamentals). Today, the concerns over exchange-rate management are limited to short-term considerations, such as the need to smooth out excessive volatility and foreclose the emergence of destabilizing speculative activities, and are usually subsumed under the overall rubric of 'financial stability'. Even though the RBI does not have a target exchange-rate band in mind, it has not hesitated from pro-active intervention to prevent undue fluctuations in the nominal exchange rate. However, such episodes of 'leaning against the wind' are becoming increasingly less frequent now, as the Indian Government is very keen to underline to the global community its commitment to financial reforms. But, as the following quotation from Mohan (2007) illustrates, India's exchange-rate policy is in a state of evolution and may undergo a substantial transformation in the foreseeable future.

> Therefore, the Dutch disease syndrome has so far been managed by way of reserves build-up and sterilisation, the former preventing excessive nominal appreciation and the latter preventing higher inflation. However, the issue remains how long and to what extent such an exchange rate management strategy would work given the fact that we are faced with large and continuing capital flows apart from strengthening current receipts on account of remittances and software exports.[7]

The above discussion should make it amply clear that a substantial opening of the capital account has already been accomplished in India. Further, the price of keeping the capital account open has been a considerable straining of the autonomy of monetary policy, a reduction in available fiscal space, and occasional bouts of volatility in foreign-exchange and equity markets. These volatility episodes have often created a penumbra of uncertainty around investment decisions, especially in the tradable sector. Sterilization operations have imposed heavy quasi-fiscal costs, while undue appreciation of currency has put severe strains on exporting units, especially the small and medium enterprises. The exact magnitude of such costs, however, has not yet been quantitatively assessed.

RETHINKING CAPITAL ACCOUNT LIBERALIZATION IN THE WAKE OF THE RECENT FINANCIAL CRISIS

The scale and duration of the current global crisis has occasioned a certain amount of rethinking within the academic community and official circles on the issue of capital controls. Most significant in this context is the revised stance of the IMF. Capital controls, which have (particularly since the 1980s) been an anathema to the IMF's thinking, are now admitted, at least as a last resort.[8] As a matter of fact, when Iceland's banking system collapsed in September 2008, a key component of the IMF reforms package was 'controls on capital outflows'. Several countries in Central and Eastern Europe (including Turkey, Russia, Kazakhstan, Ukraine, Poland and Bulgaria) and in Africa, have either introduced capital controls of some form, or are on the verge of doing so (see Buiter 2009). Academic opinion[9] is also veering towards the so-called 'saltwater' view.[10]

To review the debate on CAL in India in the light of the recent global crisis, one has to note that there is a fundamental difference between the crisis in the USA, Europe (EU as well as non-EU) and India. In the USA, the crisis originated endogenously within the financial system and subsequently spread from Wall Street to 'Main Street'. In the European economies, the financial system crisis was more by contamination from the US system than endogenous, while in India the primary source of contagion has been the trade channel. This has meant that the crisis has been largely confined to the real (tradable) sector, leaving the banking and financial institutions relatively unscathed.[11] Hence, the crisis has not affected India with the same intensity that it has, for example, the Central and Eastern European economies. The context of the debate on capital account controls in India therefore need not be guided by the immediate urgency of the situation (as in several countries of Central and Eastern Europe) but by the longer term considerations outlined in the second section of this chapter.

As we have seen, these longer term considerations do not offer any unequivocal evidence in favour of the CAL strategy. There are several further issues specifically germane to the Indian situation. First, a substantial opening of the capital account has already taken place over the past decade and, since (even as its advocates cannot be unaware of) CAL can convey only short-term growth effects (see Henry 2007), whatever benefits of CAL that were due must have already been realized (see also BIS 2009: 3). Any further opening up of the capital account can convey only marginal benefits, while substantially increasing the risk of financial instability. Second, as the Indian fiscal stimulus kicks in and the Indian economy shows signs of recovery, foreign capital will inevitably flow in. Since there has been a phenomenal injection of liquidity across the globe, the longer the recovery is delayed in the USA and the EU, the higher are the chances that this liquidity will not be absorbed domestically but seek profitable avenues in EMEs. Thus, EMEs as a group (especially China and India) need to have strategies in place not only to deal with the possibility of capital outflows triggering crises, but also with capital inflow surges.

There is one additional consideration of a somewhat different kind that, in our opinion, ought to inform the deliberations on CAL in India, namely, the issue of Participatory Notes (PNs), which seem to be a speciality of the Indian equity markets. PNs are instruments similar to contract notes issued by registered FIIs to overseas clients who are not directly eligible to invest in Indian securities markets. They are issued against an underlying security, thereby helping the holder to benefit from dividends and capital gains on that security. Most of the PNs are issued to hedge funds with opaque ownership and shifting location, and which are not registered in any country or with any regulator.[12] The reasons for Tarapore II to recommend a ban on PNs could be twofold (though these are not explicitly mentioned in the committee's report). First, the enforcement of KYC (Know Your Customer) norms is difficult in the case of PNs, because several hedge funds operate in unregulated countries behind a veil of confidentiality.[13] Second, and even more importantly, as pointed out by M.K. Narayanan (National Security Advisor, Government of India) in a speech in 2007 at the 43rd Munich Conference on Security Policy, terrorist organizations have been increasingly resorting to legitimate business enterprises and routine banking channels to fund their activities. PNs could thus be, in effect, providing a safe conduit for the movement of terrorist funding.

MEASURES FOR COPING WITH CAPITAL INFLOWS

Irrespective of whether or not India decides to go for FCAC, management of capital inflows will remain an important issue. One rational policy response would then be to examine a minimal set of capital account restrictions that will mitigate the probability of financial crises of the order of the Asian crisis (1997–98), the Long-Term Capital Management crisis (1998) or the Russian crisis (1998). I examine a few such proposals below.

Tobin taxes and its variants

Perhaps the oldest such proposal is the Tobin tax on capital flows, suggested by Tobin (1978) in an influential article. The rate of tax proposed (Tobin 1978; Summers and Summers 1990; Spahn 1996) typically ranges from 0.05 to 0.25 per cent of the transaction principal. The burden of the tax is inversely related to the length of the holding period.[14] Although the rate is small, it amounts, as shown by Dodd (2002), to a substantial proportional increase in current transactions costs, as the typical bid-ask spreads in inter-dealer markets are 0.01–0.04 per cent (of the principal). The tax can thus be expected to reduce the returns to short-term speculation. This would be a double-edged weapon, as it would simultaneously reduce the volume of speculative hot money and reduce forex volatility. Additionally, it could generate substantial revenue, which could be available for development purposes.[15] Variants of Tobin taxes include variable deposit requirements and interest equalization taxes (Haque *et al.* 1997).

In spite of its intellectual appeal, however, as a practical proposal it has not really got off the ground. There could be several reasons for this. First, the proposal would require worldwide agreement and coordination, otherwise funds will simply migrate to countries that opt out of the tax agreement.[16] Second, unless the tax is applied to both the spot capital flows and the derivative instruments (forwards, futures, options and swaps), there may be substitution from the former to the latter.

The trip wires–speed bumps (TW–SB) approach

The essence of this approach is simple. Certain basic indicators (trip wires or TWs) are defined and when these indicators deteriorate (below a threshold) certain safety measures (relating to capital account transactions) – speed bumps or SBs – are 'triggered'. The approach has been exciting increasing interest among economists in recent years (see, for example,

Ariyoshi *et al.* (2000) and Grabel (2003)). The TWs are usually simple indicators that are designed to warn policy-makers of impending risks.[17] Under the approach, whenever TWs cross pre-determined critical thresholds, various SBs are called into play.[18]

Chile is widely touted as a successful example of a financial liberalization programme, but it has to be remembered that an extremely cautious approach to capital inflows that was followed from May 1992 to October 1998 played a large role in the Chilean success story, and was an ingenious combination of the Tobin and TW–SB approaches.

Regional financial integration

EMEs like India could also try to insulate themselves from the consequences of a global financial crisis by participating in group insurance arrangements. These groups could be either fairly wide, such as the G20, or relatively narrower, centred on regional clusters. One such important regional grouping revolves around the East Asian financial integration thrust involving the Chiang Mai Initiative (CMI) (comprising the ASEAN +3 countries),[19] the Asian Bond Fund Initiative (ABFI) and the regional surveillance mechanism called ETWG (Technical Working Group on Economic and Financial Monitoring). India should try to make a serious effort to commence a dialogue with this initiative and to at least participate in the ABFI and initiate bilateral currency-swap arrangements with some important countries in the ASEAN+3 group.

Prasad (2009) has suggested a more ambitious group insurance arrangement for the G20 group as a whole. Apart from an entry fee (of between US$10 billion and US$20 billion), there would be a variable premium depending both on the level of insurance desired as well as the macroeconomic policies followed by a particular country. Participants would be offered a short-term credit line in the event of a crisis, and the surveillance authority would be the Financial Stability Forum rather than the IMF.

CONCLUSION

This chapter has argued for a cautious approach to CAL in EMEs such as India. The traditional advocacy of CAL is crucially contingent on the EMH, which is likely to overstate the benefits of CAL for economic growth. Empirical studies fail to demonstrate any clear and convincing evidence of a favourable impact of CAL on growth and, even where such effects are detected, they are circumscribed by a host of conditioning factors including level of economic development, institutional quality and sequencing of reforms. On the other hand, CAL poses very real threats to financial stability and monetary policy autonomy, especially for countries with weak regulatory mechanisms and undeveloped financial markets.

Indian policy-makers, possibly swayed by an excessive zeal to integrate with global merchandise and financial markets, have shown tremendous enthusiasm for accelerating CAL. The two committees appointed to examine the issue (Tarapore I and II) have laid out a detailed roadmap for CAC, but with inadequate attention to the pitfalls involved in the process, and a marked neglect of safeguards. It is important to stress that the line taken by several apologists for CAC[20] – that the risks of financial instability are negligible and hence more than compensated for by the benefits – ignores the magnitude of the potential costs of a crisis[21] and the fact that the poor and vulnerable sections of society have to bear a disproportionately large share of the costs.

It is difficult to speculate on what the future course of Indian reforms is likely to be, especially as it bears on CAL. But one thing is certain – Indian policy-makers have consistently subscribed to the goal of FCAC, and this commitment has been reaffirmed on several occasions. The high-powered Committee on Financial Sector Reforms, chaired by Raghuram Rajan, recommended removal of any further vestiges of capital controls in its final report (GOI Planning Commission 2009). Its major recommendations pertained to:

1. removal of restrictions on outflows by corporate entities and individuals (including mutual funds and domestic fund managers)
2. simplification of registration requirements for foreign investors
3. removal of company-wide ceilings on FPI and FDI (with some exceptions for national security reasons)
4. removal of restrictions on end-use of capital inflows
5. liberalization of restrictions on foreign investors' participation in rupee-denominated debt
6. gradual extension and ultimate elimination of ceilings on external commercial borrowings by corporate entities and banks
7. removal of regulations on insurance companies, pension and provident funds regarding portfolio diversification through investments abroad.

The financial crisis seems to have had little dampening effect on the Indian policy-makers' enthusiasm for CAL. Any doubts about the government's commitments to financial reforms (especially CAL) dithering in the face of the crisis can be safely laid aside, considering that the President of India in her inaugural address to the joint session of Parliament (4 June 2009), explicitly mentions that 'These (foreign capital) flows, especially foreign direct investment, need to be encouraged through an appropriate policy regime'. Matching action to rhetoric, the finance minister has listed seven important pending reform bills (on insurance, pension and banking reforms) for 'priority' passage by parliament. These form part of the 100-day agenda, being finalized by the Prime Minister's office.

Surprisingly, the pronounced swing of opinion against unfettered CAL that has occurred among a majority of academic economists,[22] as well as several foreign governments and multilateral institutions (the IMF not excepted) in the light of the recent financial upheavals, seems to have completely bypassed Indian policy circles. I have tried to make a case in this chapter for adopting a more cautious approach to CAL in India, drawing attention to the various pitfalls. In particular, if one has to avoid the extreme situation of having to impose stringent capital controls, it might be better to reserve options like taxes on capital inflows and TW–SBs, for adoption as a first line of defence as and when trouble looms.

NOTES

1 Director, Indira Gandhi Institute of Development Research, Goregaon (East), Mumbai 400 065, India.

2 Various proxies have been used for this entity, including quality of bureaucracy, corruption, expropriation risks, rule of law and sanctity of contracts.

3 'I'd be a bum in the street with a tin cup if the markets were efficient' is a famous remark by none other than Warren Buffet. The bulk of the econometric evidence on financial markets is also *contra* the EMH (see, for example, Shiller (1981), LeRoy and Porter (1981) and Shleifer and Summers (1990)).

4 He cites the role of exchange-rate stabilization in ending the 1920s European hyperinflation.

5 The problem is best illustrated by invoking Stiglitz's (2000) example. If a company in India, say, borrows \$500m from a US bank, then (since it may be perceived as relatively risky) an interest rate of 20 per cent may be levied. If the RBI sells bonds of an equivalent amount to maintain a stable money supply, the cost to the government of the entire operation would be \$85m – assuming that the forex reserves (of \$500m) to offset this borrowing are invested in US Treasury bills carrying 3 per cent interest. The actual costs to the economy are likely to be even higher, given two additional considerations that apply strongly in LDCs and EMEs: first, the fact that government investment is often complementary to private investment, and second the overall dominance of the domestic debt market by government bond issues (which greatly accentuate the 'crowding-out' effect).

6 These restrictions were grouped according to the sector that they were applied to to, namely, (i) corporates (domestic/resident), (ii) corporates (foreign/non-resident), (iii) banks (domestic/resident), (iv) banks (foreign/non-resident), (v) non-bank financial institutions (resident), (vi) non-bank financial institutions (non-resident) or what are now popularly called FIIS (foreign institutional investors), (vii) individuals (residents), (viii) individuals (non-residents) and (ix) financial markets.

7 The introduction of the MSS (Market Stabilization Scheme) in April 2004 assumes significance in this context as an important tool for short-term liquidity management.

8 '[T]he country could, as a last resort regulate capital transactions – though these carry significant risks and long-term costs' (Ghosh *et al.* 2009: 9). Incidentally, capital controls are permissible under IMF Article VI (Section 3) provided they do not interfere with payments for *current* international transactions.

9 To cite but two opinions from a long list. First, Paul Krugman (2009b) has this to say on capital controls 'I have a bit of personal history here – and it has some bearing on broader economic policy issues right now. Back in 1998, in the midst of the Asian financial crisis, I came out in favor of temporary capital controls

... At the time it was regarded as a horribly unorthodox and irresponsible suggestion – and I had a long, very unpleasant phone conversation with a Senior Administration Official who berated me for my anti-market ideas. Today, that wild and crazy idea is so orthodox it's part of standard IMF policy'. Second, in a recent lecture De Long (2009) talks about 'the intellectual bankruptcy of the Chicago School'.

10 In the words of Krugman (2009a) '... macroeconomics has divided into two great factions: "saltwater" economists (mainly in coastal U.S. universities), who have more or less Keynesian vision of what recessions are all about; and "freshwater" economists (mainly at inland schools), who consider that vision nonsense.'.

11 This is not to deny that that there has been considerable erosion of value in the equity markets (accompanied by some erosion in the real estate market) but both financial and physical asset markets are showing strong signs of recovery in recent months. Similarly, net investment by FIIs, which had been negative over April 2008–March 2009 (US$ –9.84 billion), turned positive in the next quarter (April–June 2009) to the tune of US$6.43 billion

12 PNs currently constitute about 25 per cent of net portfolio investment.

13 Even reputed institutions often operate through subsidiaries in countries with loose regulations and a stonewall on provision of information.

14 For example, a tax of 0.10 per cent implies that a twice-daily round trip carries an annual rate of interest of 146 per cent, whereas the same figure for a twice-weekly round trip reduces sharply to about 21 per cent.

15 D'Orville and Najman (1995) estimate that a Tobin tax of 0.25 per cent would globally fetch a revenue of US$140 billion, whereas Felix and Sau (1996) predict the revenue generation at over twice this amount (for the same rate).

16 The phenomenal rise of the Eurodollar market in the 1980s should serve to remind us of the scale of transactions that can occur outside a system of central bank clearing.

17 Among suggested TWs we may prominently mention (i) ratio of official reserves to total short-term external obligations (foreign portfolio investment and total – i.e. private plus public short-term hard-currency denominated foreign debt), (ii) ratio of foreign currency denominated debt to domestic currency denominated debt (appropriately weighted by maturity), (iii) ratio of short-term debt to long-term debt and (iv) ratio of total cumulative foreign portfolio investment to gross equity market capitalization.

18 SBs could take several forms including (i) requirements on borrowers to unwind positions involving geographical/maturity mismatches, (ii) curbs on foreign borrowings, (iii) restrictions on certain types of FPI (foreign portfolio investment) and (iv) import curbs (in exceptional circumstances).

19 The CMI aims at providing liquidity support for member countries that experience short-run balance of payments difficulties and also includes 16 bilateral currency-swap arrangements.

20 In all fairness, both Tarapore I and II committee reports refrain from this line of argument.

21 As given in Mohan (2007), recapitalization of banks (subsequent to the financial crises of the 1990s) cost 55 per cent of GDP in Argentina, 42 per cent in Thailand, 35 per cent in Korea and 10 per cent in Turkey. The total welfare costs would have been substantially higher.

22 To give one leading example, Willem Buiter in the *Financial Times* (18 February 2009) notes that: 'For countries with a minor-league currency (every currency except for the US dollar, the euro and the yen) an open capital account will always be a mixed blessing. The joys of an open capital account – the undoubted benefits from decoupling domestic capital formation from national saving and

from unrestricted portfolio diversification and risk trading – cannot be enjoyed without the pain: the risk of its domestic financial institutions, capital markets, non-financial enterprises, consumers and public finances becoming the flotsam and jetsam on massive and mindless killer waves propelled by an out-of-control global financial storm.'

REFERENCES

Aghion, P., P. Bacchetta and A. Banerjee (2000) 'Currency crises and monetary policy in an economy with credit constraints', *CEPR Discussion Paper*, No. 2529, Cambridge, MA: Center for Economic Policy Research, Harvard University.

Ariyoshi, A., K. Habermeier, B. Laurens, I. Otker-Robe, J.I. Canales-Kriljenko and A. Kirilenko (2000) 'Capital controls: country experiences with their use and liberalization', *IMF Occasional Paper*, No. 190. Washington, DC: International Monetary Fund.

Arteta, C., B. Eichengreen and C. Wyplosz (2003) 'When does capital account liberalization help more than it hurts?', in E. Helpman and E. Sadka (eds) *Economic Policy in the International Economy: Essays in Honour of Assaf Razin*, Cambridge, UK: Cambridge University Press.

Bernanke, B.S. (2005) 'Monetary policy in a world of mobile capital', *Cato Journal*, 25(1): 1–12.

Bhalla, A.S. and D.M. Nachane (2001) 'The economic impact of the Asian crisis in India and China', in H. Chang, G. Palma and D.H. Whittaker (eds) *Financial Liberalization and the Asian Crisis*, New York: Palgrave.

BIS (Bank for International Settlements) (2009) 'Capital flows and emerging market economies', *Committee on the Global Financial System (CGFS) Paper*, No. 33, Basel: BIS.

Boughton, J. (1997) 'From Suez to Tequila: the IMF as crisis manager', *IMF Working Paper*, No. WP/97/90, Washington, DC: International Monetary Fund.

Buiter, W. (2009) 'The return of capital controls', *Financial Times*, 18 February 2009.

Calvo, G. (2008) 'Systemic sudden stops: the relevance of balance sheet effects and financial integration', *NBER Working Paper*, No. 14026, Cambridge, MA: National Bureau of Economic Research.

Calvo, G., L. Leiderman and C. Reinhart (1993) 'Capital inflows and real exchange rate appreciation in Latin America', *IMF Staff Papers*, 40, 108–151, Washington, DC: International Monetary Fund.

Calvo, G. and C. Reinhart (2000) 'Fear of floating', *NBER Working Paper*, No. 7993, Cambridge, MA: National Bureau of Economic Research.

Corbo, V. and L. Hernandez (1996): 'Macroeconomic adjustment to capital inflows: Lessons from recent Latin American and East Asian experience', *The World Bank Research Observer*, 11(1): 61–85.

De Long, J.B. (2009) 'What has happened to Milton Friedman's Chicago School?', *6th Singapore Economic Review Public Lecture*, 7 January 2009.

Demirguc-Kunt, A. and E. Detragiache (1998) 'Financial liberalization and financial fragility', *IMF Working Paper*, No. 98/83, Washington, DC: International Monetary Fund.

Dodd, R. (2002) 'Lessons for Tobin tax advocates: the politics of policy and the economics of market micro-structure', *FPF Special Report*, No. 7, Washington, DC: Financial Policy Forum.

Dornbusch, R. and A. Warner (1994) 'Mexico: stabilization, reform and no growth', *Brookings Papers on Economic Activity*, No. 1, 253–315.

D'Orville, H. and D. Najman (1995) *Towards a New Multilateralism: Funding Global Priorities*, New York: United Nations.

Edison, J.H., R. Levine, L. Ricci and T. Slok (2004) 'Capital account liberalization and economic performance: synthesis and survey', *IMF Staff Papers*, 51(2): 220–256, Washington, DC: International Monetary Fund.

Felix, D. (1995) 'Financial globalization versus free trade: the case for the Tobin tax', *UNCTAD Discussion Paper*, No. 108, Geneva: United Nations Conference on Trade and Development.

Felix, D. and R. Sau (1996) 'On the revenue potential and phasing in of the Tobin tax', in M. Haq, I. Kaul and I. Grunberg (eds) *The Tobin Tax: Coping with Financial Volatility*, New York: Oxford University Press.

Fernandez-Arias, E. and P. Montiel (2009) 'Crisis response in Latin America: is the "rainy day" at hand?', *Working Paper*, No. 686, Washington, DC: Inter-American Development Bank.

Fischer, S. (1998) 'Should the International Monetary Fund pursue capital account convertibility?, *Essays in International Finance*, No. 207, Princeton, NJ: Princeton University.

Fitzgerald, E. and G. Mavrotas (1997) *International Capital Flows, Investment and Employment in Developing Countries*, Geneva: International Labour Organisation.

Ghosh, A.R., M. Chamon, C.W. Crowe, Jun Il Kim and J.D. Ostrey (2009) 'Coping with the crisis: policy options for emerging market countries', *Staff Position Note*, No. 2009/08, Washington, DC: International Monetary Fund.

GOI (Government of India) Planning Commission (2009) *A Hundred Small Steps: Report of the Committee on Financial Sector Reforms (Chairman: Raghuram Rajan)*, Delhi: Sage Publications.

Goldstein, M. (1998) *The Asian Financial Crisis: Causes, Cures and Systemic Implications*, Policy Analyses in International Economics, No. 55, Washington, DC: Peterson Institute for International Economics.

Grabel, I. (2003) 'Averting crisis: Assessing means to manage financial integration in emerging economies', *Cambridge Journal of Economics*, 27(2): 317–336.

Haque, N.U., D. Mathieson and S. Sharma (1997) 'Causes of capital inflows and policy responses to them', *Finance and Development*, March: 3–6.

Henry, P.B. (2007) 'Capital account liberalization: theory, evidence and speculation', *Journal of Economic Literature*, 45(4): 887–935.

Honig, A. (2008) 'Addressing causality in the effect of capital account liberalization on growth', *Journal of Macroeconomics*, 30(4): 1602–1616.

Huberman, G. and T. Regev (2001) 'Contagious speculation and a cure for cancer: a non-event that made prices soar', *Journal of Finance*, 56(1): 387–396.

Kaminsky, G.L. and S.L. Schmukler (2002) 'Short-run pain, long-run gain: the effects of financial liberalization', *Policy Research Working Paper Series*, No. 2916, Washington, DC: World Bank.

Klein, M.W. (2005) 'Capital account liberalization, institutional quality and economic growth: theory and evidence', *NBER Working Paper*, No. 11112, Cambridge, MA: National Bureau of Economic Research.

Kose, A.M., E.S. Prasad and M.E. Terrones (2009) 'Does openness to international financial flows raise productivity growth?', *Journal of International Money and Finance*, 28(4): 554–580.

Krugman, P. (2009a): 'How did economists get it so wrong?', *The New York Times*, 6 September.

—— (2009b) 'The conscience of a liberal', *The New York Times*, 12 September.

LeRoy, S.F. and R.D. Porter (1981) 'The present value relation: tests based on implied variance bounds', *Econometrica*, 49(3): 555–574.

Mohan, R. (2007) 'Capital account liberalisation and conduct of monetary policy: the Indian experience', paper presented at a seminar on *Globalization, Inflation and Financial Markets*, Banque de France, Paris, 14 June 2007.

Nachane, D.M. and N. Raje (2007) 'Financial liberalization and monetary policy', *Margin – The Journal of Applied Economic Research*, 1(1): 47–83.

Narayanan, M.K. (2007) Speech at the 43rd Munich Security Conference, 11 February 2007, available at http://asiantribune.com/node/4582.

Nayyar, D. (2008) *Trade and Globalization*, New Delhi: Oxford University Press.

Prasad, E.S. (2009) 'Some new perspectives on India's approach to capital account liberalization', at http://ideas.repec.org/p/nbr/nberwo/14658.html.

Reddy, Y.V. (2005) *Annual Policy Statement for the Year 2004–05*, New Delhi: Reserve Bank of India.

Reinhart, C.M. and V.R. Reinhart (2008) 'Capital flow bonanzas: An encompassing view of the past and present' in J. Frankel and F. Giavazzi (eds) *NBER International Seminar in Macroeconomics*, Chicago, IL: University of Chicago Press.

RBI (Reserve Bank of India) (1997) *Report of the Committee on Capital Account Convertibility (Tarapore I)*, New Delhi: Reserve Bank of India.

—— (2006) *Report of the Committee on Fuller Capital Account Convertibility (Tarapore II)*, New Delhi: Reserve Bank of India.

Rodrik, D. (1998): 'Who needs capital account convertibility?', *Princeton Essays in International Finance*, No. 207: 55–65.

Russel, P.S. and V.M. Torbey (2002) 'The efficient market hypothesis on trial: a survey', *Business Quest Journal*, January: 1–19.

Sargent, T. (1982) 'The ends of four big inflations', in R. Hall (ed.) *Inflation: Causes and Effects*, Chicago, IL: University of Chicago Press.

Shiller, R.J. (1981) 'Do stock prices move too much to be justified by subsequent changes in dividends?', *American Economic Review*, 71(3): 421–436.

Shleifer, A. and L.H. Summers (1990) 'The noise trader approach to finance', *Journal of Economic Perspectives*, 4(1): 19–33.

Singh, A (2002) 'Capital account liberalization, free long-term capital flows, financial crises and economic development', *Working Paper*, No. 245, ESRC Centre for Business Research, Cambridge, UK: University of Cambridge.

Spahn, P.B. (1996) 'The Tobin tax and exchange rate stability', *Finance and Development*, 33(2): 24–27.

Stiglitz, J.E. (2000) 'Capital market liberalization, economic growth and instability', *World Development*, 28(6): 1075–1086.

Summers, L. (2000) 'International financial crises: causes, prevention and cures', *American Economic Review: Papers and Proceedings*, 90(2): 1–16.

Summers, L. and V. Summers (1990) 'The case for a securities transactions excise tax', *Tax Notes*, 13 August.

Tobin, J. (1978) 'A proposal for international monetary reform', *Eastern Economic Journal*, 4: 153–159.

Vargas, H. and C. Varela (2008) 'Capital flows and financial assets in Colombia: recent behaviour, consequences and challenges for the central bank', in Bank for International Settlements (ed.) *Financial Globalisation and Emerging Market Capital Flows*, 44: 153–184, Basel: BIS.

Vegh, C. (1992) 'Stopping high inflation: an analytical overview', *IMF Staff Papers*, 39: 626–695, Washington, DC: International Monetary Fund.

Williamson, J. and Z. Drabek (1999) 'Whether and when to liberalize capital account and financial services', *Staff Working Paper*, No. ERAD-99-03, Geneva: Economic Research and Analysis Division, World Trade Organization.

9 Financial integration in Asia

Regional and Japanese perspectives[1]

Shinji Takagi[2]

INTRODUCTION

This chapter discusses the current state and future prospects of financial integration in Asia, a topic on which considerable work has already been done (see, for example, Eichengreen and Park (2004), Cowen *et al.* (2006), Pisani-Ferry and Cohen-Setton (2008)). The interest shown in the topic reflects the recognition, substantiated later in this chapter, that Asia's so-called market-driven economic integration has yielded a lopsided outcome, in the form of asymmetry between trade and finance. Kim *et al.* (2006), for example, show that, in contrast to extensive trade links, financial links in Asia are limited and are almost entirely related to trade.[3] In some sense, this outcome should be expected. Gains from trade in goods and services are tangible and visible. Moreover, in trade, distance matters critically. Even with tariff and non-tariff barriers, the law of comparative advantage is a powerful force in promoting exchanges of goods and services across a region consisting of countries that offer different factor endowments, relative cost structures and technological frontiers. In Asia, intraregional trade has expanded in recent years, not only in final goods, but also, and more importantly, in parts and components, as multinational firms created production networks that cut across national borders.

The same argument does not hold, at least to the same extent, for finance. Imperfect information explains more of the pattern of financial transactions. As a result, in finance, government policy matters more, as it determines the quality of institutions, which dictates, in turn, the nature of transactions that take place. Financial transactions also involve smaller transaction costs, compared with trade. There are hardly any transportation costs to speak of, and legal and other fees are largely fixed, so that the costs become negligible as the amount increases. Thus, even if government policy removes impediments to cross-border transactions, there is no guarantee that finance is more integrated regionally than globally. Money should flow to a financial centre that offers the smallest intermediation costs and to a country that offers the highest risk-adjusted returns, regardless of the location. In any case, given the limited development of financial markets and institutions, not to mention their reluctance to fully open the capital account, most Asian countries have not reached the stage where significant financial integration could be expected, whether globally or regionally.

These considerations do not change the fact that regional financial integration remains an important unfinished agenda for Asia. The asymmetry of trade and financial integration shows how far the region must go to achieve the quality of markets and institutions commensurate with the level of economic development being attained. While there is no theoretical case for preferring regional to global financial integration, there are benefits to be gained from promoting regional financial transactions. As the region integrates in trade and production, information is created through face-to-face contacts and through knowledge specific to real transactions. Given the nature of asymmetric information, such local information is more conducive to making regional financing deals than to making global ones. If markets and institutions are sufficiently developed, we should therefore expect to observe some 'home bias' within Asia, favouring regional financial transactions, even in situations where global transactions would offer absolute advantages in the absence of asymmetric information. The lack of home bias, even within the context of limited overall financial integration, suggests the possibility that there are unmet financing needs in Asia.

The chapter's focus is to identify the gaps that need to be filled in order to further promote financial integration in Asia. To that end, the next section discusses the concept of financial integration and how Asia's current level of financial integration can be characterized. The third section assesses Asian financial integration from the point of view of Japan, the region's largest creditor country that is closely integrated with the world's leading financial centres. The fourth section then attempts to explain why financial integration lags behind real integration in Asia, by considering major domestic determinants of cross-border capital flows in individual countries. The fifth section offers some conclusions.

Throughout the chapter, Asia for the most part includes the ten member countries of the Association of Southeast Asian Nations (ASEAN),[4] plus China, Japan, Korea and India, which we collectively call 'ASEAN+3 and India', though data limitations occasionally dictate that one or more of these countries is excluded in specific instances (typically one or more of the so-called BCLMV countries—Brunei, Cambodia, Laos, Myanmar and Vietnam). As appropriate, Hong Kong and Taiwan, and Australia and New Zealand in fewer instances, are included in the discussion when helpful to draw additional inferences for the whole Asia–Pacific region.

AN OVERVIEW OF FINANCIAL INTEGRATION IN ASIA

Concepts and measures of financial integration

Kenen (1976: 9) defines financial integration as 'the extent to which markets are connected' or 'the degree to which participants in any market are enabled and obliged to take notice of events occurring in other markets'. The concept may be straightforward, but it has multiple meanings in practice. Broadly, there are three ways in which the term financial integration has been operationally defined.[5] First, financial integration can be a de-jure measure. For example, two economies can be defined as perfectly integrated if there are no legal or regulatory restrictions on cross-border financial transactions. But lack of restrictions does not guarantee that financial transactions actually take place freely. In the terminology of Le (2000), it may well be a measure of financial openness, but it is certainly not a sufficient condition for financial integration; it may not even be a necessary condition for a *high* degree of financial integration. This is not the concept we have in mind when we talk about regional financial integration in Asia.

Second, one set of de-facto measures is based on price differentials, usually deviations from such no-arbitrage conditions as covered interest parity, uncovered interest parity and real interest parity, the last one of which incorporates both financial and real integration (Frankel 1992). The problem with using arbitrage conditions to measure financial integration is that it is often difficult to find financial instruments in two or more economies with comparable risk, liquidity and other characteristics. Alternatively, we may define financial integration in terms of correlation of broad market indices, such as stock market price indices, benchmark interest rates and the like. But the correlation can be influenced by many factors, including the choice of exchange-rate regime in place, monetary policy and business cycles. Moreover, all of these price-based measures are problematic for Asia, because they do not distinguish between global and regional integration. For example, even if a price-based measure indicates high integration for two countries, they may be linked only through a third market.

Finally, another set of de-facto measures relates to quantities, typically flows or stocks of financial instruments; they can be stated in either net or gross terms. While different concepts of financial integration address different aspects of how economies are financially linked, quantity measures appear to be the most relevant concept in the context of Asia. A quantity measure, defined in terms of either flows or stocks, can make a distinction between regional and global integration. When we are interested in the economic implications of financial links, net measures are more useful, as they correspond to a transfer of real resources across countries. But in discussing regional financial integration, gross measures may be more relevant; gross flows, in particular, are analogous to intraregional trade. When a country exports parts and components to its neighbouring country which, in turn assembles them into final products and ships them back to the home country, the volume of both exports and imports rises, though the difference between the two can be small. Increasing bi-directional flows are what we associate with trade integration. Analogously, two countries can be said to be financially integrated when they lend and borrow in both directions, even if the net balance is small.

In much of what follows, we use gross cross-border financial transactions, defined in terms of either flows or stocks, as a measure of financial integration. But the problem is that although quantity-based measures may be the most appropriate indicator of regional financial integration, they are the most difficult to obtain operationally, because of severe data limitations. The data on stocks of external assets and liabilities are not available country-against-country for all countries. The International Monetary Fund (IMF) annually publishes Coordinated Portfolio Investment Surveys (CPIS) and Coordinated Direct Investment Surveys (CDIS) for the external portfolio and direct investment positions of a number of countries, but the coverage of countries is limited. Likewise, the Bank for International Settlements (BIS) releases quarterly data on the external positions of major banks in a number of countries, but again the coverage of countries is not exhaustive on the creditor side. Data limitations are even more serious for financial flows.

Measuring financial integration in Asia

Subject to these caveats, we have used the IMF data to calculate the degree of regional financial integration in terms of direct and portfolio investments at the end of 2010, and compared them with the degree of trade integration during 2010 (Table 9.1). Here, we consider three relevant groups of Asian countries: (i) ASEAN, (ii) ASEAN+3 and India, and (iii) ASEAN+3, India, Hong Kong and Taiwan. Several observations can be made. First, the share of intraregional trade within ASEAN is relatively low, at around 25 per cent of global trade in 2010, whether we consider exports, imports or total trade. The intraregional trade share goes up considerably (to 35.6 per cent for exports, 43.6 per cent for imports and 39.3 per cent for total trade) if China, Japan, Korea and India are included. This increases to nearly 50 per cent, if Hong Kong and Taiwan are also included in the region. This indicates the significant roles Hong Kong and Taiwan play in the regional trade links of Asia. Second, in contrast to the high degree of trade integration, Asia's integration in foreign direct investment (FDI) is somewhat more limited. The balance of inward FDI liabilities owed intraregionally at the end of 2010 was 14.6 per cent of the balance held globally for ASEAN and 20.0 per cent for ASEAN+3 and India, although the share goes up to as much as 44.0 per cent if Hong Kong and Taiwan are included. On the assets side, the shares for ASEAN and for ASEAN+3 and India are higher (40.6 and 28.1 per cent, respectively), indicating that countries, especially those within ASEAN, tend to invest proportionately more in the neighbouring countries. Overall, intraregional direct investment is significant, but not as extensive as intraregional trade.

Third, Asia's integration in portfolio investment is considerably more limited. The balance of portfolio assets held intraregionally at the end of 2010 was no more than 13 per cent, whether or not Hong Kong and Taiwan are included. The comparable figure for the balance of portfolio liabilities owed intraregionally was 9.0 per cent for ASEAN+3 and India, and 16.7 per cent when Hong Kong and Taiwan are included. Unlike the case of intraregional trade, however, the intraregional investment shares rise

Table 9.1 Measures of trade and financial integration in Asia, 2010

	ASEAN	*ASEAN+3 and India*	*Asia, including Hong Kong and Taiwan*
Intraregional trade (per cent of global trade, 2010)			
Exports	25.40	35.60	52.39
Imports	24.18	43.57	46.15
Total trade	24.82	39.31	49.40
Intraregional foreign direct investment (per cent of total global balances, end 2010)			
Inward[1]	14.61	19.99	43.95
Outward[2]	40.59	28.11	36.80
Intraregional portfolio investment (per cent of total global balances, end 2010)			
Assets[3]	12.27	7.16	12.58
of which, equities	11.45	16.54	23.71
Liabilities[3]	11.48	9.00	16.74
of which, equities	8.04	7.63	14.19
External bank positions against Asian countries (per cent of global total, end 2010)			
Assets	2.18 (0.62)[4]	7.24	8.93
Liabilities	1.92 (0.32)[4]	5.20	7.29

Sources: Author's estimates based on the International Monetary Fund (IMF), *Direction of Trade Statistics Yearbook 2011*; IMF, Coordinated Direct Investment Survey; IMF, Coordinated Portfolio Investment Survey; Bank for International Settlements, *Quarterly Review*, June 2011.

Notes

1 Recipient countries are Indonesia, Malaysia, the Philippines, Singapore, Thailand (from ASEAN), China, Hong Kong, India, Japan, and Korea.

2 Source countries are Malaysia, the Philippines, Thailand (from ASEAN), Hong Kong, India, Japan and Korea.

3 Source countries are Indonesia, Malaysia, the Philippines, Singapore, Thailand (from ASEAN), India, Japan, Korea, and Hong Kong.

4 Figures in parentheses exclude Singapore.

to 12.3 per cent for assets and 11.5 per cent for liabilities when ASEAN alone is considered. This likely means that, in obtaining the low intraregional shares for ASEAN+3 and India, ASEAN's small absolute scale of external investment positions is overwhelmed by Japan, whose large absolute scale of external positions is mostly with countries outside the region. Significantly, for ASEAN+3 and India, with or without Hong Kong and Taiwan, the intraregional share for equities is greater on the asset side but smaller on the liability side. This reflects the fact that equity markets are generally more developed than bond markets (so that comparatively more of regional investors' stakes in neighbouring countries takes the form of equities) but, on the liability side, the intraregional flow of equity investment is overwhelmed by the far larger amount of investment from abroad.

Finally, a conjecture can be offered about the nature of integration in the banking market. Unfortunately, bilateral flow or stock data comparable to the IMF's CDIS or CPIS are not available. The best we can do is to make inferences from the BIS data on the external positions against Asia of all reporting banks. On both the asset and the liability side, the share of Asia in the external positions of banks was extremely small at the end of 2010: about 2 per cent for ASEAN alone (less than 1 per cent if Singapore is excluded), 5.2–7.2 per cent for ASEAN+3 and India, and 7.3–8.9 per cent for all of Asia, including Hong Kong and Taiwan. Although there is insufficient information to estimate precisely the degree of intraregional bank flows, the share of Asia within the global banking market is small indeed. Even if we make the highly unrealistic assumption (favourable to Asian integration) that a half of Asia's bank credit is extended within the region (and hence the intraregional share is 50 per cent), these numbers mean that Asia is totally at the periphery of the global banking market, with over 95 per cent of activity taking place outside the region. More realistically, much of the cross-border banking activity in Hong Kong, Japan and Singapore is with countries outside the region, so that regional banking integration can be considered extremely limited.

Saving–investment correlation

Saving–investment correlation does not measure financial integration as such, but can be a useful indicator of macro-economic conditions giving rise to capital flows. Saving–investment correlation, as a tool for analyzing capital mobility, was first proposed by Feldstein and Horioka (1980), who estimated the following regression equation for member countries of the Organisation for Economic Co-operation and Development (OECD):

$$(I/Y)_i = \alpha + \beta\,(S/Y)_i + \varepsilon_i \qquad (1)$$

where I is domestic investment; S is domestic saving; Y is domestic income; α and β are coefficients to be estimated; ε is a random error term; and i is a country subscript. The authors postulated that the coefficient (β) would be unity in the complete absence of capital flows, and zero under perfect capital mobility.

The validity of this approach has been challenged by a number of authors. Common to many criticisms is the notion that although zero capital mobility implies high saving–investment correlation, the converse may not be true if the two are correlated for reasons other than capital mobility (Harberger 1980; Obstfeld 1986; Bayoumi 1990). Indeed, a range of theoretical models could generate high saving–investment correlations even under perfect capital mobility (Coakley *et al.* 1998). However, empirical work based on intra-national data has consistently shown that the correlation, if any, between saving and investment across states, provinces or prefectures within a sovereign nation is far smaller than those typically found in cross-country data (Sinn 1992; Dekle 1996; Iwamoto and van Wincoop 2000; Boyreau-Debray and Wei 2002; Taki 2008). Thus, with a careful interpretation, saving–investment correlation could still contain useful information.

Equivalent to estimating the coefficient β is to plot the saving rate (*S*/*Y*) against the investment rate (*I*/*Y*) for each of the countries in Asia for which data are available (Figure 9.1). For the period 2006–10, we observe a positive correlation between saving and investment. Especially if we exclude Brunei, Malaysia and Singapore (the three countries towards the southeast corner) from the sample, the correlation appears to be extremely high (in terms of equation (1), β approaches unity). This is driven, in particular, by China's high saving and investment ratios and the equally low saving and investment ratios of Cambodia and the Philippines. Takagi and Taki (2011) show in a sample that includes Malaysia and Singapore that the estimated coefficient β was higher for ASEAN+3 than for any other major region of the world during 2000–06 (the coefficient was nearly zero for the Euro Zone). At least as a broad characterization, in Asia, high saving is associated with high investment, and low saving with low investment, so that the scope for capital mobility is more limited than elsewhere.

At the same time, it must be noted that some countries in the region show large saving surpluses. Brunei had an average surplus of 44.2 per cent of GDP during 2006–10, which means that the country was a net exporter of

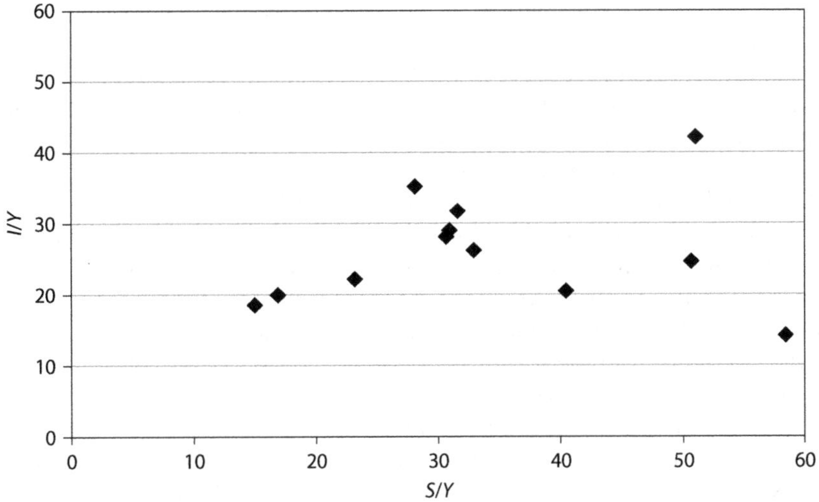

Figure 9.1 Saving and investment in Asian countries (averages for 2006–10, per cent of GDP). Source: Author's estimates based on International Monetary Fund, *International Financial Statistics*. Notes: The countries are Brunei, Cambodia, China, Indonesia, India, Japan, Korea, Malaysia, the Philippines, Singapore, Thailand and Vietnam. *I* is domestic investment, *S* domestic saving and *Y* domestic income.

capital by that amount. Likewise, the average surplus was 26.0 per cent for Singapore and 20.0 per cent for Malaysia. Even China, whose large saving was matched by its large investment, had a saving surplus of 9.0 per cent of GDP. Although the high saving–investment correlation seems to point to a comparatively limited scope for capital mobility, there is still considerable scope for external financial transactions on an absolute scale. At this stage, three reasons are offered to explain why this has not promoted regional financial integration. First, these financial flows have largely been intermediated by the public sector; they are outflows for net investment purposes and have not generated two-way capital flows. Second, a large portion of these financial flows went to the advanced markets of Europe and North America. Finally, part of the accumulation of foreign assets resulted from foreign exchange market intervention. Certainly, we do not consider a significant accumulation of foreign exchange reserves as reflecting strengthening financial links with foreign countries.

JAPAN'S EXTERNAL FINANCIAL TRANSACTIONS WITH ASIA

Another perspective of Asia's financial integration can usefully be offered by observing it from the point of view of a single country, in this case Japan. There are at least three reasons why it is useful to do so. First, Japan is by far the largest creditor country in the region (and, for that matter, in the world). The low intraregional investment share observed within Asia is, to an important extent, reflective of the limited exposure of Japanese creditors to the Asian region. Explaining why Japan does not invest in Asia more extensively thus helps us to understand why Asia's regional financial integration is limited. Second, we have access to more complete data on Japan. The available data allow a finer country breakdown, not only of Japan's international investment positions, but also of Japan's gross financial transactions with foreign countries. Finally, Japan is part of Asia. What we observe about Japan is more or less replicating the situation in which other countries in the region are placed with respect to their financial transactions with the countries in the region as opposed to those outside. We use Japan as the window through which we identify the gaps that need to be filled in order to promote regional financial integration.

Asia is by far Japan's most important trading partner (Figure 9.2). In terms of total trade (i.e. the gross value of exports and imports), the share of ASEAN in Japan's global trade is relatively small at 15 per cent in 2010, increases to 36 per cent when China, Korea and India are included, and rises further to 45 per cent with Hong Kong and Taiwan included. While not directly depicted in Figure 9.2, with Australia and New Zealand included, the share of the whole Asia–Pacific region in Japan's global trade was 50 per cent in 2010, up from 40 per cent in the early 2000s. The 10 per cent

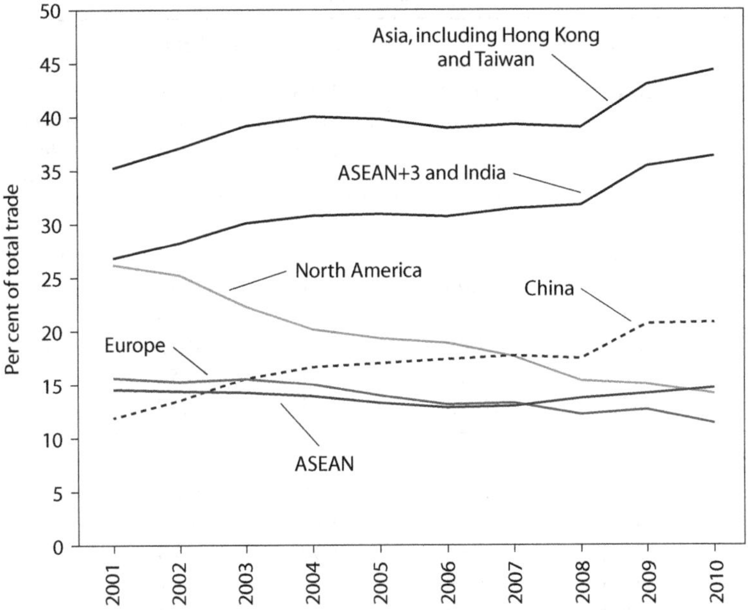

Figure 9.2 Japanese trade by major destination, 2001–10 (percentages of total trade). Source: Japan Tariff Association, *Summary Report on Trade of Japan*, various issues.

increase in the share of Asia from 2001 to 2010 is almost entirely accounted for by rising trade with China. Correspondingly, the shares of North America and Europe declined over the same period, by 12 per cent and 3 per cent, respectively. In terms of breakdown between exports and imports (not directly depicted in Figure 9.2), the share of Asia is larger on the export side (48 per cent in 2010) than on the import side (41 per cent), indicating the critical role Japan plays in supplying parts, components and capital goods for the region's production networks. Asia replaced North America as the country's most important export destination in 2001.

In contrast, the share of Asia in Japan's financial transactions is small. In terms of FDI assets, the share of ASEAN at the end of 2010 was 10.9 per cent (cf. 14.6 per cent in trade); without Singapore, the share was 7.6 per cent; with all of Asia (including Hong Kong and Taiwan), the share of Asia increases to 25.5 per cent, but still falls far short of the 44.5 per cent in trade (Table 9.2). In terms of FDI liabilities, the share of Asia is even smaller. The share of ASEAN was 6.8 per cent and a mere 0.3 per cent with Singapore excluded. Even with all of Asia included, the share increases to only 10.8 per cent. The small amount of FDI liabilities Japan owes to Asia is not surprising because most countries are small, net debtors or still poor. As the countries in the region develop and become wealthier, Japan's outward FDI may begin to expand beyond

Table 9.2 Japan's external FDI assets and liabilities, 2001–10.

Year (end)	*Global total (in trillions of yen)*	*In per cent of global total*			
		ASEAN	*ASEAN, excluding Singapore*	*ASEAN+3 and India*	*Asia, including Hong Kong and Taiwan*
Assets					
2001	39.6	9.44	6.05	14.62	17.66
2006	53.5	11.08	7.91	20.71	23.85
2007	61.9	11.23	8.02	21.13	24.22
2008	61.7	9.89	7.04	20.22	23.22
2009	68.2	10.23	7.04	20.58	23.61
2010	67.7	10.93	7.62	22.38	25.49
Liabilities					
2001	6.6	0.54	–0.06	1.08	6.65
2006	12.8	4.00	0.10	4.50	7.66
2007	15.2	3.53	0.08	4.15	7.01
2008	18.5	4.99	0.07	5.71	8.20
2009	18.4	5.50	0.19	6.34	8.67
2010	17.5	6.80	0.32	7.90	10.84

Source: Ministry of Finance, *Statistics Monthly*, various issues.

export-oriented manufacturing into wholesale, retail and other service sectors, as well as manufacturing targeted at domestic sales. At the same time, Japan's inward FDI from Asia may also increase as Asian firms seek to exploit the Japanese domestic market or to hold stake in Japanese firms. For now, Japan is a large net direct investor in the rest of Asia. Yet, the amount of FDI assets is about half of what it should be on the basis of the importance of Asia in Japanese trade.

The share of Asia in Japan's portfolio investment is even more lopsidedly smaller, compared with the case of trade, except for debt liabilities (Table 9.3). In the case of equity assets, the share of ASEAN was 2.3 per cent at the end of 2010 (1.1 per cent without Singapore); the share increases to 5.9 per cent with China, Korea and India included, and rises further to 8.9 per cent with Hong Kong and Taiwan in. The respective shares were smaller for equity liabilities, with ASEAN (without Singapore) accounting for only 0.03 per cent of foreign equity investments in Japan. As to debt assets, the shares are much smaller, suggesting that the bond markets are underdeveloped in most Asian countries. In contrast, Asia's shares in foreign portfolio investments in the Japanese bond market are considerably larger: ASEAN's share was almost 11 per cent at the end of 2010, rising to 28.1 per cent when all the countries are included. This indicates that Asian investors are active participants in Japan's large bond market. These shares fluctuate from year to year, in part reflecting valuation changes due to exchange rate movements. The recent increase may be temporary, resulting from a shift of investments from Europe following the outbreak of a sovereign debt crisis in several European countries.

The pattern of lending and borrowing we have observed from the outstanding balances of assets and liabilities is confirmed by more detailed

Table 9.3 Japan's external portfolio assets and liabilities, 2001–10.

Year (end)	*Global total (in trillions of yen)*	*In per cent of global total*			
		ASEAN	*ASEAN, excluding Singapore*	*ASEAN+3 and India*	*Asia, including Hong Kong and Taiwan*
Equity assets					
2001	30.0	0.80	0.39	1.33	3.63
2006	60.7	1.15	0.41	4.48	7.16
2007	65.4	1.78	0.65	6.43	10.06
2008	35.8	1.19	0.42	4.86	7.53
2009	54.7	1.44	0.42	5.07	8.09
2010	55.3	2.32	1.07	5.92	8.85
Equity liabilities					
2001	49. 6	2.42	0.04	2.49	4.64
2006	149.3	0.34	0.04	0.88	1.99
2007	142.0	0.37	0.03	1.96	3.11
2008	68.6	0.42	0.03	2.77	3.63
2009	76.4	0.56	0.03	0.84	1.70
2010	80.5	1.99	0.05	6.31	7.74
Debt assets					
2001	140.0	0.53	0.42	1.14	1.27
2006	218.0	0.38	0.17	0.73	0.77
2007	222.3	0.49	0.24	0.96	1.01
2008	179.9	0.42	0.25	1.04	1.10
2009	207.3	0.47	0.29	0.90	0.96
2010	217.3	0.54	0.35	1.05	1.11
Debt liabilities					
2001	38.2	9.67	3.20	14.87	16.91
2006	60.4	6.36	1.50	12.23	14.85
2007	79.5	6.58	1.46	10.99	13.01
2008	71.7	6.37	2.05	11.79	13.80
2009	65.5	10.93	5.38	17.03	18.08
2010	71.9	10.57	5.07	26.09	28.06

Source: Ministry of Finance, *Statistics Monthly*, various issues.

flow data (Table 9.4). In terms of FDI, during 2006–10 Japan invested far more than it received in investment from abroad (within Asia alone, over 2 trillion yen versus 166 billion yen on average per year). The only significant Asian direct investor in Japan was Singapore, accounting for 95 per cent of all inward FDI received from Asia during this period. On the asset side, China was an important destination for Japan's outward FDI and accounted for 90 per cent of the amount ASEAN received collectively. All in all, Asia's share in Japanese FDI was 26 per cent for outflows and 15 per cent for inflows. As to portfolio investment, while debt instruments were the predominant form of Japan's outward investment, this was not always the case with Asia. Especially in China, India, Hong Kong and Taiwan, equity investments far surpassed debt investments; the relative importance of equity investment is suggested in most of the other countries as well. This reflects the fact that, in many of the countries, the equity markets are more developed or more open to foreigners than are the bond markets. As noted previously, the reverse is true with inward debt investments. Although the share of Asia remains small, it is larger for debt liabilities than for equity liabilities. Hong Kong is virtually the only equity investor in Japan, accounting for 18.4 per cent of global equity investment in Japan and over 90 per cent of Asian equity investment.

Japanese data provide a country-by-country breakdown of external bank credits outstanding for a subset of Asian countries, with only Brunei and Cambodia missing from our sample (Table 9.5). At the end of 2010, we find that the share of ASEAN was only 3 per cent of Japan's global total, with the share increasing to 6.6 per cent with China, Korea and India included, and rising further to 8.7 per cent with Hong Kong and Taiwan in. In contrast, the share of advanced countries (according to the Bank of Japan/BIS definition) was almost 70 per cent. The share of Asia in the balance of credits extended by Japanese banks at the end of 2010 (8.7 per cent) was almost identical in magnitude to the region's share in the external positions of all BIS-reporting banks (8.9 per cent; see Table 9.1). This suggests that the behaviour of Japanese banks is similar to that of other international banks toward Asia, and confirms our earlier conjecture that intraregional banking activity is limited in Asia and that much of the little that does take place occurs with countries outside the region. Regional banking integration in Asia is indeed limited.

EXPLAINING THE LACK OF FINANCIAL INTEGRATION IN ASIA

Having established that Asia is far less integrated in finance than in trade, our next task is to offer a few reasons why this is so. The reasons may not be entirely independent of each other. Given the symbiotic relationships that often exist among different dimensions of finance, overcoming one

Table 9.4 Japan's outward and inward foreign investment flows (annual averages for 2006–10, in billions of yen; percentages of global total in parentheses).

	Global total	*Indonesia*	*Malaysia*	*Philippines*	*Thailand*	*Vietnam*	*Singapore*	*Other ASEAN*	*ASEAN*	*China*	*Korea*	*India*	*ASEAN+3 and India*	*Hong Kong*	*Taiwan*	*Asia, incl. Hong Kong and Taiwan*
Net foreign direct investment (a negative value indicates an outflow of capital from Japan)																
Net outward investment	–7,933.4	–73.6	–118.7	–72.3	–219.4	–68.0	–204.3	NA	–756.3	–679.1	–154.0	–273.2	–1,862.6	–154.3	–70.5	–2,087.4
Net inward investment	1,086.1	0.9	7.4	0.1	0.7	–0.1	153.2	NA	162.2	4.2	23.0	0.4	189.8	–30.5	6.3	165.6
Gross foreign portfolio investment (absolute value of sales and purchases of securities)																
Gross outward investment	364,027.9	269.6 (0.007)	336.4 (0.009)	167.7 (0.005)	232.7 (0.006)	13.2 (0.000)	1,268.4 (0.034)	0.9 (0.000)	2,288.8 (0.062)	2,188.4 (0.060)	1,439.9 (0.040)	764.0 (0.021)	6,681.1 (0.183)	2,071.1 (0.057)	445.9 (0.012)	9,198.1 (0.253)
Of which, equities only	50,999.3	129.5 (0.259)	120.9 (0.227)	38.6 (0.073)	103.0 (0.203)	7.4 (0.016)	571.6 (1.110)	1.0 (0.002)	972.0 (1.890)	2,145.1 (4.173)	503.2 (0.996)	654.1 (1.291)	4,274.4 (8.350)	1,915.2 (3.737)	433.0 (0.857)	6,622.6 (12.944)
Gross inward investment	847,724.7	250.1 (0.032)	195.5 (0.023)	109.7 (0.014)	7,792.2 (1.010)	3.0 (0.000)	16,833.6 (2.056)	9.5 (0.001)	25,193.4 (3.137)	5,309.3 (0.676)	679.5 (0.078)	24.7 (0.003)	31,206.9 (3.894)	103,794.1 (11.688)	134.1 (0.014)	135,135.1 (15.596)
Of which, equities only	478,435.2	0.3 (0.000)	0.3 (0.000)	0.1 (0.000)	0.7 (0.000)	0.1 (0.000)	8,398.7 (1.803)	1.0 (0.000)	8,401.2 (1.804)	3.2 (0.001)	23.9 (0.004)	0.4 (0.000)	8,428.7 (1.809)	95,705.5 (18.432)	12.3 (0.003)	104,146.6 (20.244)

Source: Japanese Ministry of Finance, *Statistics Monthly*, various issues.

Table 9.5 External credits outstanding to Japanese banks, 2006–10 (end-of-year figures).

	Percentage shares of global total, unless otherwise noted				
	2006	*2007*	*2008*	*2009*	*2010*
Indonesia	0.39	0.37	0.41	0.42	0.53
Laos	0.00	0.00	0.00	0.00	0.00
Malaysia	0.34	0.36	0.43	0.37	0.34
Myanmar	0.00	0.00	0.00	0.00	0.00
Philippines	0.14	0.18	0.17	0.15	0.17
Singapore	1.41	1.58	1.59	1.29	1.48
Thailand	0.35	0.28	0.35	0.32	0.41
Vietnam	0.05	0.07	0.10	0.11	0.13
ASEAN	2.67	2.84	3.05	2.66	3.06
China	1.10	1.17	1.09	1.17	1.25
Korea	1.06	1.22	1.45	1.46	1.53
India	0.44	0.58	0.58	0.62	0.79
ASEAN+3 and India	5.26	5.80	6.16	5.91	6.63
Hong Kong	1.54	1.48	1.39	1.23	1.77
Taiwan	0.26	0.32	0.23	0.22	0.29
Asia, including Hong Kong and Taiwan	7.05	7.60	7.78	7.37	8.69
Advanced countries	73.24	72.86	71.93	73.53	69.36
Global total (in millions of US dollars)	1,607,545	1,973,144	1,906,168	2,046,328	2,312,226

Source: Bank of Japan at http://www.boj.or.jp.

impediment to financial integration, for example, may help remove another. Some gaps are easily amenable to government policy; some take a considerable amount of time to fill; and others may require international or regional cooperative efforts to find effective solutions.

At the outset, we must not forget that many of the countries in Asia were poor, developing countries not too many decades ago; some are still far behind in terms of catching up with the level of per-capita income prevailing in the industrialized world. It is possible that much of the lack of substantial financial integration reflects the region's overall stage of development. Thus, the reasons we offer for the lack of intraregional financial integration in Asia may not necessarily be problems that need to be solved. With the passage of time, as per-capita incomes grow, household savings rise and firms expand the scale of domestic and international operations, regional financial integration is bound to deepen to a level more commensurate with trade integration.

This does not mean that Asia's policy-makers should just stand idly by while their economies continue to develop. There are things they can do to help promote regional financial integration. There are at least three broad areas where they can act: (i) capital market development; (ii) capital account liberalization; and (iii) financial services (banking) liberalization.

First, Asian policy-makers must develop their domestic capital markets further, and make them deep, liquid and efficient. This is not to deny that capital markets have grown rapidly since the financial crisis of 1997–98, in absolute terms, as a share of total financial assets and as a share of GDP in many Asian countries. According to ADB (2008), as a result, the share of bank claims in total financial assets had declined from nearly 60 per cent in 1995 to slightly over 35 per cent in 2007 in 15 Asian counties.[6] Given the rising weight of capital markets in Asia, why has not more intraregional portfolio investment taken place? The lack of significant Japanese portfolio investments in Asia when Japan trades extensively and accumulates considerable FDI assets with Asia points to a possible explanation.

We noted earlier that the share of Asia was particularly small in Japan's debt investment abroad, and conjectured that the reason lay in the generally underdeveloped bond markets. This indeed appears to be the case (Table 9.6). Except in Japan and possibly China (and perhaps Korea), there is no bond market, especially for corporate bonds, that has sufficient size to accommodate large international investors. Even India's bond market is seen to be comparatively small. The need to develop bond markets is a high priority, as is well recognized by the region's policy-makers, because debt is the predominant form of portfolio flows among the developed countries. Currently, regional initiatives to develop debt markets include the Asian Bond Markets Initiative established by ASEAN+3 and the Asian Bond Fund set up by the Executives' Meeting of East Asia–Pacific Central Banks. The acceleration of regional financial integration may not take off until such markets are firmly established.

In contrast, equity markets are well developed in most countries of the region, often with sophisticated trading platforms. In Brunei, Cambodia, Laos and Myanmar, however, they are either nonexistent or only just beginning to emerge. The lack of Japanese equity investments in Asia seems to suggest a more fundamental problem of the domestic equity markets of the region: their small size (Table 9.7). Again, except for Japan, China and India (and possibly Korea), domestic equity markets are limited in terms of capitalization and trading value. These markets therefore offer limited depth and liquidity, features that are important to attract large international investors. Foreign investors do come and participate in these markets, often very actively. But limited depth and liquidity create volatility, and the authorities therefore tend to find free equity inflows to be a source of vulnerability. To some extent, the same problem may be identified when

Table 9.6 Domestic debt securities outstanding in principal Asia–Pacific markets (end of 2010; in billions of US dollars; percentages of global total in parentheses).

	All issues	*Government*	*Private*
Japan	13,734.41 (20.45)	11,632.31 (29.86)	2,102.10 (7.46)
China	3,031.38 (4.51)	1,622.82 (4.17)	1,408.56 (5.00)
Korea	1,111.04 (1.65)	475.08 (1.22)	635.96 (2.26)
Australia	1,043.58 (1.55)	339.95 (0.87)	703.63 (2.50)
India	708.53 (1.06)	608.25 (1.56)	100.27 (0.36)
Taiwan	258.06 (0.38)	156.98 (0.40)	101.08 (0.36)
Malaysia	239.87 (0.36)	127.98 (0.33)	111.89 (0.40)
Thailand	225.50 (0.34)	166.05 (0.43)	59.45 (0.21)
Singapore	128.73 (0.19)	102.76 (0.26)	25.97 (0.09)
Indonesia	93.41 (0.14)	81.85 (0.21)	11.56 (0.04)
Philippines	64.02 (0.10)	61.73 (0.16)	2.29 (0.01)
Hong Kong	65.51 (0.10)	30.70 (0.08)	34.82 (0.12)
Memoranda: major markets outside the region			
France	3,170.18 (4.72)	1,700.42 (4.36)	1,469.76 (5.21)
Germany	2,615.88 (3.90)	1,724.43 (4.43)	891.45 (3.16)
Italy	3,000.02 (4.47)	1,933.53 (4.96)	1,066.49 (3.78)
UK	1,646.97 (2.45)	1,324.21 (3.40)	322.76 (1.14)
USA	25,349.02 (37.75)	11,151.67 (28.62)	14,197.36 (50.36)
Global total	67,153.67	38,959.92	28,193.75

Source: Bank for International Settlements, *Quarterly Review*, June 2011.

domestic bond markets are ultimately developed. It may be that, as long as the economies remain small, the home currency denominated capital markets are bound to remain small. The long-run solution to the limited size of domestic capital markets may be to create a consolidated region-wide market for all securities issued within the region.

Second, the pattern of Japanese investment activity with Asia suggests a lack of two-way flows. Japan invests much more in Asia than it receives in investment in return. In some sense, this is not surprising, insofar as Japan is a net creditor country with a large and continuing current account surplus. But in a world where finance is highly integrated a debtor can also engage in gross capital outflows. As long as cross-border financial transactions predominantly involve net flows, there is a natural limit to financial integration. To promote financial integration, there must be an environment in which gross flows are promoted. The lack of gross flows in Asia can be substantiated in terms of the stocks of external assets and liabilities (Table 9.8). A highly financially integrated country might have large gross international investment positions (as it holds both large assets and large liabilities) even though it necessarily holds a net position in one or the other

Table 9.7 Principal Asia–Pacific stock exchanges, 2010 (numbers indicate respective global rankings).

Domestic market capitalization (end of 2010; in billions of US dollars)		*Number of listed companies (of which, foreign companies)*	*Value of share trading (2010; electronic order book trades, in billions of US dollars)*		*Of which, foreign companies*
3. Tokyo	3,827.77	2,293 (12)	3. Shanghai	4,486.48	0.00
6. Shanghai	2,716.47	894 (0)	4. Tokyo	3,792.72	0.71
7. Hong Kong	2,711.32	1,413 (17)	5. Shenzhen	3,563.79	0.00
9. Bombay	1,631.83	5,034 (0)	9. Korea	1,604.55	10.89
9. India (National SE)	1,596.63	1,552 (1)	10. Hong Kong	1,496.22	7.77
11. Australian	1,454.49	1,999 (86)	13. Australian	1,061.98	49.48
13. Shenzhen SE	1,311.37	1,169 (0)	14. Taiwan	899.67	8.34
16. Korea	1,091.91	1,798 (17)	16. India (National SE)	798.64	0.00
20. Taiwan	818.49	784 (32)	22. Singapore	288.39	NA
21. Singapore	647.23	778 (317)	24. Bombay	258.57	0.00
23. Malaysia	408.69	956 (8)	25. Thailand	211.67	0.00
24. Indonesia	360.39	420 (0)	27. Osaka	179.70	0.03
29. Thailand	277.73	541 (0)	29. Malaysia	111.82	1.59
30. Osaka	271.83	1,273 (1)	30. Indonesia	103.68	0.00
34. Philippine	157.32	253 (2)	39. Philippine	21.64	0.00
Memoranda (largest four exchanges outside the region):					
1. New York	13,394.08	2,238 (451)	1. New York	17,795.60	1,736.11
2. NASDAQ	3,889.37	2,778 (298)	2. NASDAQ	12,659.20	1,178.45
4. London	3,613.06	2,966 (604)	6. London	2,749.53	265.01
5. Euronext	2,930.07	1,135 (152)	7. Euronext	2,022.21	7.78
WFE total	54,953.61	45,508	WFE total	63,077.78	

Source: World Federation of Exchanges (WFE), http://www.world-exchange.org/statistics.

direction but, except for Malaysia, Japan and Singapore, no country in Asia had a gross international investment position of more than 100 per cent of GDP at the end of 2010. Equally important, a substantial portion of the gross international investment positions is accounted for by FDI assets and liabilities, not portfolio assets and liabilities. Japan is the exception. This tendency is particularly pronounced in countries with less capital account openness or less-developed financial markets (e.g. Myanmar, Cambodia and China). FDI is a less liquid form of foreign investment, which limits the scope for two-way flows.

In terms of balance of payment flows, gross FDI flows were larger than portfolio flows in almost all countries during 2006–10 (5.6 per cent versus 4.1 per cent on average for the region), though they were smaller in the Philippines, Japan and Korea (Table 9.9). In contrast to the stock data, except in Cambodia and Myanmar (and to a lesser extent in Brunei), the flow data show a larger weight of portfolio flows. This may mean that Asian countries have been increasing their presence in the international capital markets in more recent years. Moreover, many Asian countries are seen to have been engaged in significant other capital transactions (for the most part bank flows), particularly Singapore (given its status as a regional financial centre) and Brunei (which is connected to Singapore through extensive bank flows). Among the other ASEAN countries, other capital transactions were the most significant form of external financial flows during 2006–10 in Cambodia, Indonesia, Malaysia and the Philippines. But even with increasing portfolio flows in recent years, and the greater weight of other

Table 9.8 Gross international investment positions[1] in Asian countries, 2010 (per cent of GDP)

	FDI (share of total)	*Equity*	*Debt*	*Total*
Cambodia	56.05 (94.1)	3.51	0.00	59.56
Indonesia	22.01 (50.4)	0.92	20.71	43.63
Malaysia	83.30 (54.6)	15.09	54.05	152.45
Myanmar[2]	36.18 (100.0)	0.00	0.00	36.18
Philippines	16.48 (40.5)	6.04	18.20	40.72
Singapore	342.75 (50.8)	246.21	83.91	674.87
Thailand	50.60 (60.0)	7.20	26.55	84.35
China	30.14 (78.9)	4.34	3.74	38.21
Japan	19.06 (16.7)	60.96	34.10	114.12
Korea	27.33 (31.6)	11.06	48.19	86.58
India	18.29 (62.8)	0.10	10.73	29.13

Source: Author's estimates based on International Monetary Fund, *International Financial Statistics* and *World Economic Outlook* database.

Notes
1 Gross positions represent a sum of asset and liability positions in absolute value.
2 2006 for Myanmar only.

capital transactions (for which there were no comparable stock data), during 2006–10 total gross financial transactions still accounted for a much smaller share of GDP than did gross trade (18.2 per cent versus 114.3 per cent for the region as a whole; 13.4 per cent versus 106.4 per cent for ASEAN less Singapore). Even among the advanced members of ASEAN, the GDP share ranged between 6.8 per cent (Indonesia) and 24.6 per cent (Malaysia) when the GDP share of gross trade flows ranged between 52.8 per cent (Indonesia) and 195.6 per cent (Malaysia). Relative to trade openness, Asia's average openness to financial flows is overall quite limited.

Capital account policy in part explains the pattern of financial flows that is largely defined by net flows. According to a de-jure index of capital account openness obtained from the latest issue of the IMF's *Annual Report on Exchange Arrangements and Exchange Restrictions* (Figure 9.3),[7] most countries still impose extensive controls on capital account transactions. Exceptions are Singapore (a score of 95), Japan (93) and Brunei (88).[8]

Table 9.9 Financial and trade openness in Asian countries, 2006–10 (annual averages in per cent of GDP)[1]

	Gross FDI	*Gross portfolio*	*Gross other*	*Gross total financial transactions*	*Gross trade*
Brunei[2]	1.88	1.17	11.94	14.99	101.51
Cambodia	7.48	0.14	10.24	17.85	134.37
Indonesia	2.28	2.20	2.32	6.80	52.78
Lao PDR	5.42	0.17	3.48	9.07	59.79
Malaysia[2]	7.65	6.66	10.29	24.60	195.61
Myanmar	2.67	0.00	0.07	2.74	41.08
Philippines	2.03	4.59	4.74	11.37	75.82
Thailand	4.74	3.90	6.17	14.81	136.69
Vietnam	8.44	2.85	7.18	18.47	159.57
Singapore	24.17	17.23	46.56	87.96	406.19
ASEAN[3]	6.67	3.89	10.29	20.87	136.34
ASEAN less Singapore[3]	4.73	2.41	6.27	13.41	106.36
China	4.56	2.17	3.03	9.75	61.02
Japan	1.89	6.22	6.08	14.19	32.03
Korea	2.08	7.57	4.12	13.75	95.45
India	3.79	1.88	2.68	8.36	48.04
ASEAN+3 and India [3]	5.64	4.05	8.49	18.19	114.28

Source: Author's estimates based on International Monetary Fund, *International Financial Statistics* and *World Economic Outlook* database.

Notes
1 Openness is measured by a sum of inflows (imports) and outflows (exports) divided by GDP.
2 2005–09 for Brunei and Malaysia only.
3 Simple averages.

While most countries substantially allow direct investment inflows and portfolio inflows through purchases by nonresidents of domestic securities, they continue to maintain controls on the ability of residents to invest abroad. Figure 9.3 clearly shows that the controls are tighter on outflows than on inflows, even for the advanced members of ASEAN (i.e. 76 versus 68 for Indonesia; 76 versus 40 for Malaysia; 92 versus 32 for the Philippines; and 48 versus 24 for Thailand). China and India, the two most important economies in terms of size, are among the most restrictive in the region. This in part explains the lack of two-way capital flows, and limits the potential for regional financial integration.

Finally, the cross-border activity of Asia-based banks within the region appears limited. In part, this is because, except for Japan and Korea, Asian regulators tightly restrict the entry of foreign banks, including those from within the region. For historical and other reasons associated with colonial heritage or crisis-prompted sale of failed banks to foreign strategic investors, some countries have allowed foreign banks to operate with a substantial share of the domestic market, but they are all large international banks from Western countries. Where there are transparent licensing criteria (usually based on total assets or global ranking), they also tend to favour large Western banks. It is true that a handful of Asia-based 'national champions' have operations in neighbouring countries, but the overall regional banking networks are limited, despite the fact that many of them have quite a number of branches outside the region.[9] In contrast, large Western banks have branches or subsidiaries in several of the countries in the region.[10]

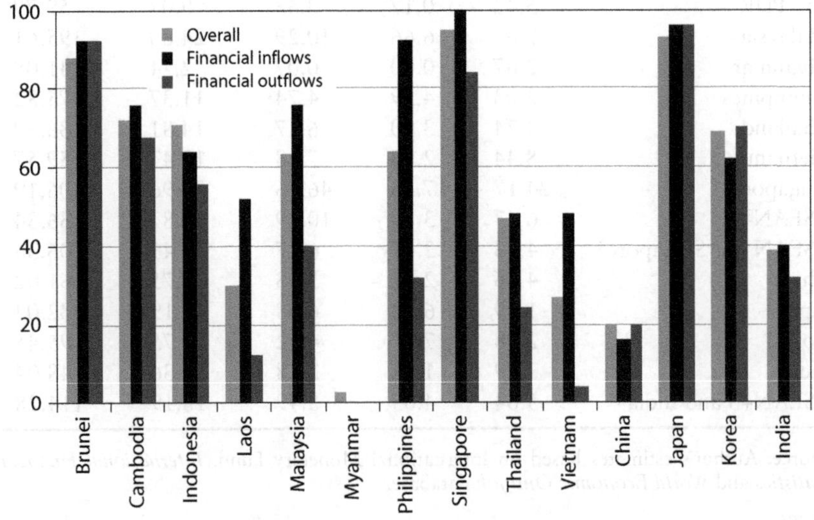

Figure 9.3 Capital account openness in Asian countries, 2010. Source: Author's assessment based on International Monetary Fund, *Annual Report on Exchange Arrangements and Exchange Restrictions*, 2011.

The policies favouring large Western banks have had the effect of strengthening the financial links of Asian countries with international financial centres, rather than with each other. While this is not in itself a bad thing, it has limited the scope for exploiting the information generated by Asia's growing trade and FDI links and face-to-face contacts, and has thereby contributed little to regional financial integration. This is unfortunate because Asia's domestic financial systems are bank-based and, given the time it will likely take to develop securities markets, banks must play the central role in intermediating intraregional financial flows. Capital account policy is also responsible for this outcome, as bank flows are the most regulated form of cross-border financial transactions in many countries, including the advanced members of ASEAN. For example, external borrowing is subject to control in Indonesia, Malaysia and Thailand, while restrictions are placed upon the ability of banks to lend abroad in Indonesia, Malaysia, the Philippines and Thailand (especially by using domestic deposits). It is no wonder that regional banking activity is dominated by large international banks from outside the region.

A high degree of regulatory harmonization is necessary for creating a unified market for financial services across the region (as has been achieved in the European Union and is now being contemplated by ASEAN).[11] But this is not the only way to promote regional banking integration. To give Asia-based foreign banks easier access is essential, but it would not be necessary to allow them to offer the same services as they do in their home markets or as provided by domestic banks. As long as Asia-based banks can operate freely across the region, thus exploiting the information generated locally through trade and FDI links, gross bank flows are bound to expand. Given the limited size of most Asia-based banks, it may be that only Chinese and Japanese (and possibly Korean) banks have the necessary internal resources to operate region-wide. On a more limited scale, however, national champions from the advanced ASEAN countries (e.g. Maybank, Bangkok Bank and UOB) and India could also play an important but more localized role. Asian financial integration in a bank-dominated system presupposes the active participation of a large number of Asia-based banks in a region-wide banking market. For this, Asian policy-makers must make concerted efforts to liberalize cross-border bank flows and to establish transparent and objective licensing standards that do not discriminate against Asia-based banks.

CONCLUSION

Asia is much less intraregionally integrated in finance than in trade. We have confirmed the limited integration of finance, relative to that of trade, in FDI, portfolio investment (both equities and debt) and bank flows by using data for the region as a whole as well as from the point of view of Japan, the region's most important creditor country. While the share of Asia in Japan's global trade was as much as 44.5 per cent in 2010 (when the broadest definition of Asia is used), it was considerably less in FDI, and even more limited in portfolio investment. For example, Asia accounted for as little as 1.1 per cent of Japan's balance of debt assets. The pattern of Japan's investment activity pointed to a few possible factors to explain the lopsidedly small share of Asia in Japan's external investment and hence the lack of regional financial integration: (i) underdeveloped and small domestic capital markets; (ii) capital account restrictions that limit the scope for two-way capital flows; and (iii) licensing and other regulatory practices that discriminate ex post against the cross-border activity of Asia-based banks in the region.

Undoubtedly, part of the overarching reason can be found in the stages of development of many of the countries in Asia. With the passage of time, as their economies grow, regional financial integration is bound to deepen to a level more commensurate with trade integration. Even so, there are things Asian policy-makers could do to help promote regional financial integration. Although there is no theoretical case for preferring regional to global financial integration, given the nature of asymmetric information, some financial transactions should be intermediated within the region as economic agents attempt to exploit the information generated locally. The lack of 'home bias' observed in the limited intraregional financial integration therefore suggests the possibility that there are unmet financing needs in Asia. Cooperative efforts may be needed to safeguard the process of capital account liberalization, relax the licensing standards for Asia-based foreign banks to operate more freely and to set common standards for domestic capital markets and cross-border transactions of financial products. In the long run, a region-wide consolidation of domestic capital markets may be necessary in order to create a market with the size, depth and liquidity that is sufficiently attractive to large international and regional investors.

NOTES

1 An earlier version of this chapter was presented at the roundtable *Asia, the G20 and Global and Regional Architecture* held at the Crawford School of Public Policy, Australian National University, Canberra, on 18 August 2011.
2 Graduate School of Economics, Osaka University, Japan.
3 By estimating a gravity model of bilateral financial asset holdings for 1999–2003, they found that an East Asia dummy had no additional explanatory power (indicating the lack of financial integration beyond what could be explained by trade).
4 That is, Brunei, Cambodia, Indonesia, Laos, Malaysia, Myanmar, the Philippines, Singapore, Thailand and Vietnam.
5 In view of the multidimensionality of the concept of financial integration, Takagi and Hirose (2004) have suggested a methodology using principal components analysis to obtain a univariate measure of financial integration from several competing ones.

6 The sample is similar to ours, except that none of the BCLMV countries are included.

7 This is calculated as a weighted average of openness with respect to personal transactions (10 per cent), financial inflows (25 per cent), financial outflows (25 per cent), exchange rate risk hedging activity (4 per cent), cross-border use of foreign and domestic currencies (5 per cent), current account transactions (12 per cent) and foreign direct investment (19 per cent). Altogether we have considered 36 separate transactions to come up with a score.

8 Brunei is virtually fully open as it is part of the common monetary area with Singapore. Given the lack of a domestic capital market, however, the country receives only limited portfolio inflows.

9 For example, no Indonesian bank has a foreign branch except in Singapore; only one Thai bank has foreign operations outside Singapore, Cambodia and Laos; the only foreign operation of Philippine banks is a representative office maintained by Metrobank (in contrast, the largest bank, Banco De Oro Unibank, has no branch or subsidiary within ASEAN although it has a presence in Europe and the USA as well as in Hong Kong, Macao and Taipei); CIMB of Malaysia is the only non-Singaporean bank with operations in Thailand.

10 For example, HSBC, Standard Chartered and Citibank have operations in at least 11 of the 14 countries of what we collectively call Asia.

11 ASEAN is currently in the process of liberalizing financial services within the region as part of creating the ASEAN Economic Community by 2015, but a radical change can hardly be expected as long as the process, in keeping with ASEAN's characteristically cautious attitude, allows 'adequate safeguard against potential macroeconomic instability and systemic risk that may arise from the liberalization process' (ASEAN Economic Community Blueprint, paragraph 32, 2007).

REFERENCES

ADB (Asian Development Bank) (2008) *Emerging Asian Regionalism: a Partnership for Shared Prosperity*, Manila: Asian Development Bank.

Bayoumi, T. (1990) 'Saving–investment correlations: immobile capital, government policy, or endogenous behavior?', *Staff Paper*, No. 37: 360–387, Washington, DC: International Monetary Fund.

Boyreau-Debray, G. and S. Wei (2002) 'How fragmented is the capital market in China?', *Working Paper*, No. 0214, Hong Kong University of Science and Technology.

Coakley, J., F. Kulasi and R. Smith (1998) 'The Feldstein–Horioka puzzle and capital mobility: a review', *International Journal of Finance and Economics*, 3: 169–188.

Cowen, D., R. Salgado, H. Shah, L. Teo and A. Zanello (2006) 'Financial integration in Asia: recent developments and next steps', *Working Paper*, No. 06/196, Washington, DC: International Monetary Fund.

Dekle, R. (1996) 'Saving–investment associations and capital mobility on the evidence from Japanese regional data', *Journal of International Economics*, 41: 53–72.

Eichengreen, B. and Y.C. Park (2004) 'Why has there been less financial integration in Asia than in Europe?', *Staff Paper*, No. 28, Monetary Authority of Singapore.

Feldstein, M. and C. Horioka (1980) 'Domestic saving and international capital flows', *Economic Journal*, 90: 314–329.

Frankel, J.A. (1992) 'Measuring international capital mobility: a review', *American Economic Review*, 82(2): 197–202.
Harberger, A. (1980) 'Vignettes on the world capital market', *American Economic Review*, 70: 331–337.
Iwamoto, Y. and E. van Wincoop (2000) 'Do borders matter? Evidence from Japanese regional net capital flows', *International Economic Review*, 41: 241–269.
Kenen, P.B. (1976) 'Capital mobility and financial integration: a survey', *Princeton Studies in International Finance*, No. 39, Princeton, NJ: Princeton University, Department of Economics.
Kim, S., J. Lee and K. Shin (2006) 'Regional and global financial integration in East Asia', *Discussion Paper Series*, No. 0602, Seoul: Korea University, Institute of Economic Research.
Le, H. (2000) 'Financial openness and financial integration', *Working Paper*, No. 00-4, Canberra: Australian National University, Asia Pacific School of Economics and Management.
Obstfeld, M. (1986) 'Capital mobility in the world economy: theory and measurement', *Carnegie–Rochester Conference Series on Public Policy*, 24: 55–104.
Pisani-Ferry, J. and J. Cohen-Setton (2008) 'Asia–Europe: the third link', *Economic Papers*, No. 352, Brussels: European Commission, Directorate-General for Economic and Financial Affairs.
Sinn, S. (1992) 'Saving–investment correlations and capital mobility: on the evidence from annual data', *Economic Journal*, 102: 1162–1170.
Takagi, S. and K. Hirose (2004) 'A multivariate approach to grouping financially integrated economies', in G. de Brouwer and M. Kawai (eds) *Exchange Rate Regimes in East Asia*, pp. 131–152, London and New York: RoutledgeCurzon.
Takagi, S. and T. Taki (2011) 'Financial integration in Asia and around the world', *Osaka Economic Papers*, 61(1): 1–12.
Taki, T. (2008) 'Indicators of financial integration: tests based on country and Japanese regional data', *Osaka Economic Papers*, 58(3), 41–61. [In Japanese with an English summary]

10 Strategies for Asian exchange-rate policy cooperation

Yiping Huang[1]

INTRODUCTION

Asian economies have undergone significant transformation since the 1997–98 financial crisis. In order to reduce risks of a balance-of-payments crisis, Asian policy-makers introduced a number of reforms, including promotion of current account surpluses, accumulation of foreign reserves and some regional cooperation initiatives. These changes strengthened Asia's external sector fundamentals and helped Asia's ability to withstand external shocks.

However, Asia is not immune from the current global financial crisis. The performance of Asian currencies since the onset of the US subprime crisis has shown significant variation. Some currencies, such as the Korean won and Indonesian rupiah, have collapsed by more than 20 per cent against the US dollar since mid 2008, while others, such as the Chinese yuan and Japanese yen, have been either stable or have made some gains.

Different currency performance across the region was attributable to a combination of several factors, including exchange rate policy, economic openness and external sector resilience. Generally more flexible exchange rate regimes after the 1997–98 crisis implied greater currency volatility, given the region's very open economy. On the other hand, perceived high external sector weakness also increased vulnerability of some regional currencies, especially the Korean won, Indonesian rupiah and Indian rupee.

This was unfortunate given Asia's tremendous policy efforts during the past 10 years. Merely 2 years ago, many regional central bankers believed that their accumulated foreign-exchange reserves were too high. This assessment led to the creation of the Korean Investment Corporation (KIC) and China Investment Corporation (CIC) and proposals for setting up similar sovereign wealth funds (SWFs) in the other economies. Capital market investors, however, did not agree with the above assessment, as indicated by currency market experiences during the current financial crisis.

This raises a critical question about future options for Asia's exchange rate system. Should Asia pursue closer monetary integration? If the answer is positive, then what should be the next step – creating a regional currency or strengthening policy coordination? At the centre of this policy deliberation, policy-makers must carefully weigh benefits and costs of exchange rate flexibility versus stability, taking into account current economic conditions in the region.

In this chapter, I argue that currency integration should be the long-term goal for Asia. However, it is best to leave it to the market to decide whether the future currency system will be dominated by an 'Asian dollar', Japanese yen, Chinese yuan, Indian rupee or a dynamic basket of currencies. While currency stability is valuable for emerging economies in Asia, some flexibility across regional currencies may still be necessary, given different levels of development, different stages of macro-economic cycles and different macro-economic fundamentals. Premature implementation of currency integration could make macro-economic management exceedingly difficult.

Monetary integration in Asia might follow a three-stage approach:

- a first stage involving expansion of the foreign reserve fund and creation of an Asian central bank forum (or expansion of the Asian Financial Stability Dialogue) for both administration and policy dialogue;
- a second stage focusing on improvement and standardization of macro-economic policy-making across the region; and
- a final stage integrating the regional currencies.

Depending on economic and political development, the last stage of monetary integration might or might not happen.

A more urgent task is, however, for Asia to play a greater role in reform of the global monetary system. Asian economies should coordinate themselves better, to project a clear voice in the G20, including in discussions about reform of the International Monetary Fund (IMF). As the rising power of the world economy, Asia has a strong vested interest in facilitating a smooth transition of the global currency system. In the meantime, Asian economies should also supplement regional integration with policy reforms at the national level. Internationalization of the Chinese yuan, for instance, will be a critical step towards enhancing regional exchange rate policy coordination in the near term.

This chapter is organized as follows. The next section reviews key reforms and macro-economic changes after the 1997–98 financial crisis. Section three discusses impacts of the US subprime crisis on Asia, with a special focus on the regional currency market. Section four assesses the question about how much foreign reserves are sufficient to support capital and currency market stability. Section five discusses the three-stage strategy toward monetary integration in Asia proposed in this study. The final section offers thoughts on key directions for policy cooperation in the near term.

RESPONSES TO THE 1997–98 ASIAN FINANCIAL CRISIS

In retrospect, the Asian financial crisis was essentially a balance-of-payments crisis, although in some economies, such as Korea, it started from a domestic financial crisis. In the years preceding the crisis, most Asian economies experienced strong economic growth, supported by extraordinary investment booms. In 1996, investment shares of GDP reached 44.6 per cent in Malaysia, 41.8 percent in Thailand, 39.0 per cent in Korea and 30.7 per cent in Indonesia.

As a result, the external account positions deteriorated sharply. All four crisis-affected economies – Indonesia, Korea, Malaysia and Thailand – suffered steady current account deficits before the crisis (Figure 10.1). External debts also stayed at relatively high levels. In particular, short-term debts accounted for more than one-third of their total external debts (Figure 10.2).

In July 1997, Thailand was forced to abandon its currency peg to the US dollar. This signalled the beginning of the Asian financial crisis. In the following months, Asian central banks were forced to accept exchange rate shocks one after another. Within the following year, the real effective exchange rate of the Indonesian rupiah crashed by almost 70 per cent, while those of the Malaysian ringgit (MYR), Korean won and Thai baht (THB) had declined by about 40 per cent at their troughs (Figure 10.3). The Philippine peso and Taiwan dollar also weakened during the crisis, but the changes were somewhat smaller (Figure 10.4).

The only major currencies that did not show significant weakening during the Asian financial crisis were the Chinese yuan and Indian rupee. The Indian rupee's exceptional performance was mainly because of its distance from the epicentre of the crisis. India's degree of economic openness was much lower than that of East Asian economies. In particular, its economic linkage with East Asian economies was quite weak at that time.

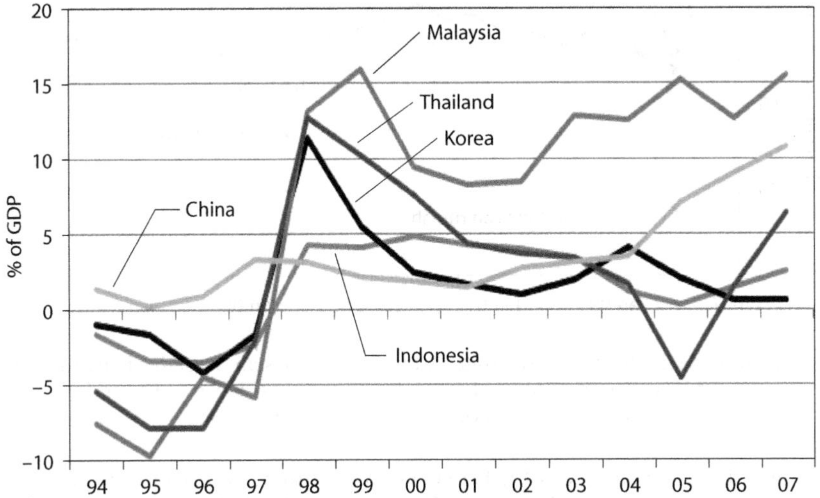

Figure 10.1 Current account balances (% of GDP) in Indonesia, Korea, Malaysia, Thailand and China, 1994–2007. Source: Citigroup estimation.

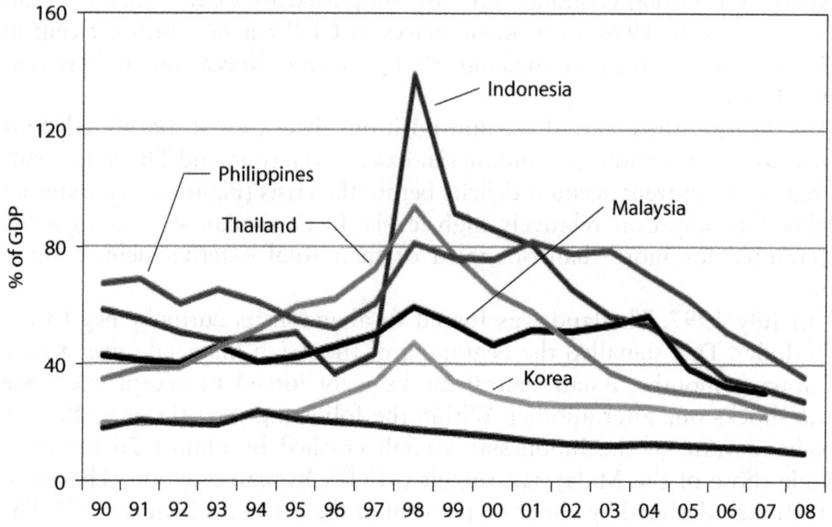

Figure 10.2 External debt (% of GDP) in Indonesia, Malaysia, Korea, Thailand and Philippines, 1990–2008. Source: Citigroup estimation.

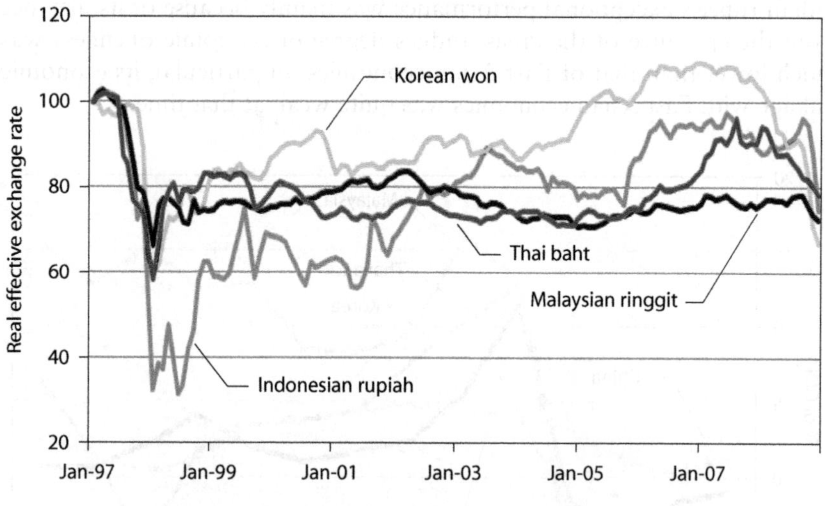

Figure 10.3 Real effective exchange rates of Indonesian rupiah, Korean won, Malaysian ringgit and Thai baht, January 1997 – December 2008 (January 1997=100). Source: Citigroup estimation.

The Chinese yuan (CNY), however, was under significant pressure to devalue in the wake of the crisis. China first unified the official and swap market CNY/US dollar (USD) rates to 8.7 at the beginning of 1994. The currency then experienced a period of slow but steady appreciation.

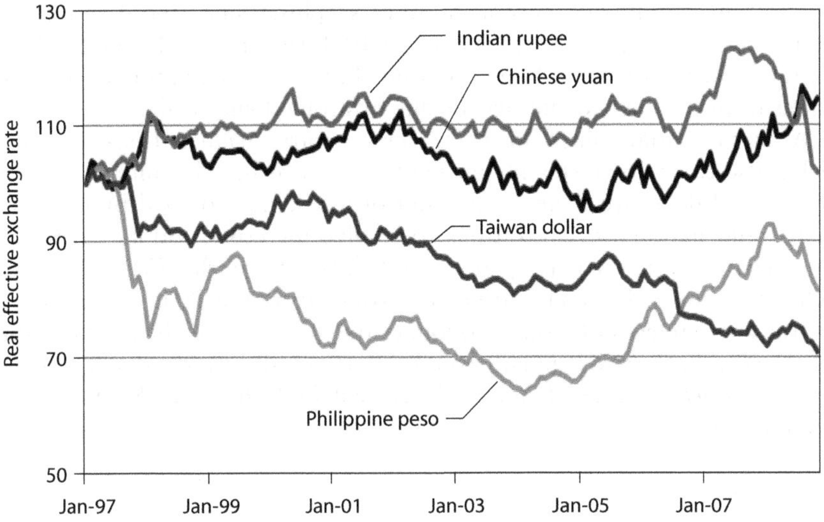

Figure 10.4 Real effective exchange rates of Chinese yuan, Indian rupee, Philippine peso and Taiwan dollar, January 1997 – December 2008 (January 1997=100). Source: Citigroup estimation.

The CNY/USD rate reached 8.27 at the end of 1997. Amidst the height of the Asian financial crisis, the authorities decided to peg the CNY/USD rate at 8.27 in order to avoid competitive devaluation in the region. Malaysian authorities also pegged the MYR/USD at 3.8 around the same time.

In the following years, Asian economies undertook a series of policy actions that may be termed as 'Asian Consensus' policies, in order to significantly lower risks of a balance-of-payments crisis. The essence of that policy strategy is to gradually build defence lines through key measures including:

- adopting more flexible but still conservative exchange rate policies;
- promoting exports and achieving current account surpluses;
- accumulating foreign-exchange reserves;
- reducing reliance on external borrowing, especially short-term borrowing;
- cautiously liberalizing the capital account; and
- introducing initiatives for regional policy cooperation.

These policies have been largely effective, at least for the time being. With the exceptions of the Chinese yuan and Indian rupee, however, the real effective exchange rates of most Asian currencies stayed weaker than their respective levels at the beginning of 1997. The Korean won strengthened temporarily, exceeding its January 1997 level between early 2005 and early 2007.

Except for Thailand in 2005, the crisis-affected economies all have successfully maintained current account surpluses since the Asian crisis. China's current account surplus reached 10.8 per cent of GDP in 2007, an extraordinary level for a large economy. India and Vietnam continued to suffer from current account deficits due to strong domestic demand.

After the initial spikes during the crisis years, Asian nations' external debts also came down steadily during the past decade. The initial increases in external debts were largely a result of financing provided by multinational and national organizations to resolve the crisis. Indonesia, Korea and Thailand, nevertheless, all repaid funds from the IMF ahead of schedule, while Malaysia had not borrowed from the IMF. More importantly, governments of Asian economies quickly lowered their proportion of short-term borrowing. The average share of short-term debts in total external borrowing fell from 32.9 per cent in 1996 to 17.5 per cent in 2000 (Figure 10.5).

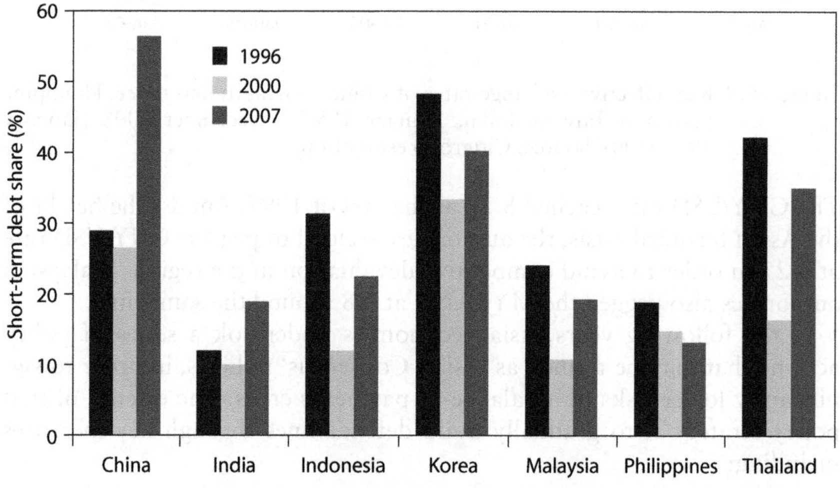

Figure 10.5 Shares of short-term debt (%) in total external debt in selected Asian economies, 1996, 2000 and 2007. Source: Institute of International Finance and Citigroup.

The most visible progress is, perhaps, rapid accumulation of foreign-exchange reserves. In 1996, emerging Asia as a whole owned only US$485 billion in reserves, whereas by the end of 2008 total reserves had reached US$3.5 trillion (Figure 10.6). The fastest accumulation occurred in China, Indonesia, Korea and Malaysia during that period. This rapid growth of foreign-exchange reserves can be attributed to increasing current account surpluses and growing capital inflows. However, the fundamental contributing factor was conservative exchange rate policies across the region.

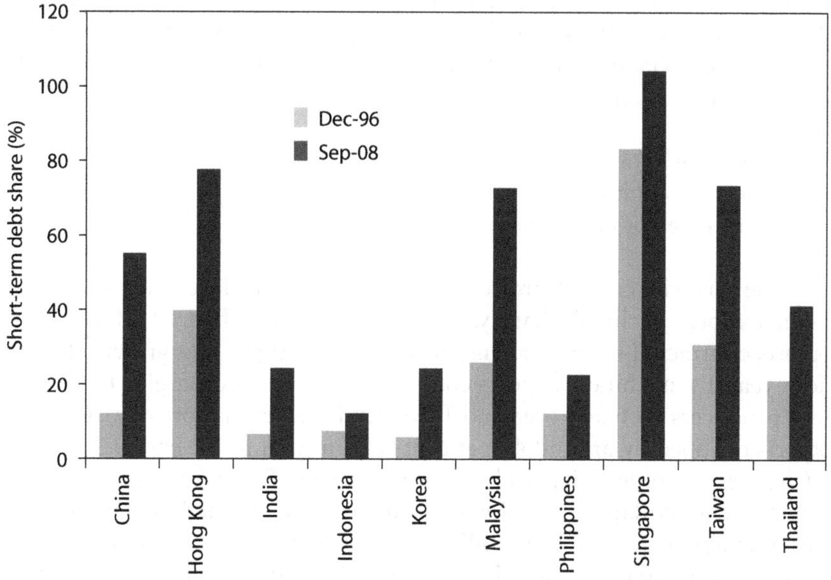

Figure 10.6 Shares of short-term debt (%) in total external debt in selected Asian economies, 1996, 2000 and 2007. Source: Institute of International Finance and Citigroup.

WEATHERING THE GLOBAL FINANCIAL CRISIS

Soon after the US subprime crisis began, the hope that Asia could remain unscathed faded greatly. The once very popular decoupling thesis quickly lost credibility. The decoupling argument suggests that, since Asian economies became highly interdependent, they could maintain strong performance regardless of conditions in the industrial economies. Such an argument, while tempting, overlooks the deep economic interactions existing between Asia and rest of the world.

One of the arguments often cited to support the decoupling thesis is the development of intra-regional trade in Asia. Intra-regional trade grew rapidly in recent years, especially after China joined the WTO. Intermediate goods, however, accounted for more than 70 per cent of total intra-regional trade in Asia in recent years. The Tech Industry provides a good example. In the years immediately following China's WTO entry, many Tech factories moved to China to take advantages of its open markets and cheap production costs. These factories, nevertheless, still imported intermediate goods from other Asian economies such as Singapore, the Philippines, Malaysia, Korea and Taiwan. However, since the majority of the end users are still in developed economies, the growing intra-regional trade in intermediate goods did not mean Asia had become decoupled from the USA or Europe.

In fact, intra-regional trade could disappear quickly if demand by end users of these products collapses. This was exactly what happened during 2008.

The global financial crisis affects Asian economies through at least the following three interrelated channels:

- collapse of exports;
- reversal of capital flows; and
- loss of investor confidence.

As the financial crisis depressed consumption in the developed economies, Asian exports declined sharply. During the second half of 2008, Asian exports contracted by 20 per cent, in contrast to 20 per cent growth the previous year. Even Chinese exports contracted by a similar margin. Traditional Tech producers such as Korea and Taiwan suffered even more damage. Their exports dropped by around 40 per cent year-on-year at the end of 2008.

Changes in trade balances have been uneven. This was mainly because imports also collapsed as domestic demand weakened. Compounding this, a sharp decline in commodity prices significantly improved terms of trade for many Asian economies, most of which are commodity importers. Taking China as an example, its average trade surplus actually rose from about US$20 billion a month during the third quarter of 2008 to about US$40 billion towards the end of the year. China's trade balance, however, deteriorated sharply at the beginning of 2009 as the decline in its exports rapidly worsened. But this may not be the end of the story. Its trade balance could worsen even more later in 2009 when domestic demand picks up as a result of the domestic stimulus policies.

Felt probably even more rapidly were the impacts of the global financial crisis on regional capital markets. During the whole of 2008, Asian equity prices fell by an average of 50 per cent. This was even greater than falls in many industrial economies. The debt markets also underwent similar changes. The average spread of Asian sovereign bonds went up by more than 660 basis points, an increase of 500 per cent, between mid 2007 and the end of 2008.

There were probably several reasons behind sharp adjustments of asset prices in Asia. First, global financial institutions invested in Asian markets were forced to de-leverage by selling their assets overseas in order to repair their domestic balance sheets. Second, as part of the emerging markets, Asian assets are perceived as high risk, especially at times when the global risk appetite recedes rapidly. And, finally, despite the popular decoupling thesis, investors probably still saw strong economic and market linkages between the USA and Asia and, therefore, significant downside risks for Asian economies.

As a result of the combination of the above factors, capital left the region. During the whole of 2008, there was a net outflow of about US$20 billion of global institutional funds from Asian equity markets, which completely offset the net inflows of the previous 2 years. These flows, however, are highly volatile (Figure 10.7). In early 2009, for instance, we saw strong capital inflows, especially to the China markets. Confidence was boosted by the massive stimulus packages announced by the government.

Asian exchange rates have experienced a rocky period since risks of a financial crisis emerged in early 2008. The US dollar strengthened significantly during the crisis, despite the fact that the USA is the epicentre of the event (Figure 10.8). This is mainly attributable to the fact that the US dollar is the world currency. Also, US dollar assets are perceived as low risk, especially US Treasuries. The US institutions hit by the crisis were also forced to withdraw investment from overseas to repair their balance sheets. Ironically, these led to capital inflows into, not outflow from, the USA. How long this strength lasts depends in part on economic policies in the USA and in part on the evolution of the global financial risks. The recent decision by the US Federal Reserve to purchase long-term Treasury bonds, for instance, caused dips in the US dollar as investors began to worry about inflationary effects of money printing.

The Japanese yen surged as a result of an unwinding of carry trade, which refers to investors' previous practice of borrowing low-interest yen and investing in high-yield currencies such as the New Zealand dollar and Indonesian rupiah. Therefore, recent strengthening of the yen in no way reflected investors' perception about the macro-economic fundamentals of the Japanese economy.

The Chinese yuan also appreciated. Investors are probably less worried about defensibility of the yuan exchange rate, given China's close to US$2 trillion foreign reserves. Decisive stimulus policies also played an important role in supporting investor confidence in the Chinese economy

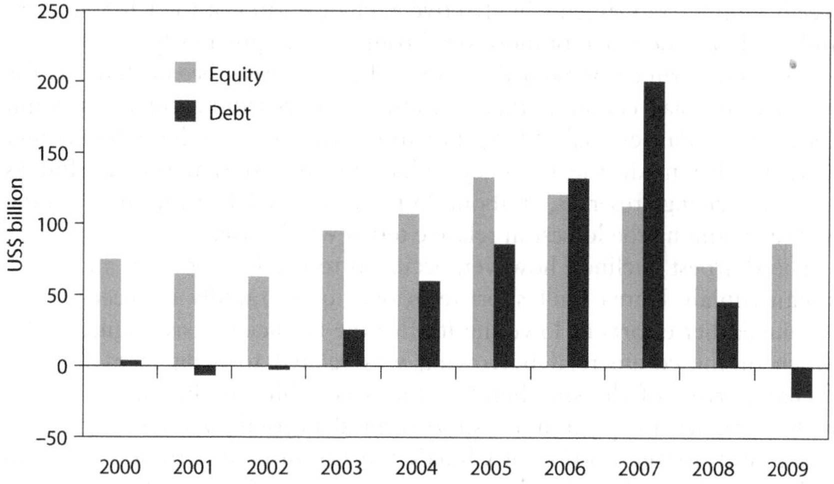

Figure 10.7 Net private capital flows (US$ billion) to emerging Asia, 2000–09. Source: Institute of International Finance.

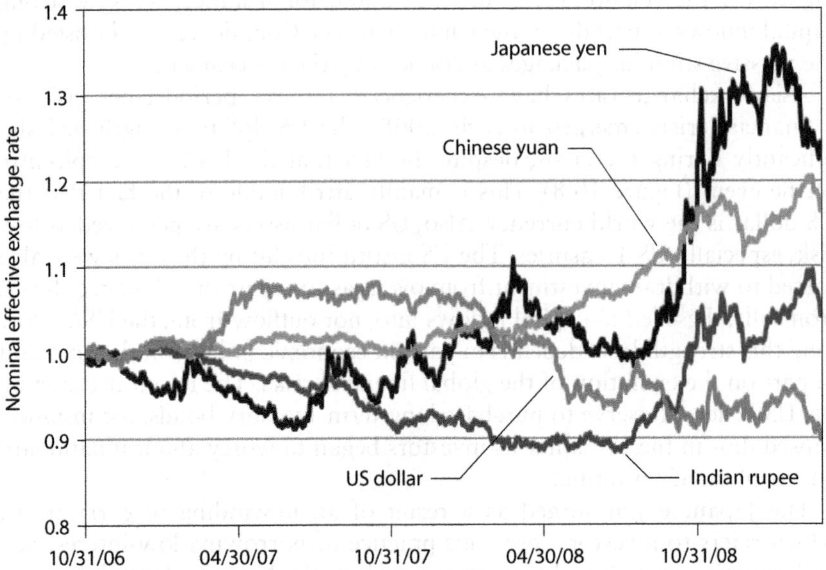

Figure 10.8 Nominal effective exchange rates of US dollar, Japanese yen, Chinese yuan and Indian rupee, October 2006 – March 2009 (31 October 2006=1.0). Source: Citigroup. Note: USD = US dollar; JPY = Japanese yen; CNY = Chinese yuan; INR = Indonesian rupiah.

and its currency. But, most importantly, the People's Bank of China appeared to have returned to an implicit currency peg to the US dollar, with CNY/USD rate fluctuating within a narrow range of 6.8–6.9. In fact, in recent months, movements in effective exchange rates of the Chinese yuan and US dollar looked a lot more synchronized than previously.

The Indian rupee weakened steadily after the crisis began. India is the only major Asian economy that constantly suffers from a current account deficit. Potential reversal of large portfolio investment in the Indian equity markets also made the currency vulnerable to external shocks. India's foreign-exchange reserves, at about 25 per cent of GDP at the end of 2008, were also among the lowest in relative terms within Asia.

The sharpest declines, however, occurred to the Korean won and Indonesian rupiah. Korea built short-term debt quite rapidly in recent years, despite earlier efforts of lowering it after the financial crisis (Figure 10.9). Much of the commercial borrowing was related to hedging of foreign-exchange risks of the ship-building industry. China is the only economy with a higher proportion of short-term debt/total external debt than Korea. But a large portion of China's short-term debt is trade credit and is therefore less vulnerable than commercial borrowing. Significant foreign portfolio investment in domestic capital markets also added pressures on the Indonesian rupiah.

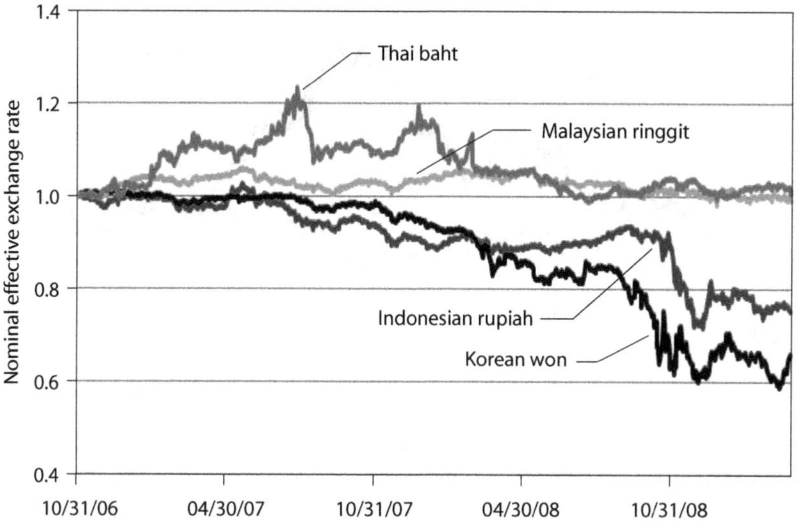

Figure 10.9 Nominal effective exchange rates of Indonesian rupiah, Korean won, Malaysian ringgit and Thai baht, October 2006 – March 2009 (31 October 2006=1.0). Source: Citigroup. Note: IDR = Indonesian rupiah; KRW = Korean won; MYR = Malaysian ringgit; THB = Thai baht.

The effective exchange rates of both the Malaysian ringgit and Thai baht remained surprisingly stable during the current crisis. In Malaysia, the central bank (Bank Negara Malaysia) probably intervened in the foreign-exchange markets, stabilizing the MYR/USD rate at around 3.6. In Thailand, the Bank of Thailand, due to serious concerns about unwanted currency strength and the possible reversal of capital flows, previously imposed restrictions on capital inflows. This probably reduced shocks of capital outflows during the current crisis. Thailand also entered the crisis with stronger macro-economic conditions, with a current account surplus at around 5 per cent of GDP.

The Singapore dollar has been largely stable in the past year, a result of the city state's managed float regime with reference to a basket of currencies (Figure 10.10). The Hong Kong dollar showed a trend of strengthening, given its currency board arrangement. The Taiwan dollar weakened over time, largely due to its large exposure to the global markets. Surprisingly, however, the Philippine peso managed some gains from the end of 2008, although it weakened quickly during much of 2008. The recent gains probably reflected relatively more resilient worker remittances and improved fiscal conditions.

Altogether, Asian currencies moved significantly during the current global financial crisis, but their changes were by no means synchronized. The sharpest declines occurred to the Korean won, Indonesian rupiah, Indian rupee, Thai baht and Philippine peso (Figure 10.11).

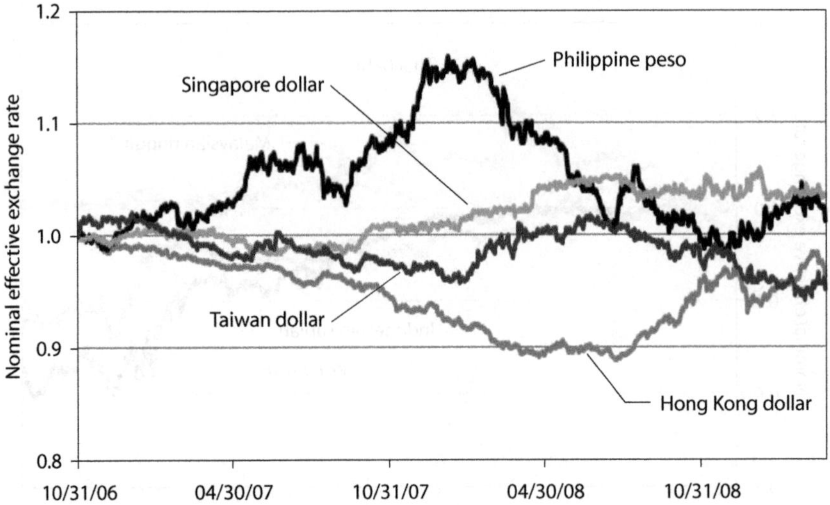

Figure 10.10 Nominal effective exchange rates of Hong Kong dollar, Philippine peso, Singapore dollar and Taiwan dollar, October 2006 – March 2009 (31 October 2006=1.0). Source: Citigroup. Note: HKD = Hong Kong dollar; PHP = Philippine peso; SGD = Singapore dollar; TWD = Taiwan dollar.

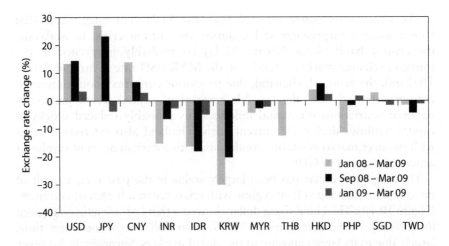

Figure 10.11 Changes (%) in nominal effective exchange rates of US dollar and selected Asian currencies, January 2008 – March 2009, September 2008 – March 2009 and January 2009 – March 2009. Source: Citigroup. Note: USD = US dollar; JPY = Japanese yen; CNY = Chinese yuan; INR = Indonesian rupiah; IDR = Indian rupee; KRW = Korean won; MYR = Malaysian ringgit; THB = Thai baht; HKD = Hong Kong dollar; PHP = Philippine peso; SGD = Singapore dollar; TWD = Taiwan dollar.

FOREIGN RESERVES: HOW MUCH IS ENOUGH?

Significant differences in performance of Asian currencies during the current financial crisis are an important phenomenon deserving close attention. In the past, there was an expectation among investors that Asian currencies might begin to move together even without explicit currency arrangements.

A number of related mechanisms could contribute to this expected synchronization of Asian exchange rates. First, economic integration, particularly trade integration, deepened significantly among Asian economies in recent years. This could lead to synchronization of macro-economic cycles across the region. Second, increasing adoption of inflation targeting by regional central banks could lead to more synchronized monetary policies in Asia. And, finally, while the US dollar is still the most important reference currency, CNY exchange rate is gradually becoming an important indicator for currency flexibility around the region.

For several reasons, however, this market-based synchronization mechanism of Asian exchange rates has yet to materialize. Asian currency regimes still show significant differences in terms of exchange rate flexibility. At the one end, exchange rates of the Korean won, Indian rupee and Philippine peso are relatively free to move, although the central banks also intervene from time to time. At the other extreme, exchange rates of the Hong Kong dollar, Singapore dollar and Vietnamese dong are tightly controlled. The Chinese yuan and Malaysian ringgit sit somewhere in between.

Asian economies also differ significantly in terms of their openness. Export shares of GDP, for instance, are greater than 100 per cent in Hong Kong and Singapore, while for India the corresponding statistic is around only 20 per cent. The economies of Korea and Taiwan are more deeply integrated into the international supply chain of the Tech Industry, while the economies of Indonesia, Malaysia and Vietnam are relatively more exposed to the commodity markets. Capital accounts are tightly controlled in some countries, such as China, but relatively open in others, such as Korea.

The most important difference, however, probably lies in the strength of the external sector. Most Asian economies maintained current account surpluses in recent years, but India and Vietnam suffered from persistent deficits. One important factor that determined currency performance during the past year was foreign-exchange reserves.

In most Asian economies, foreign-exchange reserves seem already peaked, at least in the near term. In some smaller economies, such as Pakistan and Sri Lanka, foreign reserves have been down 50 per cent from their peaks (Table 10.1). In other Asian economies, such as Malaysia, Korea and India, foreign-exchange reserves also declined, because of either investment losses or policy interventions. The only economies that maintained relatively

Table 10.1 Latest levels of foreign-exchange reserves in selected Asian economies and changes from their peaks

	Foreign reserves (US$ billion)	*Forward book (US$ billion)*	*Changes from peak (%)*	*Peak time*
China	1,946.0	n.a.	0.00	December 08
India	251.5	−0.5	−17.30	May 08
Indonesia	50.9	n.a.	−16.10	July 08
Korea	201.7	−6.9	−23.70	March 08
Malaysia	91.3	0	−39.00	May 08
Pakistan	6.9	−1.9	−51.40	February 08
Philippines	39.2	2.3	0.00	January 09
Singapore	167.1	37.1	−5.80	March 08
Sri Lanka	1.8	n.a.	−50.70	July 08
Taiwan	292.7	n.a.	0.00	January 09
Thailand	112.3	5.5	0.00	January 09

Sources: CEIC Data Company and Citigroup.
Note: Latest data are for end of March wherever possible.

stable foreign reserves are China, the Philippines, Thailand and Taiwan. Even in these economies, future development could become less certain if the global recession continues to deepen.

Before the current crisis, many Asian central bankers, and even investors, felt that Asia had probably accumulated too much foreign-exchange reserves. Some economies, such as Korea and China, started to set up new vehicles for more commercial investment. Others, such as Taiwan, Indonesia and Malaysia, began to contemplate similar ideas. Such perceptions, however, were proven overoptimistic soon after the global financial crisis began.

What level of reserves is sufficient? Traditionally, the minimum requirement of foreign-exchange reserves is the country's short-term debt. In this sense, the main purpose of accumulating foreign reserves is to cope with risks of the sudden stop of financial flows. In cases of external shocks, financial flows could terminate abruptly. If a country does not have enough foreign reserves, it would be forced to default its foreign debts. Therefore, short-term foreign debt plus long-term debt that would mature in the coming year constitute the narrowest definition of required foreign reserves.

The medium definition is a country's total external financing needs, including both retiring debts and current account deficits. Current account deficits normally need to be balanced by capital flows. Should financial flows stop suddenly, the country needs to finance the current account deficits in order to continue regular economic activities.

The broadest definition of required foreign-exchange reserves includes not only total external financing needs but also mobile foreign capital in the country. Mobile foreign capital refers to portfolio investment by foreign investors in domestic equity and debt markets. Portfolio investment is highly mobile and can flow across borders quickly as investment risks rise and fall, which often leads to significant fluctuation of the exchange rate.

Obviously, foreign reserves covering mobile foreign capital have a different purpose from foreign reserves covering external financing needs. The latter would be drawn to maintain regular economic order in cases of sudden cessation of financial flows. The former would normally not be used to fill the gaps left by mobile foreign capital but to guard against speculative attacks on the currency.

Application of the above three definitions of 'sufficient foreign reserves' generates three foreign reserve cover ratios: foreign reserves/retiring debts, foreign reserves/total external financing needs, and foreign reserves/total external financing needs plus mobile foreign capital (Table 10.2).

Clearly, of the 11 emerging Asian economies examined, most of them had enough foreign reserves to cover retiring debts at the end of 2008 (cover ratio greater than 1). The sole exception was Sri Lanka. Most economies also had enough foreign reserves to meet total external financing needs. According to both measures, Korea barely had enough foreign reserves to cover either retiring debts or total external financing needs (Korea's cover ratio for retiring debt is greater than that for external financing needs because it had a current account surplus). This picture of generally sufficient foreign-exchange reserves across the region was a result of the policy reforms introduced after the 1997–98 crisis.

However, when both external financing needs and mobile foreign capital are included in the calculation, the cover ratios fell below one in Indonesia, Korea, Pakistan and Sri Lanka. India's cover ratio is only marginally above one. In fact, with the exceptions of China and Thailand, all cover ratios were below two. These are consistent with the broad weakening of Asian currencies when risk premiums rose during the current financial crisis. The Korean won, Indonesian rupiah and Indian rupee experienced sharpest declines.

PURSUING ASIAN MONETARY INTEGRATION

After the 1997–98 financial crisis, Asia is already moving quickly from trade integration to monetary and financial cooperation. ASEAN+3 has focused its efforts on regional economic surveillance (Economic Review and Policy Dialogue), regional short-term arrangements (Chiang Mai Initiative) and local currency bond market development (Asian Bond Markets Initiative) (de Brouwer 1999; Bergsten and Park 2002; Ghosh 2006).

The ASEAN+3 Finance Ministers' agreement on reserve pooling in May 2008 was a very positive step. In January 2009, ASEAN+3 raised the size of foreign reserve funds from US$80 billion to $120 billion. A recent Asian Development Bank (ADB) study on emerging regionalism also recommended

Table 10.2 Foreign-exchange (forex) reserve cover ratios for selected Asian economies (US$ billion).

	Forex reserve (1)	*Short-term debt by remaining maturity (2)*	*Current account deficit (in 2009 fiscal) (3)*	*Total external finance required (2+3)*	*Forex reserve / short-term debt by remaining maturity (1/2)*	*Forex reserve/total external finance required (1/(2+3))*	*Foreign hold of stocks (7)*	*Foreign hold of bonds (8)*	*External finance + mobile capital (9)*	*Forex reserve/ (external finance + mobile capital) (1/9)*
China	1,946	250	–427.0	–177.0	7.8	n.a.*	30		–147	n.a.
Indonesia	50.9	33.2	–1.9	31.3	1.5	1.6	18	7.1	56.4	0.9
India	251.5	91.9	23.0	114.9	2.7	2.2	94	6.7	215.6	1.2
Korea	201.7	191.1	–13.0	178.1	1.0	1.1	111	27	316	0.6
Malaysia	91.3	42.4	–21.3	21.1	2.2	4.3	22.3	11.8	55.2	1.7
Pakistan	6.9	3.2	10.2	13.4	2.1	0.5	1.3	0	14.7	0.5
Philippines	39.6	14.3	–4.7	9.7	2.8	4.1	11.6	0.6	21.9	1.8
Sri Lanka	1.75	3.3	3.3	6.6	0.5	0.3	0	0.1	6.7	0.3
Thailand	112.3	35.1	–14.5	20.7	3.2	5.4	30.7	1.7	53.1	2.1
Taiwan	292.7	99.1	–30.0	69.1	3.0	4.2	101	1.1	171.2	1.7
Vietnam	22.0	7.1	4.8	11.9	3.1	1.9	2.1	0.5	14.5	1.5

Source: Chua (2009).

two new institutions, including an Asian Financial Stability Dialogue and an Asian Secretariat for Economic Cooperation (ADB 2008). ADB has also initiated efforts at creating an Asian Currency Unit (Kawai 2008).

Asia's experiences during the current crisis, however, suggest that these regional initiatives were not sufficient in supporting regional economic and market stability when facing external shocks. Excessive currency volatility in some regional economies was particularly worrisome as it causes difficulties for not only trade and investment activities but also macro-economic policy-making. Asian policy-makers, therefore, need to make more efforts to either strengthen the existing frameworks or find new ways of developing regional monetary policy cooperation.

Expected changes of the international monetary system further necessitate regional cooperation in Asia. Since 1944, the US dollar has dominated the international economic system as the major global currency. Although the US dollar will likely remain a key reserve currency for some time, its importance will probably decline and its value will likely fall after this global crisis. The US dollar should stay as the most important currency for accounting and transaction in international economic dealings, but its function of value stocking has already diminished and will likely diminish further (Figure 10.12).

Such change poses important challenges for Asia. The world currency system may evolve into a new system based on a basket of global currencies and this implies greater exchange rate uncertainty in the future. This is particularly so for Asian economies whose central banks traditionally pay much closer attention to the US dollar than any other currencies in the world.

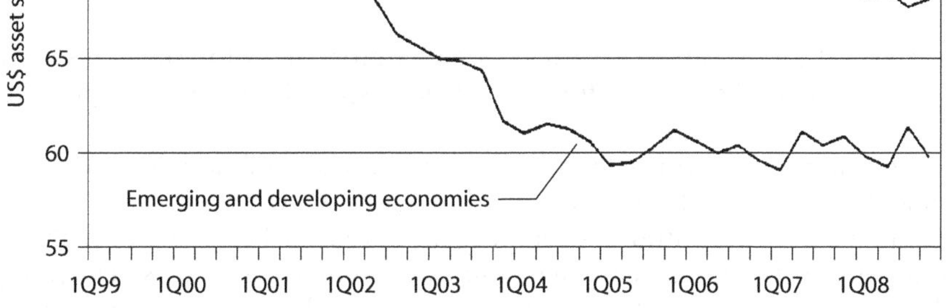

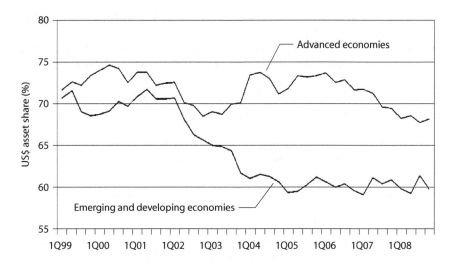

Figure 10.12 Shares (%) of US dollar assets in official foreign-exchange reserves, first quarter 1999 – fourth quarter 2008. Source: International Monetary Fund.

Asia's monetary policy cooperation should focus on:

- contributing to reforms of the international currency system;
- initiatives promoting regional exchange rate coordination; and
- efforts to improve the quality of macro-economic policy-making in individual economies.

The central issue facing Asian policy-makers collectively is the form of monetary integration they must pursue. In the long run, it may be ideal to unify the regional monetary system under one currency, like the EU economy under the euro. But the question about which currency will dominate the future regional financial system should be left open for the time being. It could be an Asian dollar, Japanese yen, Chinese yuan, Indian rupee or even a combination of some of the regional currencies. This decision can be sensibly made only in the future.

In the near term, it may be difficult to immediately pursue EU-type monetary integration. Unlike the EU at the beginning of monetary integration, Asia comprises economies at very different stages of economic development, with very different sizes, very different macro-economic cycles and very dynamic economic weights. It is difficult to fit all these economies under one exchange rate regime. Lack of a successful resolution of historical differences also points to difficulties in achieving political consensus on a high degree of integration.

Taking currency unification as the ultimate goal, Asia's monetary integration may follow a three-stage approach:

- Stage 1: building regional foreign reserve funds and conducting policy surveillance and dialogue;
- Stage 2: standardizing macro-economic policy framework across the region, such as independent monetary policy and inflation targeting; and
- Stage 3: integrating regional monetary system under a regional central bank with one regional currency.

Stages 1 and 2 can be regarded as preparatory steps for Stage 3. Given the current conditions, the first two stages, especially Stage 2, might take some decades.

An important reason why monetary integration in Asia will take more time than that in Europe is the differences between emerging Asian economies. Asian central bankers face an old but delicate question about trade-offs between currency flexibility and stability. For most emerging Asian economies, free float is probably not the best option, considering potential damage of exchange rate volatility (and thereby possible excessive speculations) to investors' and exporters' expectations and financial institutions' risk management.

Asia's own experiences before the 1997–98 crisis also confirmed that a fixed exchange rate regime is also not a preferred option, as it forces all economic adjustments to domestic monetary policies. Individual economies also need to maintain some flexibility against other regional currencies, given their different stages of economic development and macro-economic cycles.

The best option is probably a managed float, which is the most common regime in Asia today. But it needs to be supplemented by certain market mechanisms to avoid excessive speculation and currency volatility.

The purpose of first-stage policy efforts is to strengthen the region's collective macro-economic fundamentals in order to promote stability of regional exchange rates. It is also a continuation of earlier policies introduced after the 1997–98 financial crisis. The previous policies aimed at building foreign reserves by individual economies in order to reduce risks of balance-of-payments crises. However, necessary foreign reserves expanded as Asian economies opened up their capital markets. Therefore, building enough foreign reserves by individual economies is neither practical nor efficient.

However, Asia as a whole has already accumulated large volumes of foreign reserves. Collectively, these reserves are probably sufficient to support stability of regional currencies. The current foreign reserve fund, at US$120 billion, is too small to be effective. Ideally, they will probably need to be increased by 8–10 times. But that will have to happen over time.

A more challenging task is administration of the foreign reserve funds. In the region, there is already an operating ASEAN+3 framework. This needs to be expanded to include other important regional players such as India and possibly even Australia. And, for the purpose of monetary policy integration, the region needs to create an Asian Central Bank Forum (ACBF; or, alternatively, an expansion of the Asian Financial Stability Dialogue, AFSD), alongside the existing Finance Ministers' Meeting.

The ACBF or AFSD can then act as a central point for dialogue among regional monetary policy-makers and for fostering macro-economic policy surveillance across the region. ACBF should also maintain a close link with global financial institutions, such as the IMF, but should not act as a regional central bank, at least not during this early stage.

The purpose of the second stage is to enhance monetary policy-making in Asian economies and to eventually reduce gaps in economic development and even induce synchronization of macro-economic cycles. This is a critical preparatory step for the ultimate integration of the regional currency system.

During this stage, the role of ACBF or AFSD should be expanded from a forum for policy dialogue and administration of the Foreign Reserve Funds to more active coordination of monetary policies, especially the policy-making approaches, across the region. For instance, all participating central banks will need to gradually become independent from the government systems and adopt a common set of indirect policy instruments. Managed float exchange rates and inflation targeting could be examples of common policy instruments.

The purpose of the last stage is to establish a regional currency system. One possibility is to adopt a regional currency like the Euro Area. However, this Asian regional currency can be either a new currency or an existing currency such as the Japanese yen or Chinese yuan. If Asia successfully moves to this stage, then ACBF can become a regional central bank. Integration of the monetary system will be conditional on a certain degree of political integration, and it is entirely possible that Asian monetary integration will halt at Stage 2. But that would nevertheless remain a positive outcome.

CONCLUDING REMARKS

Asian economies underwent significant transformation after the 1997–98 crisis. Policy-makers implemented a set of changes in order to strengthen external sector fundamentals and reduce the risks of a balance-of-payments crisis. Exchange rate regimes became more flexible but remained relatively conservative in order to promote exports growth, external account surplus and foreign reserve accumulation. As a result, current accounts turned from deficits to surpluses and foreign reserves grew rapidly. Asian leaders also introduced a number of regional cooperation initiatives, such as Asian Bond Funds and Asian Reserve Funds.

These changes put Asia on a much stronger footing to withstand external shocks. During the US subprime crisis, emerging Asia weathered much better than many other emerging economies. Despite collapse of the export sector and significant capital outflows, Asian economies stayed relatively resilient. Most Asian governments are able to take aggressive stimulus measures to boost domestic demand.

But currency performance varies widely across the region. During the five quarters between the first quarter of 2008 and the first quarter of 2009, the nominal effective exchange rate of the Korean won collapsed by 30 per cent. Both the Indonesian rupiah and Indian rupee weakened by about 16 per cent. And the Philippine peso and Thai baht depreciated by 11–13 per cent. Meanwhile, the Japanese yen strengthened by 27 per cent and Chinese yuan by 14 per cent.

Differences in currency performance probably reflected differences in a number of factors, including openness and exchange rate flexibility. But a critical factor is the individual economy's level of foreign reserves. There are three criteria judging whether or not an economy's foreign reserves are sufficient: the narrowest compares only with debt amortization; the medium compares with total external financing needs (debt amortization plus current account deficits); and the broadest compares with the sum of external financing needs and mobile foreign capital.

Most Asian economies' foreign reserves are sufficient to cover external financing needs. However, as Asian capital markets gradually became more open, mobile foreign capital grew. And according to the broadest criteria, Korea, Indonesia and India face higher capital flow risks. This is probably why their currencies suffered the greatest damages during the current crisis, while their central banks thought, less than 2 years ago, that they had built enough reserves.

Application of the broadest definition, however, means every economy will need to accumulate massive foreign reserves in order to support investor confidence and maintain currency stability. But this would be neither practical nor efficient. Since Asia has collectively accumulated large reserves, a better option is probably to enhance regional cooperation in this area. Asia currently has a Foreign Reserve Fund of US$120 billion. This fund needs to be increased in order for it to play a meaningful role in regional financial markets.

Strengthening of the reserve fund should only be a small part of the broad efforts of regional monetary integration, which could follow a three-stage approach. The first stage would involve expansion of the foreign reserve fund and creation of Asian central bank forum (or expansion of the Asian Financial Stability Dialogue) for both reserve administration and policy dialogue. The second stage would focus on improvement and standardization of macro-economic policy-making across the region. And the final stage would integrate the regional currencies. Depending on economic and political development, the last stage of monetary integration might or might not happen.

While a single currency may be viewed as a long-term goal, it is best to pursue in Asia a different form of integration from that in Europe. Some exchange rate stability is helpful for most emerging Asian economies, but a certain degree of flexibility is also critical for macro-economic management in individual economies given their different stages of economic development and macro-economic cycles. This is why Asian monetary integration should probably focus on enhancing the reserve funds and improving policy-making, not on specific currency arrangements.

But Asia also faces an important and urgent task. Asia must contribute to the reform of the international monetary system. Asia has the world's second- and third-largest economies and five of the G20 members. If the USA and Europe represent the old power of the world economy, Asia represents the rising new power. Yet, Asia doesn't have a single and consistent voice in either G20 or IMF discussions. Asia has a strong vested interest in facilitating a smooth improvement of the global currency system.

Finally, regional integration efforts should also be accompanied by policy reforms by individual countries. Regional dialogue or forums may provide some guidance, but the initiatives must come from the national governments. One critical condition for potential monetary integration is synchronization of macro-economic cycles. This requires adoption of transparent and consistent monetary policy frameworks such as inflation targeting, in addition to deeper economic integration.

Exchange rate policy reform is also critical. In particular, internationalization of the Chinese yuan should help promote regional monetary cooperation, given the Chinese yuan's importance in regional exchange rate decisions. For more than 10 years, China has been preparing for currency convertibility under the capital account. It is now time for China to speed up this process. Cautious but swift realization of Chinese yuan convertibility is likely to prove beneficial to not only China but also the region as a whole.

NOTE

1 China Center for Economic Research, Peking University, Beijing, China. Email: yhuang@ccer.edu.cn.

REFERENCES

ADB (Asian Development Bank) (2008) *Emerging Asian Regionalism: a Partnership for Shared Prosperity*, Manila: ADB.

Bergsten, F. and Y.C. Park (2002) 'Toward creating a regional monetary arrangement in East Asia', *ADBI Research Paper Series*, No. 50, Tokyo: Asian Development Bank Institute.

Chua, J. (2009) 'Asia macro views: Asia – reassessing FX reserve adequacy', 23 February 2009, Hong Kong: Citigroup.

de Brouwer, G. (1999) *Financial Integration in East Asia*, Cambridge, UK: Cambridge University Press.

Ghosh, S.R. (2006) *East Asian Finance: the Road to Robust Markets*, Washington, DC: World Bank.

Kawai, M. (2008) 'Toward a regional exchange rate regime in East Asia', *Pacific Economic Review*, 13(1): 83–103.

Index